T0247591

LINCOLN'S GOD

LINCOLN'S
GOD

HOW FAITH

TRANSFORMED

A PRESIDENT

AND A NATION

JOSHUA ZEITZ

VIKING

VIKING
An imprint of Penguin Random House LLC
penguinrandomhouse.com

Copyright © 2023 by Joshua Zeitz
Penguin Random House supports copyright. Copyright fuels creativity,
encourages diverse voices, promotes free speech, and creates a vibrant culture.
Thank you for buying an authorized edition of this book and for complying
with copyright laws by not reproducing, scanning, or distributing any part of
it in any form without permission. You are supporting writers and allowing
Penguin Random House to continue to publish books for every reader.

LIBRARY OF CONGRESS CATALOGING-IN-PUBLICATION DATA
Names: Zeitz, Joshua, author.
Title: Lincoln's God : how faith transformed a president and a nation / Joshua Zeitz.
Other titles: How faith transformed a president and a nation
Description: [New York, New York] : Viking, [2023] |
Includes bibliographical references and index.
Identifiers: LCCN 2022040227 (print) | LCCN 2022040228 (ebook) |
ISBN 9781984882219 (hardcover) | ISBN 9781984882226 (ebook)
Subjects: LCSH: Lincoln, Abraham, 1809–1865—Religion. |
Presidents—Religious life—United States. | Christianity and politics—United
States—History—19th century. | United States—History—Civil War,
1861–1865—Religious aspects—Christianity. | United States—Religion—19th century.
Classification: LCC E457.2 .Z46 2023 (print) | LCC E457.2 (ebook) |
DDC 973.7—dc23/eng/20220920
LC record available at https://lccn.loc.gov/2022040227
LC ebook record available at https://lccn.loc.gov/2022040228

Printed in the United States of America
1st Printing

Book design by Daniel Lagin

For Carl Zeitz and Larry Snowhite

and in memory of Elaine B. Zeitz and Deede Snowhite

CONTENTS

PREFACE

From the moment of Abraham Lincoln's assassination on Good Friday 1865, many Americans remembered their sixteenth president as an almost Christlike figure. Josiah Holland, the deeply pious editor of the Springfield, Massachusetts, *Republican*, wrote one of the earliest and most popular hagiographies, in which he portrayed Lincoln as an "eminently Christian president"—a Bible-quoting evangelical whose hatred of slavery flowed from an eschatological belief that "the day of wrath was at hand." "I know that liberty is right, for Christ teaches it and Christ is God," Holland imaginatively quoted the future president, who almost certainly said nothing of the sort. It hardly mattered. In a deeply religious country just recently touched by four years of war and fratricide, the reading public eagerly bought up one hundred thousand copies, making it an overnight bestseller. Americans *needed* to memorialize Lincoln as a Christian martyr.

Successive generations of amateur Lincoln biographers would continue in this vein. They claimed that Ann Rutledge, his first love, lent him her mother's Bible and that young Abe circled passages from the Song of Solomon; that he was converted at a Methodist camp meeting in 1837; and that he once confided in a close friend, "When I left Springfield, I asked the people to pray for me. I was not a Christian. When I buried my son, the severest trial of my life, I was not a Christian. But when I went to Gettysburg and saw the graves of thousands of our soldiers, I then and there consecrated myself to Christ. Yes, I do love Jesus." None of this was true. But as a newspaperman noted ruefully at the time, the fatal bullet that John Wilkes Booth fired at Ford's Theatre in April 1865 "made it impossible to speak the truth of Abraham Lincoln hereafter."

But was Abraham Lincoln in fact a religious man? If so, did he regard himself as an evangelical Christian? Or was he, like Thomas Jefferson and other members of the founding generation, a deist who believed more vaguely in a controlling influence that guided human events?

Does it even matter?

The truth about Lincoln's beliefs was of course considerably more complicated than these saccharine fabrications. Abraham Lincoln was not a "technical Christian," his wife, Mary Todd Lincoln, offered a year after her husband's death. His beloved stepmother, Sarah Bush Lincoln, recalled that Abe "had no particular religion." A friend claimed that a minister in Springfield, Illinois, attempted to convert Lincoln as late as 1858 but "couldn't do it." Jesse Fell, a close friend and ally throughout the pitched political wars over slavery in the 1850s, developed a more charitable assessment: "His religious views were eminently practical and are Summed up on these two propositions. 'The Fatherhood of God, and the Brotherhood of Man.'" To William Herndon, his law partner and friend, Lincoln was "simply a Theist—an un-believer in Christianity," an "infidel . . . in the orthodox sense of the term." Herndon was appalled by popular attempts to apotheosize Lincoln. He was by no means a disinterested party. But he was in a position to know.

That Lincoln rejected formal religion is at once easy to understand and difficult to reconcile with the myth surrounding him. Raised in a strict Calvinist household, he learned from an early age to associate his father's crude belief in predestination with narrow ambition and a sharply limited worldview. It seemed to Lincoln that his father's complete lack of drive—a quiet resignation that flowed naturally from his theological rejection of personal agency—consigned Thomas Lincoln for all time to the hardscrabble existence of a semiliterate dirt farmer. It was a life from which the son was determined to break free. From an early age, Abe displayed what his White House secretaries called a "fixed and inflexible will to succeed," and the more that he learned to hate manual labor—cutting down trees with his famed ax, breaking the prairie dirt with a hand-drawn plow, enduring a never-ending cycle of planting and harvesting—the more that he came to resent Thomas and everything that Thomas represented, which included Calvinism.

But discarding religion as a part of social and familial flight does not necessarily mean that he should have rejected *all* religion. Coming of age in an era of intense evangelical revivalism, Lincoln could have—in theory, *should* have—followed millions of his fellow strivers into the Baptist, Methodist, Congregational, or Presbyterian churches, where a new Arminian (and non-Calvinist) spirit taught that humans *did* have agency—*did* control their own destinies—and *could* secure their own salvation through good works, faith, and a personal relationship with Jesus Christ. It was an ethos well suited to a noisy democracy and bustling market economy in which Americans understood themselves to be masters of their own fate—equally free to choose what church to worship in, what profession to ply, what goods to purchase, or which candidate to vote for, as how (or even whether) to secure their own eternal salvation. Lincoln's Whig Party, whose political base was inseparable from mainline churches and reform movements, was popularly known as "the Christian party." Its closely intertwined relationship with Protestant social reform movements—with their emphasis on the moral uplift of both individuals and the nation—reflected an ascendant premillennial strain in American thought, which anticipated the country's role in ushering in one thousand years of peace before Christ's return. But Lincoln, unlike most of his political brethren, kept organized Christianity at arm's length for most of his life. He never joined a church and even when president only sometimes attended Sunday services with his wife. Before the war, he had been, in his own way, a vaguely "religious man," Mary acknowledged, but his spirituality was abstract and informal, marked by skepticism of rigid dogma rather than categorical belief. Certainly he did not consider himself an evangelical Christian in even the loosest reading of the term.

That changed during the war. As was true for millions of his fellow citizens, Lincoln underwent a spiritual renewal. Typical of a man who was, by his own admission, "rather inclined to silence," and not easily pulled along by the tug of popular convention, Lincoln followed his own religious path. His transformation was quiet, subtle, understated, and iconoclastic. It nevertheless left a profound mark on his presidency and on the Union's understanding of the Civil War.

Gallons of ink have been spilled in contemplation of Lincoln's ideological evolution, political talents, mastery of power, inner life, and military genius. But to understand Lincoln's performance as president—his eerie self-possession in the face of political turmoil and military setbacks, his sangfroid in the face of unspeakable death, his ability to muster political support for causes like abolition, which were unpopular, and for

a war that many fellow citizens wanted to abandon in the dark days of
1862 and 1863—it is essential to follow his spiritual journey from skeptic
to believer.

⚜

LINCOLN'S JOURNEY WAS NOT UNIQUE. AMERICA ITSELF UNDERWENT A
profound religious transformation in the first half of the nineteenth century. Shedding their Puritan forebears' sturdy faith in predestination,
millions of Americans flocked to new evangelical churches, which held
that through belief, repentance, and a personal relationship with Christ,
individuals could find grace in this life and the next. The profusion of
Protestant churches, denominations, and sects in the early years of the
new century—a sharp break with the colonial era, when a small number
of established churches dominated the religious landscape—reflected the
emergence of a noisy democratic culture. In the same way that Americans
in the age of Jefferson and Jackson embraced a radical, leveling spirit in
politics, in the first decades of the nineteenth century they asserted their
right to make individual decisions about doctrine and liturgy. It was an
ethos also well suited to the emergence of a modern market economy
in which people forged associations that extended beyond local communities and embraced an economic worldview that vaunted individual choice, autonomy, and responsibility. It would be a mistake to argue
that economic change drove religious developments, or vice versa. The
two trends occurred in tandem and reinforced each other. Church membership exploded in these years. The ranks of the clergy swelled. Tract
societies and evangelical newspapers became key staples of public culture. Evangelical Christianity, with its perfectionist strain, inspired a
wave of reform movements that bridged otherwise disparate causes like
temperance, public education, and abolitionism. It was the nation's lingua

franca, especially for a rising generation of urban professionals—
lawyers, doctors, editors and writers, merchants, businesspeople—for
whom political, religious, and economic ideology were of a piece.

By numbers alone, organized Protestant churches were arguably the
most influential public institutions in the United States. On the eve of the
Civil War, the number of active Methodist clergymen roughly equaled
the number of postal workers nationwide (a significant benchmark, as
before the war, the post office was the largest federal agency and the
branch through which most Americans experienced a direct relationship with the federal government). By some estimates, the total receipts of
all churches and religious organizations were almost equal to the federal
government's annual revenue. Among the country's roughly four hundred
colleges, almost every last one was affiliated with a church.

The coming of the Civil War sharply changed the substance and tenor
of evangelical culture in America. For one, it rent the major denominations in two, as Baptists, Methodists, and Presbyterians from the North
and the South went their separate ways, dividing up church property
and dissolving their bonds of Christian fellowship, each side firm in the
belief that its side was just. In the North, the war also transformed organized Protestantism, which in the decades before the 1860s had focused
on winning converts to Christ and regenerating sinners in anticipation of
the millennium—the thousand years of peace that would precede Christ's
Second Coming. Before the war, lay and religious leaders largely remained
aloof from politics and observed an unspoken division between the sacred and the secular. Their mission was moral suasion—winning souls
and saving sinners. After 1861, Northern churches and clergy threw
themselves into the work of raising local regiments, furnishing Army
camps with chaplains and Bible tracts, and establishing medical and
hygienic services for the government. In time, they effectively became

adjuncts to the Republican-dominated government in Washington and in Northern state capitals. Shedding their earlier rejection of politics, prominent leaders lent their full-throated support to the Union and its political leadership, and they came to associate engagement in political and military affairs as an imperative of their faith.

Protestants in the North also turned to religion to make sense of a national tragedy that eventually killed 750,000 American men and left many thousands more permanently wounded and disabled. Religion was not a fixed matter. Mass death compelled Christians, as well as those of other faiths, or none, to develop new ideas about heaven and the afterlife.

The war also changed ways of thinking about slavery, as Protestants came to view the peculiar institution not just as a matter of individual sin, but as a collective, national transgression that God intended them to erase from the face of the earth.

Northern evangelicals also grew accepting of state power and coercion—including violence—in the service of preserving the Union and eradicating slavery. Religious men and women who once favored pacifism and moral suasion now embraced the gun, the ballot box, and instruments of government control, including censorship, martial law, and the expropriation of rebel property. In their quest to confirm America's place as God's new Canaan, they came to view the pulpit and the state as twin instruments in the same divine project. In effect, the war transformed Protestantism in America every bit as much as Protestantism bolstered the Union in its time of gravest need and distress.

For Northerners, evangelical Christianity was just one—albeit one very powerful—building block of people's identities. Not all evangelical Christians experienced the war in the same way or shared a uniform religious experience as a result of the pain and loss that the war inflicted. Black Christians had long gravitated toward the Old Testament's prophetic tradition and did not require the same jolt to their system to find religious justification and biblical precedent for the use of violence in the service of liberation. Many soldiers found that their faith sustained them in battle, but just as many found Christianity wanting as a means to understand the conflict or steel one's nerves for the fight. Counterintuitively, home front religiosity was often more bellicose and certain than the lived experience of Union soldiers. Recognizing these various distinctions is critical to understanding the powerful but dynamic role of faith in shaping the North's encounter with the Civil War.

EARLY IN HIS PRESIDENCY, WITH THE DREAD SPECTER OF DISUNION HOVering over the nation, Lincoln began invoking biblical imagery to explain what was at stake. In speeches along his journey from Springfield to Washington, he appealed to "Divine Providence," "the Providence of God," "that God who has never forsaken this people," "without whose aid we can do nothing." He gestured to "the Almighty," in whose hands the fate of the Union rested. But it was not until the civil conflict began to claim thousands of lives weekly, and until death touched the Lincoln household in an awful, intimate way, that religion became a commanding force in his personal and public lives. Lincoln's spiritual turn combined a deep and probing exploration of divine intent and human agency, and stark political realism.

Abraham Lincoln, the erstwhile skeptic, was the first president to understand and channel the spiritual and institutional power of the evangelical churches. Over a century before Jimmy Carter became the first born-again resident of the White House and Ronald Reagan declared before the Religious Roundtable, "I know you can't endorse me, but I want you to know that I endorse you," Lincoln assiduously courted the Protestant clergy. He warmly embraced and cultivated mass-readership Protestant publications and corresponded regularly with religious reformers and tract society publishers, even bringing them into the official embrace of government through wartime organizations like the Sanitary Commission. He also frequently entertained visiting church delegations. Evangelical Protestants became the sturdiest layer of the Republican Party's foundation and, by Lincoln's design, a critical engine of its electoral success in the 1863 off-year elections and the critical 1864 national campaign. From thousands of pulpits across the country, each Sunday, evangelical clergy sustained support for the war effort even when the Union seemed lost and more sober voices called for an honorable settlement with the South. Lincoln's pursuit of the religious community is an underappreciated feature of his presidency. "You may depend upon it, the Lord runs Lincoln," a prominent Methodist layman proclaimed.

Lincoln's personal faith and growing political reliance on evangelical voters deepened in tandem and led him over time to frame the meaning of the Civil War with words and cadences reminiscent of the King James Bible, a book he had memorized almost chapter and verse early in life, even before he was anything proximate to a believer. The translation with which most Americans were then familiar, published in 1769, was a revision to the original edition published in 1611. It knowingly invoked Elizabethan English—*Shakespearean* English, with its poetic rhythms and antediluvian verb formations, often ending in "-th." Long a devotee of Shakespeare's plays and sonnets, Lincoln gravitated naturally to the melodic formations of the King James Bible as he struggled to come to terms with the butcher's bill he had asked the country to pay.

But Lincoln remained, as always, an iconoclast. Whereas evangelical leaders increasingly asserted that the Union was on God's side, and God was on the Union's side, Lincoln remained unsure. Unlike most evangelical Northerners, he did not believe in a personal God. Rather, he perceived God as a distant and unknowable force, his will mostly indiscernible to men and women. The war, Lincoln told Americans, was in some fashion divine retribution for the sin of slavery. Whether God willed that the North should win that war was another matter, and one of which he could not be certain.

As the fighting bore on, Lincoln came to view himself as God's "instrument" on earth, meant to prosecute total war against the South until one side or the other lost. He reverted, ironically and profoundly, to the fatalism of his father's religion—to a belief that the scope for human agency was limited. He had a role to play, one that had been divinely predetermined and from which he was powerless to break free. But he was genuinely unsure whether his was God's favored side.

WHAT FOLLOWS IS THE STORY OF ABRAHAM LINCOLN'S RELIGIOUS TRANS-formation, set against the backdrop of a nation's spiritual awakening and transformation. Religion helped millions of Northerners interpret the carnage and political upheaval of the 1850s and 1860s. It gave them a way to understand the role that they would play in events as momentous and historic as the biblical tales of the Old Testament, and the language and framework to perceive the national tragedy they endured.

Rather than trace the war's battles and personalities, I'm interested in the social impact of the war on Northerners' spiritual worldview, and the impact of that worldview on the war effort itself. This is not a comprehensive biography of Lincoln or a broad account of the Civil War. Instead, it is the story of how religion and, more specifically, the rise of evangelical Protestantism, influenced the familiar political, economic, and military narrative. Living as we do in a highly polarized country, some readers may find it unintuitive that most Americans in the mid-nineteenth century often viewed secular events through a spiritual lens. Other readers may be startled at how much American Christianity itself was shaped and transformed by secular developments. The truth is that evangelical Protestantism was a dynamic and constantly evolving faith from the time of its inception until long after the war. Religion— specifically evangelical Christianity—played an instrumental role on the battlefield, on the home front, and inside the corridors of government. The war, in turn, transformed Protestantism.

This story does not diminish the profound importance of religion to the growing number of Jewish and Catholic Americans, congregants of non-evangelical and nonconforming Christian churches, and members of other spiritual movements. The same social, economic, and political forces that interacted with evangelical Protestantism also influenced, and were influenced by, non-evangelical religion. But the vast majority of Americans in the era of the Civil War were Christians, and among Christians, evangelicalism was the predominant spiritual and intellectual framework.

Abraham Lincoln's own spiritual journey was distinct from that of most Americans, but he understood better than most the organizing and galvanizing power of evangelical Christianity. His faith, and his appeal to the faith of others, in no small way determined the outcome of the war.

PART
I

CHAPTER 1

UNDISTINGUISHED FAMILIES

In early 1860, John Locke Scripps, publisher of the *Chicago Tribune*, asked candidate Abraham Lincoln to furnish details of his ancestry and childhood. The newspaperman was preparing a brief campaign biography for the state's favorite son and dark horse presidential aspirant but realized that he knew almost nothing of his background. "Why Scripps," Lincoln replied, "it is a great piece of folly to attempt to make anything out of my early life. It can all be condensed into a single sentence, and that sentence you will find in Gray's Elegy: 'The short and simple annals of the poor.' That's my life, and that's all you or any one else can make of it." Other politicians might genuinely have valued their humble origin story and made good use of it, as indeed Republicans sought to do at the Illinois nominating convention later that year, when Lincoln's cousin, John Hanks, strode up the center aisle to boisterous cheers, hauling two wooden rails that he and his famous kinsman purportedly had cut from raw timber three decades earlier. But Abraham Lincoln was inflexibly tight-lipped about his childhood. "There is not much of it," he said to rebuff another inquiry, "for the reason, I suppose, that there is not much of me."

"My parents were both born in Virginia of undistinguished families," he would explain, "second families, I should say." His father, Thomas, had been born to a reasonably prosperous household but was reduced to "a wandering laboring boy" at age eight when, while he was planting corn in the field with his brothers, Indian assailants sneaked up on the group and killed their father. Mordechai, the oldest son, who was fifteen at the time, picked up a rifle and shot one of the attackers dead, just before he could approach Thomas, who had sprinted to his father's side and knelt by his body. Mordechai would go on to inherit his father's land and become a wealthy farmer and horse breeder in Kentucky, while Thomas, in the words of his son, the sixteenth president, led the narrow and itinerant life of a small dirt farmer who "grew up literally without an education" and "never did more in the way of writing than to bunglingly sign his own name." "Uncle Mord," Lincoln is said to have remarked in jest, "had run off with all the talents of the family." Of his mother, the only point he thought worthy of mention was that her name was Nancy Hanks, and that she died in the autumn of 1818, when he was nine years old. His father remarried the next year.

As an adult, Lincoln seldom spoke of his parents—or of his older brother, who had died in infancy, or of his sister, Sarah, with whom he had shared a very close relationship, and whose death during childbirth in 1828 left the future president profoundly bereaved. While riding in a coach in the 1850s with his law partner, en route to try a court case, he shared his understanding that his mother had been born out of wedlock, "the illegitimate daughter of [his grandmother] Lucy Hanks and a well-bred Virginia farmer or planter." Whether Lincoln's suspicion was true has eluded historians since, but if Herndon is to be trusted as a credible source, Lincoln appears sincerely to have believed it and posited that the offspring of such unions were "oftentimes sturdier and brighter than those born in lawful wedlock." "God bless my angel mother," Lincoln ostensibly said on another occasion. "All that I am or ever hope to be I owe to her." That now-famous line, frequently invoked as an expression of a son's love for his mother, was in fact Lincoln's way of proposing that he owed his natural gifts and drive to his real grandfather—that unknown Virginia planter—but certainly not to Tom Lincoln, the untaught farmer, or even to his "angel mother" (a term meant to distinguish her from his stepmother, who was very much still alive), who had left him with seemingly little but a secret pedigree.

MUCH OF LINCOLN'S SILENCE ABOUT HIS YOUTH AND UPBRINGING SPRANG from a decades-long, conscious effort to break free not only from his parents but also from the world they inhabited—a world of hardscrabble subsistence farming, extended kinship networks, constrained ambition, and strong Calvinist faith that held people largely powerless to change their lot in this life or the next. Like many young men of his generation, Lincoln ardently embraced an emerging economy in which, courtesy of roads, canals, and, later, railroads, people enjoyed access to faraway markets. They now had an opportunity to produce and sell agricultural surplus for profit, rather than for subsistence. The new market economy also gave rise to artisans and urban professionals. It encouraged greater individualism, personal agency, and self-improvement, qualities that Lincoln found decidedly lacking in his family. Straddling two eras in American history, Thomas and Abraham Lincoln had trouble understanding each other from the earliest days of their relationship.

To be sure, Tom was a man who experienced more than his share of bad luck—or, by the uncharitable assessment of one of his in-laws, made his own bad luck. He was "very careless about his business, a poor Manager, at time[s] accumulated considerable property which he always managed to make way with about as fast as he made it, & was what is generally called an unlucky Man in business." Having bought three successive farms in Kentucky, but failing to secure a clear title to any of them—a fault that lay as much with the state's tangled patchwork of surveys and property laws as with Tom himself—Lincoln's father moved the family across the Ohio River in 1816 to land nestled by Little Pigeon Creek in Spencer County, Indiana. The heavily wooded tract was thick with trees and rocks and filled with dangerous animals that terrified young Abe. He captured that raw fear in a poem some thirty years later:

When first my father settled here,
'Twas then the frontier line.
The panther's scream, filled the night with fear
And bears preyed on the swine.

The woods needed to be cleared, first to make way for the construction of the family's cabin, and then for planting. Abe had an ax "put into his hands" at an early age, he later wrote in the third person, "and from that till within his twentythird year, he was almost constantly handling that most useful instrument—less, of course, in plowing and harvesting seasons." The work was arduous, and the material circumstances in which the family labored were primitive. That winter, the ground froze through, preventing Thomas from pulling enough clay and grass to plug the gaps between the logs in the family's new cabin, exposing the Lincolns—Tom and Nancy, Sarah and Abe—to bitter cold at night. Until enough area was cleared for cultivation, they relied on what they could kill for food.

At age eight, Abe picked up a rifle and shot a wild turkey dead, but he did not have the stomach for hunting and "ha[d] never since pulled a trigger on any larger game."

Matters seemed to take a better turn when Nancy's aunt and uncle, Elizabeth and Thomas Sparrow, purchased a nearby tract of land and erected their own homestead, bringing with them Nancy's cousin, eighteen-year-old Dennis Hanks. But the Little Pigeon community was soon ravaged by a milk sickness epidemic: cows left to roam in the woods ate poisonous white snakeroot plants and passed their deadly toxin to humans through their milk. Thomas and Elizabeth Sparrow were the first to be stricken. Tom Lincoln built coarse wooden coffins from timber that he had sawed himself. Nancy Hanks was next. She succumbed after several days of high fever, nausea, and stomach distress. Dennis Hanks would remember how "she knew she was going to die & Called up the Children to her dying side and told them to be good & kind to their father—to one an other—and to the world."

Abe left no record of his loss or grief, though Dennis Hanks, who moved in with the family after the Sparrows' deaths, remembered that Sarah, aged twelve and now responsible for managing the small household, would cradle herself by the fire and cry. The following year, recognizing the impossibility of raising his children alone while also providing for the family, Thomas Lincoln made a trip to Kentucky, where he courted and married Sarah Bush Johnston, a widow whom he had known in earlier years. When she returned to Indiana with her new husband—as well as with her children, Elizabeth, John D., and Matilda, who ranged from eight to thirteen years old—Sarah Johnston found Abe and his sister "ragged & dirty," living in squalor. She promptly "Soaped—rubbed and washed the Children Clean so that they looked pretty neat," Dennis Hanks wrote, "sewed and mended their Clothes," and compelled her

—

7

new husband and the boys, Abe and John D., to build a proper wood floor, roof, and door for the cabin, which she then furnished with belongings she had brought with her from Kentucky: real bedding, a bureau, table and chairs, and cutlery. In an era when many children lost a parent early in life—even by the early twentieth century, over 35 percent of all American families still experienced the death of a parent when their children were still minors—it was no foregone conclusion that stepparents and stepchildren would take to each other. But Abe and Sarah Johnston developed a quick and easy affection. "His mind & mine—what little I had seemed to run together—move in the same direction," she told Herndon, shortly after Lincoln's assassination. "He was dutiful to me always—he loved me truly I think."

In Indiana, the Lincolns lived much like their neighbors, cultivating only a small portion of their land to grow corn and vegetables and raise hogs and cattle, leaving the rest fallow and overgrown. A cousin who lived for a time in the extended household later remarked that Thomas "was like the other people in that country. None of them worked to get ahead. There wasn't no market for nothing else unless you took it across two or three states." Though he attempted on several occasions to take pork and corn by flatboat to New Orleans, in the absence of roads and canals, and with large parts of the Ohio and Mississippi Rivers largely unnavigable, the cost of transportation all but erased the profit margin. Without a market for goods, and in the absence of a developed cash economy, most families did what was logical, producing enough for home consumption and little more, perhaps selling a small surplus to neighbors, bartering for goods and services, manufacturing clothing and other necessities at home, and purchasing what few items they could not produce themselves—sugar and other dry goods, glass for windows—from a nearby country store. Thomas was a trained, if rudimentary, carpenter and hired himself out in the cold months to build shelves, tables, doors, and window casings for his neighbors. But on the edge of the Indiana frontier, brute reality afforded little reward for greater industry and ambition. Neither did it offer much scope for individual success. Survival demanded a collective outlook. Like other families, the Lincolns relied on a growing kinship network of cousins and in-laws who established small, adjoining homesteads and built an informal system of cooperative farming, home production, and bartering.

Like many of their neighbors, Thomas and Sarah were "Hard Shell" (known also as antimission or Separate) Baptists. In Kentucky, they had belonged to the Little Mount Separate Baptist Church. In Indiana, they waited three years to join the independent Little Pigeon Creek Church, relenting only when the congregation aligned itself with the Separates. Thomas ultimately helped construct its new building. Strongest in Virginia and Kentucky, and in areas, like Southern Indiana, with its heavy contingent of Kentucky-born settlers, Hard Shell Baptists resisted the perfectionist strain that many churches were slowly adopting, as well as the rising Methodist movement's faith in free will and universal salvation. They hewed instead to the Westminster Confession, which affirmed the Calvinist doctrine of predestination and election—the belief that only a small number of people were born as God's elect, chosen for salvation, while the greater lot of humanity was not. Only God's will determined one's eternal fate; neither good works nor an acceptance of Christ as savior could alter that reality. Hard Shell Baptists bitterly rejected the idea, in the words of the Delaware River Baptist Association, that "human measures" were legitimate "criterions by which to decide Christian character and standing in the sight of God." Ultimately, declared another group of antimission Christians, "regeneration . . . is exclusively the work of the Holy Ghost performed by His divine power at His own sovereign pleasure according to the provisions of the everlasting covenant." At Thomas and Sarah Lincoln's own Little Pigeon Creek Church, congregants proudly believed "in Election by grace given us in Christ Jesus. Before the world began & God Cawls, generates and sanctifies all who are made meat for Glory by his special grace."

Theirs was in many ways a profoundly democratic theology. The Hard Shells distrusted seminary-trained theologians and believed that God could speak through ordinary laypeople at least as well as through college-educated elites. They had little use for ecclesiastical authority. They did not hire salaried ministers. They strongly rejected frills of religious ceremony that could not directly trace back to Paul's teachings. In Maryland, antimissionists rejected Sunday schools—a favorite project of evangelical reformers—for their misplaced faith in the potential of "conversion, or regeneration, if produced by impressions made upon the natural mind by means of religious sentiments instilled into it." They scorned seminaries and other religious educational institutions for elevating "the revelation of God on a footing with mathematics, philosophy, law," and other "human sciences." In politics, many Hard Shells, including, it seems, Thomas Lincoln, gravitated to Andrew Jackson's populist political movement by the 1820s. Their critics, like one Rhode Island missionary who tried but failed to find converts to the evangelical cause, looked down their noses at the "old travelers" of the inland South who were intimidated by "new men and new measures" and "disturbed at being left behind." They were, by the estimation of their evangelical critics, "thick-skinned Antinomians"—successors to the seventeenth-century Puritans of New England, who held no brief for the concepts of free will or human agency in securing eternal election. Above all, they deplored social reformers who, with Bible in hand, extolled against this or that sin. The outspoken Hard Shell John Taylor of Kentucky derided their "Female Societies, Cent Societies, Mite Societies, Children Societies, and even Negro Societies," each urging a favored road to perfectionism and salvation, be it temperance, anti-gambling laws, or even abolition. Given this theological stance, it is little surprise evangelical missionaries who preached salvation through individual choice found their message falling on deaf ears among the citizens of Little Pigeon Creek and places like it. Theirs was not a dour faith. If anything, Hard Shells resented the incessant moralizing of evangelical missionaries—their strict Sabbatarianism, advocacy of temperance, and other efforts to instill Christian (and capitalist) discipline among the general population. But in a protomarket environment where most people farmed for subsistence and enjoyed little control over their fortune, being at the mercy of the weather, sickness and disease, and crop failure, a personal theology that held individuals powerless to influence their fate made a great deal of sense.

How deeply Lincoln absorbed his parents' hyper-Calvinist theology is unknown. Certainly he would have attended sermons and church meetings with his parents, and from one of the first books he absorbed, *The Kentucky Preceptor*—a handbook on Christian morality and oration— he learned that "every occurrence in the universe is *Providential* . . . to select individual facts, as more directed by the hand of Providence than others, because we think we see a particular good purpose answered by them, is an infallible inlet to error and superstition." However far he traveled from organized Christianity, that idea seemed to stick with him until his death.

✦

LINCOLN WOULD LATER DISMISS PIGEON CREEK AS "A WILD REGION. . . .
There were some schools, so called," but they conferred little knowledge "beyond 'readin, writin, and cipherin,' to the Rule of Three. If a
straggler supposed to understand latin, happened to so-journ into the
neighborhood, he was looked upon as a wizzard. There was absolutely
nothing to excite ambition for education." Yet for a few years, at least,
he appeared genuinely to enjoy living in a boisterous, blended household
with stepsiblings, a stepmother who cared for him and encouraged—
perhaps even ignited—his passion for books, and playmates from nearby
homesteads, some of them cousins or in-laws who followed Thomas
into Indiana. Returning to the area in 1846, the year of his election to
Congress, Lincoln took time to scribble out a poem in which he acknowledged to himself, if to no one else, his conflicted feelings about his
upbringing:

> My childhood-home I see again,
> And gladden with the view;
> And still as mem'ries crowd my brain,
> There's sadness in it too. . . .
> . . . .
> Now twenty years have passed away,
> Since here I bid farewell
> To woods, and fields, and scenes of play
> And school-mates loved so well.
> Where many were, how few remain
> Of old familiar things!
> But seeing these to mind again

The lost and absent brings.
The friends I left that parting day—
How changed, as time has sped!

By his teenage years, though, Lincoln began to chafe against his father's limited ambition and imagination. As Abe discovered a passion for reading that far outstripped what little interest he took in farming— he "was not Energetic Except in one thing, he was active & persistent in learning, read Everything he Could," his stepsister Matilda observed— he found himself in frequent conflict with Thomas, who expected his son to pull his weight in chopping, planting, harvesting, and tending to the land. John Hanks, who lived with the family in Indiana for several years and worked with Thomas on the farm, remembered that when he and Abe returned "to the house from work," Abe "would go to the Cupboard—Snatch a piece of Corn bread—take down a book—Sit down on a chair—Cock his legs up high as his head and read. Abrm read Constantly when he had an opportunity." Sarah Bush Johnston later told Herndon that her husband, who could "read a little & could scarcely write his name," supported his son's efforts to attend school and to attain literacy. "As a usual thing Mr. Lincoln never made Abe quit reading if he could avoid it." But John B. Helm, who had known the family in Kentucky, where Abraham and his sister spent several months at a makeshift ABC school—known also as "blab" schools, where students learned the basics of reading by rote recitation of texts—disagreed, remembering that Thomas, "being a day laborer and without education," regarded "time spent in school as doubly wasted." It is possible that Sarah Bush Johnston changed her husband's mind on the matter, or that she later glossed over the tensions within her family, although even she would acknowledge that Abe, though a "good boy," "didn't like physical labor—was diligent for Knowledge." By Dennis Hanks's telling, Abe constantly had his head in a book—a spelling primer, *Robinson Crusoe*, Parson Weems's *Life of Washington*, *Aesop's Fables*, *Pilgrim's Progress*. He was a "constant and I may Say Stubborn reader," so much so that Thomas would have "sometimes to slash him for neglecting his work by reading. Mr. Lincoln—A's father—often said I had to pull the old sow up to the trough—when speaking of Abe's reading & how he got to it, then now he had to pull her away."

There were other sources of conflict too. Abe was a precocious teen-ager, increasingly too big for his britches, intellectually confident bordering on arrogant, and sometimes "a little rude," Dennis remembered. "When strangers would ride up along & up to his fathers fence Abe always, through pride & to tease his father, would be sure to ask the stranger the first question, for which his father would sometimes knock him a rod." Cousin Sophie Hanks reported the same pattern of impudence and punishment, noting that Thomas would normally wait until guests left the premises before administering a beating, as he did on one occasion when Abe mocked a barefoot, impoverished neighbor. He would "very often correct his father in talking when [Thomas] was telling how anything happened," usually earning him a slap across the face. Most of these accounts were handed down years after the fact and, in some cases, secondhand, but they tell a consistent enough story. When whipped by his father, according to Dennis, Abe would retreat into stoic resistance—"never bawled but dropt a kind of silent unwelcome tear, as evidence of his sensations—or other feelings." Even on the morning of the family's departure for their new home in Illinois, when Abe, then twenty-one years old, arrived late for the journey, an in-law watched with dread as Thomas—visibly angered by the delay—approached his son with an ox whip in hand. "Watch old Tom flail him," the in-law purportedly muttered under his breath, by then familiar with the plot-line. Instead, Tom quietly handed his son the whip and instructed him to lead the trail of carriages.

Thomas would regularly hire his son out for manual labor, as was custom in the local cooperative economy and his legal right until Abraham came of age. Though endowed with considerable strength and athleticism, the son resented life as a hired hand, with wages directed to his father. Cousins and neighbors would later describe him as "awful lazy," "always reading & thinking" or at the very least apt to "laugh and talk and crack jokes & tell stories all the time" when he was otherwise intended to be "farming, grubbing, hoeing, making fences." These memories were an overstatement. Lincoln was good and diligent at the work, if wont to grouse about it and eager to escape it. As he told one family friend, his "father taught him to work but never learned him to love it."

When a neighbor to whom he was regularly lent out compelled Abe to work three full days at hard labor to compensate for minor damage to a book he had borrowed, and then docked his wages and forced him to work extra days when Abe was just a few minutes late in arriving each morning, the boy allegedly retaliated with a series of songs, doggerel, and short-form prose mocking the neighbor's miserliness and large nose. On another occasion, after cutting cords of wood, Abe expected to be paid in cash but was disappointed to find that his compensation came in the form of store credit.

Years later, as his deep moral antipathy toward slavery came into focus, Lincoln wrote to a friend, "Through life I have been in no bondage, either real or immaginary from the thraldom of which I so much desired to be free." He may very well have had this experience in mind.

Just as Abe gradually came to reject a life of manual labor, he appears also to have rejected his family's religious worldview. His sister, Sarah, was baptized and became a full member of Little Pigeon Creek Church at age nineteen, but "Abe had no particular religion—didn't think of that question at that time, if he ever did," his stepmother later told Herndon. "He never talked about it." Seeking to counter the tendency to apotheosize Lincoln in the months following his death, she conceded that he "read the Bible some, though not as much as said; he preferred more congenial books." He did, however, enjoy mimicking, even satirizing, the Hard Shell preachers whom he encountered at his parents' church. His stepsister Matilda remembered that when Thomas and Sarah Bush Johnston traveled the mile and a half to services and left the children behind, Abe, then a teenager, "would take down the bible, read a verse—give out a hymn." When he attended church, he would return home, gather the other children, mount a tree stump, and repeat with dramatic flourish the entirety of the sermon—doing it "well and accurately," according to Dennis—much as he committed to memory important speeches and orations that he read in the few books and newspapers to which he enjoyed access. Predictably, Thomas disapproved of these displays, perhaps considering them blasphemous, or just further evidence of his son's indolence. He would "make him quit [and] send him to work," Matilda recalled.

Cousin Sophie Hanks would later say that "Abe always had a natural idea that he was going to be something." So it is little surprise that his parents' strict, predestinarian Baptism—a theology that reflected and reinforced the economic and social environment in which they lived— held little interest for Lincoln. He was not satisfied with what meager life God had chosen for him. While his cousin's memory was surely clouded by his later rise to prominence, the testimony of other cousins and stepsiblings confirm that Tom Lincoln's son strove from an early age to break free of his parents' world. His was not an unfamiliar story. Families in this period frequently experienced clashes between fathers rooted in the old ways of subsistence farming, home economy, and extended kinship networks, and sons attracted by the entrepreneurial opportunities and promise of individual autonomy that a capitalist society offered. Often these disagreements manifested themselves through arguments about education. One young man—typical of his age, and nearly echoing Lincoln—lamented that his "education had been sadly neglected. [He] could hardly read or write intelligibly." Historian Joyce Appleby surmised that by "rendering their fathers as failures," young people like Abraham Lincoln were "burning their bridges to a past—a past, moreover, that had prized continuity."

Other relatives and neighbors remembered Thomas Lincoln more charitably. He was a strong and sturdy character. Sociable, fond of telling stories and jokes, devoted to his community—"a good quiet citizen, moral habits . . . sound judgement," "lively and cheerful"—he likely bequeathed more of his good qualities to his son than Abe was ever willing to admit. Abe's disdain notwithstanding, Tom was as hard a worker as most in the community ("not a lazy man," an in-law remembered, if not especially lucky). His fortunes certainly declined over the years. In Kentucky he had owned 826.5 acres at one point, then 160 acres in Indiana, and 80 acres in Illinois. But that was true of many of his fellow frontiersmen. He was, by the estimation of a neighbor and in-law, a "good citizen and a worthy intelligent farmer and a devout Christian of the Baptist order." When Abe lamented that Uncle Mordechai had "run off with all the talents of the family," he failed to remember that, courtesy of Kentucky's primogeniture laws, Mordechai had also run off with all of the family's *land*, leaving Tom to scratch out a living and oversee decades of chain migration that drew an extended community of friends and kin into what was in all reality as successful a life as most people of his generation knew.

Shortly after helping his family move to Illinois in 1830, Abraham Lincoln burned his bridges and scarcely looked back. He rarely saw his parents or relatives after staking out on his own. Neither Thomas nor Sarah would ever meet Abe's wife or children or visit his home in Springfield. When asked whether "Abe loved his farther Very well or Not" or "Card for his Relations," Dennis replied that "when he was with us he Seemed to think a great Deal of us but I thought Sum times it was hipocritical But I am Not Shore." It seemed to rankle Abe that his father formed a close and lasting bond with John D. Johnston, his stepbrother. In 1848, while completing his one term in Congress, Lincoln replied to letters from Thomas and John D. (his stepbrother penned Thomas's note by his own hand). The elder Lincoln asked his son for twenty dollars to settle a lien against his farm. Abe "cheerfully" sent the money but lectured his father condescendingly, finding it "singular that you should have forgotten a judgment against you" and suggesting that "before you pay it, it would be well to be sure you have not paid it; or, at least, that you can not prove you have paid it."

To his stepbrother's request for eighty dollars, he was less generous. "You are not *lazy*, and still you *are* an *idler*," he scolded John D. "I doubt whether since I saw you, you have done a good whole day's work in any one day. You do not very much dislike to work; and still you do not work much, merely because it does not seem to you that you could get much for it." Abe advised John D., who had remained Thomas's loyal partner in planting and harvesting through the seasons, to hire himself out and pay off his debts. "You say if I furnish you the money you will deed me the land, and, if you dont pay the money back, you will deliver possession. Nonsense! If you cant now live *with* the land, how will you then live without it? You have always been [kind] to me, and I do not now mean to be unkind to you. On the contrary, if you will but follow my advice, you will find it worth more than eight times eighty dollars to you."

According to Dennis Hanks, Johnston "thought that Abe did not Do a Nuff for the old people [and] they Be Cum Enemies for a while on this ground." (Hanks also believed that Lincoln "Dun more for John than he deserved.") Whatever the case, Lincoln so thoroughly distanced himself from his family that even his friends knew little of his upbringing. A year after Lincoln's assassination, Leonard Swett, one of Lincoln's closest political and legal associates and a chief architect of his nomination in 1860, fell into possession of both letters. "I never knew Mr. Lincoln had a brother," he admitted to Herndon. "It is perhaps a little singular, but I never heard him speak of any relative, except as connected with his boy history."

Their differences notwithstanding, when Thomas fell gravely ill the following year, John D. wrote urgently to his stepbrother. The elder Lincoln "Craves to See you all the time & he wonts you to Come if you ar able to get hure," he told Abe, adding that he was Thomas's "only child that is of his own flush & blood." Augustus Chapman, an in-law, also implored Lincoln to make haste and visit. Thomas was "very anxious" to see his son and meet his grandchildren before he died. "I am told that His Cries for you for the last few days are truly Heart-Rendering," Chapman continued. The family was prepared to "do all we can to render your stay agreeable." Abe did in fact make way to his parents' farm in Coles County—alone, and not with his wife or sons in tow—before receiving word that his father had recovered from his illness. What transpired during their visit is lost to history.

In late 1850, Johnston wrote twice to inform his stepbrother that Thomas was once again seriously ill. Abe returned neither letter, prompting Dennis's daughter Harriet, who had lodged with the Lincolns for a time in Springfield, to contact him of her own accord. Abe finally responded. "I received both your [letters, and] although I have not answered them, it is no[t because] I have forgotten them, or been uninterested about them," Lincoln told John D., "but because it appeared to me I could write nothing which could do any good." Lincoln had no "desire that neither Father or Mother shall be in want of any comfort either in health or sickness while they live; and I feel sure you have not failed to use my name, if necessary, to procure a doctor." But as business concerns tied him to Springfield, and his wife, Mary, was ill, a visit was out of the question. "Say to him that if we could meet now, it is doubtful whether it would not be more painful than pleasant," Lincoln continued, "but that if it be his lot to go now, he will soon have a joyous [meeting] with many loved ones gone before; and where [the rest] of us, through the help of God, hope ere-long [to join] them."

Thomas passed away within the week.

The physical distance between Springfield, where Abe lived, and Coles County, where his parents continued to farm, was scarcely more than one hundred miles. Lincoln traveled that distance regularly as a circuit lawyer. But he had worked for two decades to shake free of Thomas's world. He told John D. that he hoped his father would, in his final days, "call upon, and confide in, our great, and good, and merciful Maker; who will not turn away from him in any extremity. He notes the fall of a sparrow, and numbers the hairs of our heads; and He will not forget the dying man, who puts his trust in Him." Those were probably the words of a son telling his religious family what he wanted to hear. There is nothing to suggest Abe actually believed what he wrote. His convictions lay with "reason, cold, calculating, unimpassioned reason," he intoned several years after leaving the family homestead.

And still, throughout his life, Abraham Lincoln never did quite shake the fatalism of his parents' religion.

CHAPTER 2

EVERY SOUL IS FREE

In rejecting his parents' faith, Abraham Lincoln swam against the currents. America in the first half of the nineteenth century was a deeply Christian and predominantly evangelical nation. Mason Locke Weems (remembered today as Parson Weems), an itinerant Bible salesmen and author whose hagiographies of George Washington and other leading figures fused public enthusiasm for democratic politics and religious revivalism, captured the popular spirit when he declared it "the very season and age of the Bible. Bible Dictionaries, Bible tales, Bible stories—Bibles plain or paraphrased, Carey's Bibles, Collin's Bibles, Clarke's Bibles, Kimptor's Bibles, no matter what or whose, all, all will go down—so wide is the crater of public appetite at this time. God be thanked for it." That Americans bought Bibles in bulk was merely one gauge of the country's spiritual wakening, a trend that moved in parallel with the growth of democratic institutions and a national market economy. By the mid-nineteenth century, the United States was unique in its enthusiasm

---

for liberal capitalism, a boisterous representative democracy, and millennial fervor. One could not be disentangled from the others.

It had not always been so. Notwithstanding a brief moment of Puritan zeal in New England from the 1630s through the 1660s, and early attempts to plant the Church of England in the Tidewater region, religious decline was a marked feature of early eighteenth-century colonial life. By the late 1690s, fewer than 15 percent of adults in many New England towns claimed church membership; in Virginia, where the Church of England represented the predominant faith, some 85 percent of children were unbaptized. Most colonies had an established church, but the establishment excited little passion. An Anglican minister in Maryland may have overstated the point when he complained that in his colony "the Lord's day is profaned, religion is despised, and all notorious vices committed . . . it is become a Sodom of uncleanliness and a pest house of iniquity." But in the main, religious observance, even in parts of North America that had been founded in furtherance of a spiritual mission, was on the wane in colonial America.

Spiritual torpor gave way in the decades preceding the American Revolution to a new spirit of religiosity, partly owing to a surge of non-English immigrants who imported an active and diverse faith to the New World. Before 1690 roughly 90 percent of all congregations in the colonies were either Congregationalist (Puritan churches primarily in New England and the middle colonies) or Anglican (Church of England, primarily in the southern Tidewater region). By the eve of the Revolution, a wave of settlement from France, Scotland, Ireland, and Germany had transformed the religious landscape of British North America. Presbyterians from Scotland. Baptists and Quakers from both England and Wales. German Lutherans, German Reformed, Mennonites, Moravians, and Bavarian Catholics. English Methodists. French Huguenots. Sephardic Jews. They built churches and synagogues and greatly changed the nation's spiritual demography, such that by the time of the Revolution, no one denomination accounted for more than 20 percent of the population.

Even as newcomers imported religious enthusiasm to the colonies, a wave of revivals, later termed the First Great Awakening, attracted colonial subjects, old and new alike, who were living in a time of rapid population growth and movement, economic expansion, and political instability. George Whitefield, an Anglican minister from England who pioneered the revivalist style, conducted seven tours of the North American colonies, drawing large crowds. Where most Protestant ministers read their sermons in monotone from a written page, Whitefield committed his homilies to memory and delivered them with flair—arms gesticulating, tone rising and falling for effect. Jonathan Edwards, a Congregationalist minister from Massachusetts and perhaps the best known of the revivalists, held listeners rapt as he described in vivid prose the eternal punishment that awaited sinners—who, given his Calvinist moorings, greatly outnumbered those whose souls God would save. "Your wickedness makes you as it were heavy as lead," he thundered in his sermon "Sinners in the Hands of an Angry God," "and to trend downwards with great weight and pressure towards hell: and if God should let you go, you would immediately sink and descend into the bottomless gulf." Notably, the Great Awakening was as ecumenical as it was short-lived. It animated the spirit of Calvinists like Edwards, but also Anglicans, Dutch Reformed, Baptists, and Methodists—the latter, a rising movement within the Church of England that sharply rejected predestinarian doctrine. By the eve of the Revolution, the awakening had run its course.

As dramatic as the mid-eighteenth-century revivals were, they were a mere precursor to the Second Great Awakening, which convulsed the new republic between the 1790s and the 1830s. Especially resonant among the nation's largest Protestant denominations—Methodists, Baptists, and Disciples of Christ—as well as smaller movements, including Presbyterians, Congregationalists, and Evangelical Lutherans, the awakening was longer lasting and distinctly evangelical in nature. By numbers alone, it wrought unprecedented religious growth. In the mid-eighteenth century, some 1,800 clergymen attended to the spiritual needs of colonists. By 1845 the clerical profession numbered 40,000, cutting the ratio of clergy to layman from one per 1,500 to one per 500. By the mid-nineteenth century, roughly 40 percent of all white Americans belonged to a church, with many others—including Abraham Lincoln, after his marriage to Mary Todd—attending less frequently.

The spark that lit the tinder came in 1797, when James McGready, a Presbyterian minister in south-central Kentucky, gathered several dozen neighbors outdoors over four days. His preaching resulted in emotional rites of repentance and conversion—a forerunner to what followed four years later at Cane Ridge, Kentucky, just north of Lexington, where upwards of twenty-five thousand people gathered for what was then the largest and most affecting religious revival in the United States. Immersed in days of prayer and sermonizing, attendees wept openly and broke into spontaneous dance and convulsions. Some even fell prostrate and barked like dogs, so great was the spirit that overcame them. Peter Cartwright, a Methodist circuit rider who attended a follow-on revival nearby and whose political career would intersect with Lincoln's, described some participants as "being under deep convictions; their heart swells, their nerves relax, and in an instant they become motionless and speechless. . . . It comes upon others like an electric shock, as if felt in the great arteries of the arms or thighs. The body relaxes and falls motionless; the hands and feet become cold, and yet the pulse is as formerly. . . . They are all averse to any medical application. . . . They continue in that state from one hour to twenty-four."

The awakening was not confined to the old southwest. Methodists, who preached a radically Arminian strain of Christianity, inviting ordinary people to choose redemption—to repent for their sins, form a personal relationship with Christ, and lead a godly life that would secure their salvation—converted people in every part of the country. A minority influence in the colonies before the Revolution, the Methodist Episcopal Church—which began as the Wesleyan movement within the Church of England but became independent of the Anglican Church in 1784—claimed roughly 1.74 million members in the United States by the eve of the Civil War, more than double the denomination's strength just twenty years earlier. Under the stewardship of Francis Asbury, an English-born evangelist who devised an elaborate system to recruit and assign circuit riders, who in turn staged dramatic camp meetings ("the battle ax and weapon of war," Asbury declared, designed to "break down walls of wickedness, part of hell, superstition, [and] false doctrine"), an army of itinerant preachers vastly expanded the church's membership. Critics deplored what they saw as the crude and emotive appeal of Methodist proselytizing—the "brutal attempts to excite passions," the overwrought response of converts, whose "fainting, shouting, yelling, crying, sobbing, and grieving" seemed a wholly new feature of religious expression. But to hundreds of thousands of believers, the church—with its promise of sanctification, deliverance, and a personal relationship with Christ—proved a resonant source of faith, stability, and community in a changing world.

Not far behind the Methodists in numbers, regular Baptists, who had also been a minority denomination in the colonial era, claimed over one million members by the start of the Civil War. Supplemented by Free-will Baptists, who wholly rejected predestinarian doctrine, as well as antimission Baptists, the broader movement emerged as the second-largest evangelical community in the United States. Though they shared Calvinist origins with their Congregationalist and Presbyterian brethren, most regular Baptists also came to embrace the doctrinal belief that humans could determine their own spiritual outcomes, reflecting a broader gravitational pull toward "Arminianized Calvinism." Well behind the Methodists and Baptists in numbers, but still a strong presence, were Presbyterians and Congregationalists—the progenitors of New England's original Christian communities—and Episcopalians, who once held favored status as the established church throughout much of British North America. Alongside new movements like the Disciples of Christ, whose adherents observed a back-to-basics approach to Bible reading and worship, the ascendant evangelical churches represented a break with the nation's colonial past—in the way they organized their congregations, the theology they preached, the relationship they forged between laity and clergy, and the role they envisioned for faith communities beyond the church walls.

All told, by 1855 approximately four million Americans, out of a total population of between twenty-three million (1850 census) and thirty-two million (1860 census), belonged to Protestant denominations, the vast majority of whom identified as evangelicals. These numbers, though staggering, vastly undercounted the number of people who regularly attended church. In most denominations, congregants were required to make public attestations of their Christian faith to attain full membership. Many people, for varying reasons, were not prepared to do so. By some estimations, for every member of an evangelical church, there were between four and five "hearers"—people who attended services frequently or infrequently, but who were not in full communion. Many Americans also identified with non-evangelical or even non-Christian denominations and movements ranging from Episcopalians and Catholics to Mormons, Lutherans, and Jews. But if correct, these approximations suggest that well over half of Americans embraced evangelical Christianity to some degree of commitment and intensity. James Dixon, a Methodist from England, captured the nuance well when he observed that "Christianity pervades the United States in vigorous action. This is seen in the numbers attending public worship, in the extent of church communion, in the observance of the sacraments of the Church, in the respect paid to the Sabbath, in the number and variety of religious and charitable institutions." Christianity, he maintained, "touches and influences the entire social and political state. It is not meant that every individual is a pious Christian, but that the spirit of the evangelical system is in sufficient power to give to religious opinion and sentiment the complete ascendant in society."

Though they hotly contested matters of theology and splintered even within their own denominations (New School versus Old School Presbyterians; antimission, Freewill, and Regular Baptists), most converts to evangelical Protestantism shared a foundational set of beliefs: faith in a Trinitarian God; acceptance that humans were born depraved, sinful, and condemned; and certainty that through repentance and faith, people could achieve regeneration and find salvation in the moment of final judgment. The last point was new and distinctive. Robert Baird, a Presbyterian minister from New Jersey, noted that despite their doctrinal differences, most evangelical Christians "ought to be viewed as branches of one great body" that "believe there is such a thing as being 'born again.' And very few, indeed, admit the doctrine that a man who is not 'converted,' that is, 'renewed by the spirit,' may come without sin to that holy ordinance." Evangelicals believed that Jesus Christ died for all humankind's sins—not merely the unconditional elect—and that grace could be fully given and universally accepted. Individuals were empowered to achieve a new birth. A New School Presbyterian church in Peoria, Illinois, captured a full range of evangelical conviction in 1857 when its minister explained, "We believe in the absolute sovereignty of God, and in the free will and responsibility of man. We cannot take such a view of the Divine Sovereignty, as should involve the denial of human responsibility; nor, on the other hand, such a view of human ability, as should involve the denial of our dependence. We believe that Christ died for all men, and that some will be saved according to the eternal electing purpose of God. We believe that grace is free; and is offered sincerely to all men; and that all who repent and believe will be justified and saved. We believe that the ability to sin implies the ability to repent; and that the sinner is responsible for not repenting."

The notion that people could freely embrace Christ and choose rebirth, or redemption, broke with the rigid predestinarian faith shared by earlier generations of Americans. The Puritans of old New England, who left a seemingly indelible stamp on the nation's religious consciousness, had devoted enormous efforts to these questions. They believed that people were born either with God's grace or without it. Those born with it were few. Most people were sinful and depraved. Puritans worried a great deal about their own condition, knowing they could not change it. In the seventeenth century, Michael Wigglesworth, a tutor at Harvard—the school Massachusetts Puritans built to train ministers—fretted over his "carnal" leanings. "I am often slothful and lay down the weapons of my warfare and do not fight, cry [and] strive as I should against," he wrote. If outward signs of sin were likely a sign that one was unregenerate, could an outward show of piety be a sign that one was elect? A person could not buy his or her way to heaven through good deeds or good works. But "invisible saints" probably *did* lead upstanding lives, as a reflection of their own salvation. How, then, could one distinguish between church members who were truly among the elect, and those who were, even subconsciously, attempting to project the right image in hopes they might be saved? The question seems circular, but it was enormously important to the early settlers, and to their intellectual descendants, who still debated these questions in the halls of the nation's most prestigious divinity schools—at Yale, Princeton, and, always, Harvard. Ordinary laypeople also continued to grapple with the problem of predestination in their individual spiritual journeys. Caleb Rich, an early founder of the Universalist movement, remembered that when he was a child in rural Massachusetts, his local Congregational minister taught that Christ would win scant few "trophies in his Mission into the world, but his antagonist would have his countless millions." Shook by the seeming inevitability of his damnation, Rich found that his "situation appeared more precarious than a ticket in a lottery, where there was an hundred blanks to one prize."

No denomination rejected this tradition so unreservedly as the Methodists, whose message of sanctification left far greater scope for personal agency. Upon hearing Jesse Lee, one of the movement's early leaders in America, assail the old Calvinist conception of "unconditional election," a congregant exclaimed, "Why, then, I can be saved! I have been taught that only a part of the race could be saved, but if this man's singing be true, all may be saved!"

Lorenzo Dow, one of the church's most electrifying itinerant evangelists, openly scoffed at the remnants of Puritan theology. When a heckler demanded whether the unschooled and emotive preacher could even define Calvinism, Dow replied, "Yes!"

> You can and you can't,
> You will and you won't;
> You'll be damned if you do,
> And you'll be damned if you don't.

The doggerel was probably not his, originally. Charles Grandison Finney, a Presbyterian-turned-Congregationalist minister and perhaps the nation's preeminent evangelist, often invoked it to make the same point. As he barnstormed the northeast and, later, the Old Northwest with his message of Christ's love, Finney insisted that "God has made man a moral free agent," free to choose good over evil, charity over greed—and salvation over damnation. "It should in all cases be required now to repent, now to give themselves up to God, now to say and feel, 'Lord here I am, take me, it's all I can do,'" read an outline to one of Finney's sermons. "And when the sinner can do that . . . his conversion is attained." Finney did not promise that "God's mind is changed by prayer" alone, but he held that "prayer produces such a change *in us* as renders it consistent for him to do otherwise." Even Lyman Beecher, a sometimes antagonist of Finney who preached a moderate strain of Calvinism, embraced the same lexicon, declaring that "men are free agents, in the possession of such faculties, and placed in such circumstances as render it practicable for them to do whatever God requires." When a theological opponent insisted that one could not repent for his or her sins until influenced by the Holy Ghost—an occurrence that would logically only come to those among God's elect—Finney replied with a shout, "You lie! You can repent and be converted immediately."

In his famous "New Heart" sermon, Finney captured the emotional and democratic appeal of evangelical revivalism. It was folly, he declared, for individuals to "sit quietly and wait for some invisible hand to be stretched down from heaven and perform some surgical operation, infuse some new principle, or implant some constitutional taste; *after* which they suppose they shall be *able* to obey God." Rejecting the "abstract doctrines [and] metaphysical subtleties" of Calvinism, he bade his listeners to repent, choose redemption, and make "new hearts." It was as simple as that. In fact, it was imperative. "Another moment's delay and it may be too late forever." For many evangelicals, personal agency was not simply the ability to accept Christ and earn redemption, but also to discern God's wisdom independently. A former lawyer who experienced a spiritual crisis and converted to a life of ministry, Finney had been ordained and licensed as a Presbyterian minister before he even bothered to read the Westminster Confession. After consulting the text, he was "absolutely ashamed of it" and "could not feel any respect for a document that would undertake to impose on mankind dogmas such as those." Rejecting what he viewed as arcane and highbrow religious scholarship and preaching, Finney embraced a personal, emotive relationship with God. Having found little solace or reason in the Confession, or any other work of religious exegesis, he found "nowhere to go but directly to the Bible and the philosophy or workings of [his] own mind." Believing that "reason was given us for the very purpose of enabling us to justify the ways of God" by individual divination. "I gradually formed views of my own," he remembered, "which appeared to me to be unequivocally taught in the Bible."

Barton Stone, a Presbyterian evangelist who played a hand in organizing the Cane Ridge revival, and who later broke free of his church to help found the Christian movement, of which the Disciples of Christ became a preeminent influence, placed the new theology in sharp relief: "We urged upon the sinner to believe *now*, and receive salvation—that in vain they looked for the Spirit to be given them, while they remained in unbelief . . . that no previous qualification was required, or necessary in order to believe in Jesus, and come to him."

It was not only that one could choose to be saved, or that one could achieve salvation without the intercession of learned biblical scholars and experts. One could choose the church or religious denomination that best suited his or her beliefs and the style of worship he or she preferred, much as people felt emboldened to select political candidates who appealed to their sensibilities. A visitor from Sweden marveled that there "are no sects in America, no Dissenters, no seceders—or, whatever other terms may be employed to designate the position and standing of a Christian society. They are all alike considered as Christians; and adopting, according to the judgement of charity, with equal honesty the common charter of salvation, the word of God, they are treated as equal, and as possessing similar and indefeasible rights. This is certainly a new aspect of living and visible Christianity."

HELPING DRIVE THE POPULAR EMBRACE OF EVANGELICAL THEOLOGY, IN which Arminian conceptions of free will were generally prominent, was a rising tendency of Americans, elite and non-elite alike, to assert their right and qualification to read and understand the Bible absent the controlling intervention of experts. Barton Stone rejected the theological "labyrinth" of Calvinism; he preferred a back-to-basics approach of reading the Bible—the only scripture truly inspired by God—and drew his own conclusions about its meaning. Two of his fellow Christian movement leaders in Kentucky captured this defiant spirit when they declared,

"We are not personally acquainted with the writings of John Calvin, nor are we certain how nearly we agree with his views of divine truth; neither do we care." Many evangelists—particularly Baptists, but certainly Disciples of Christ and to some degree Methodists—embraced a popular form of Christianity that lent more credence to authentic, emotive prayer and Bible reading than to clerical authority and scholarly exegesis. Elias Smith, who left the Baptist church after foreswearing belief in election and the Trinity, and who not coincidentally left the Federalist Party for Thomas Jefferson's Democratic-Republican Party around the same time, urged his neighbors to think for themselves in all matters political and spiritual. "Let us be republicans, indeed," he implored. "Many are republicans as to government, and yet are but half republicans, being in matters of religion still bound to a catechism, creed, covenant or a superstitious priest. Venture to be as independent in things of religion, as those which respect the government in which you live." Smith's personal journey followed just this path. After "meditating" on the respective merits of Calvinism and Universalism, he heard a "gentle whisper" that instructed him, *Drop them both and search the Scriptures.*

Writing in 1809, Smith captured the broader currents that shaped his own religious awakening, and that of millions of other Americans. It had been just two decades since Americans ratified their Constitution, and in that short space of time, much had changed in Americans' political expectations. The nation's founding generation had structured the country to operate as a "republic," not a democracy. Indeed, many architects of the new government feared the proliferation of "democracy"—a term that implied factions of self-interested men, not necessarily of the highest intellectual or social caliber, competing in the political sphere over crass material concerns. By contrast, republican ideology held that society was organic and unified: All persons shared the same fundamental interests and outlook, regardless of region, profession, income, or background. Such thinking delegitimized popular politics. In a republican society, men of education and achievement would serve as neutral stewards of the common good—as civic leaders as well as in churches and religious societies. Such men were "disinterested," meaning they owned their own land, owed no debts, and enjoyed economic independence.

Though republicanism always reflected more myth than reality, it had been easy in the mid-eighteenth century for Americans to convince themselves of its broad applicability. In a nation of small, coastal towns populated mostly by farmers—relative to later years, homogenous in ethnic and religious background—the idea of a single commonweal made sense. But the country was not the same in the 1830s as it had been in 1787. It grew more ethnically diverse, with a large influx of German and Scotch Presbyterian immigrants pushing the frontier ever westward, up to and across the Allegheny and Appalachian Mountains. More people were engaged in manufacturing and trade. There were more landless farmers, more regional economic interests, more diversity. When in 1786 the Pennsylvania legislature debated whether to recharter a state bank, a legislator from the western part of the state—William Findley, a Scotch Irish immigrant and former weaver—challenged claims by the state's eastern elites that they, not he, could speak to the broader common good, given their higher degree of achievement and economic independence. In fact, Findley argued, the bank's advocates were stockholders—they "feel interested in it personally, and therefore by promoting it [are] acting as judges in their own cause."

Far from deriding his opponents for pursuing parochial concerns, Findley argued that politics *should* operate as a system by which to broker competing interests. "Any others in their situation . . . would do as they did," he claimed. Rather, his objection was that the eastern elites refused to drop their republican pretense. They continued to insist that men of good breeding and high achievement were somehow the only legitimate guardians of public virtue. They should admit that "it is their own cause they are advocating." In fact, Findley argued, there wasn't just one public good; there were many public goods, and each had to be balanced against the other.

In the opening decades of the nineteenth century, the country continued to grow economically, regionally, and ethnically diverse in ways that made the idea of an organic, monolithic community less plausible. Between the American Revolution and Lincoln's election to Congress in 1846, the American population increased almost tenfold, from 2.5 million to 20 million, as the United States expanded from a loose assembly of colonies that hugged the Atlantic coast to a sprawling empire that would soon extend from the Atlantic to the Pacific—as far west as California and Oregon, as far south as present-day Texas, and into the Old Northwest, comprising present-day Minnesota and Wisconsin. Twin revolutions in transportation (first brought about by the canal craze of the 1820s and, later, the growth of railroads) and information (inspired by the United States Post Office, which subsidized the delivery of newspapers and magazines, and after 1848, the telegraph) drew disparate communities into closer connection with each other and with an emerging market economy that relied on credit, surplus production, and trade. In such a world, a self-styled "disinterested" elite class—always acting in the interest of the common good, never in its own narrow self-interest—could no longer credibly claim to speak for everyone.

Notably, in these years many states began a longer process of loosening voting requirements; whereas states originally permitted only landowning men to participate in elections, most gradually extended the ballot to white men who paid taxes or satisfied residency requirements. This trend accelerated as new territories sought to attract settlers in order to achieve statehood (and, conversely, as older states attempted to retain their residents). Consequently, elite actors gradually lost their lock on government. "The direct action of great minds on the character of our community is unquestionably less at the present period, than in former days," observed one self-styled "great mind."

Jeffersonian Republicans, including the political convert Elias Smith, tended to encourage this democratic spirit—a spirit that also enlivened a broader sense of self-determination on the part of individuals. If elites were not the guardians of a fictitious public good, they equally had no lock on truth or fact. In parallel with the democratization of politics and government, over the first half of the nineteenth century, professions like the law, medicine, and the ministry underwent a similar dramatic democ- ratization, with states loosening educational and licensing requirements. Not everyone approved of these developments. A college president in Pennsylvania anticipated with worry book titles like *Every Man his own Lawyer*, *Every Man his own Clergyman and Confessor*, or *Every Man his own physician*. "Truth," grumbled a concerned Federalist, "has but one side and listening to error and falsehood is indeed a strange way to discover truth." Another opponent of this new hyperdemocratic, relativist spirit warned against a world in which "the unalienable right of private judgment involves the liberty of thinking as we please on every subject."

Yet once unbottled, the democratic spirit was tough to recapture. Americans, as Herman Melville would later write with derision, would no longer take elite opinion at face value, for "nothing but their own eyes could persuade such ignorance as theirs." The French visitor Alexis de Tocqueville, whose travel chronicles provide a vivid account of po- litical culture in Jacksonian America, went so far as to propose that the "character of Anglo-American civilization . . . is the result (and this should be constantly kept in mind) of two distinct elements, which in other places have been in frequent disagreement, but which the Americans have succeeded in incorporating to some extent with the other and combining admirably. I allude to the *spirit of religion* and the *spirit of liberty*."

For some people, the democratization of both politics and religion posed a frightening development. Looking back on an earlier age, David Daggett, a United States senator and scion of a famous family of clergymen, lamented that in his youth, "the minister, with two or three principal characters were supreme in each town," but as a more democratic spirit came to define the political culture of the young nation, "knowledge has induced the laity to think and act for themselves." Richard McNemar, an early leader of the Shaker movement—an English religious sect that took root in the United States in the early nineteenth century— looked more favorably on this trend:

Ten thousand Reformers like so many moles
Have plowed all the Bible and cut [it] in holes
And each has his church at the end of his trace
Built up as he thinks of the subjects of grace

With a more dispassionate and scholarly eye, a midcentury theologian surveyed the country's evolving religious landscape and found that most Protestant denominations privileged "private judgement" over dogma, leaving each man to study and divine scripture "in a direct way for himself, through the medium simply of his own mind."

Some Americans worried that the profusion of new denominations and offshoot churches offered too much choice. But others had faith in common people's ability to divine truth for themselves. Such thinking befitted the democratic spirit of the times. "I said in my heart that there was not then upon earth the religion which I sought," remembered Lucy Smith, whose son, Joseph, tried many variants of Protestant faith before founding the Church of Jesus Christ of Latter-day Saints. "I therefore determined to examine my Bible, and taking Jesus and the disciples as my guide to endeavor to obtain from God that which man could neither give nor take away . . . The Bible I intended should be my guide to life and salvation." Such thinking could lead to radical ends—the rise of a new religion or, in the case of the Disciples of Christ, an anticlerical movement that rejected most forms of religious authority. "Every member shall be considered as possessing in himself or herself an original right to believe and speak as their own conscience," wrote an elder of the Christian movement, "between themselves and God, may determine; without being called into question by man." Two Presbyterian ministers who briefly flirted with the Christian movement ultimately gravitated back to their church—with its synods, seminaries, and doctrinal certainties—after having come to believe that when the "Bible was the only Confession of our Faith . . . no man could be tried, or judged heretic, who professed faith in the scriptures, however heterodox he might be in his sentiments."

More often than not, existing religious structures learned to tolerate and embrace the predominant faith in people's ability to read the Bible and choose for themselves: which church to join, which creed to adopt and which to discard, the right way to salvation—whether one even chose to be saved at all. Charles Finney, who converted Americans by the tens of thousands, described his own journey away from Calvinism. A lawyer who felt the call of God and studied for the Presbyterian ministry, Finney found that he was "utterly unable to accept [predestinarian] doctrine on the ground of authority . . . I had nowhere to go but directly to

the Bible, and to the philosophy of workings of my own mind. I gradually formed a view of my own which appeared to me to be unequivocally taught in the Bible." William Smythe Babcock, a leading Free Will
Baptist, was fond of repeating a verse—later adapted into an interdenominational hymn popular among evangelicals of the time—that he
attributed to a nine-year-old girl in his congregation:

> Know then that every soul is free
> To choose his life and what he'll be
> For this eternal truth is given
> That God will force no man to heaven.
> He'll draw persuade direct him right
> Bless him with wisdom love and light
> In nameless ways be good and kind
> But never force the human mind.

Of course, the United States in the antebellum period was a profoundly inegalitarian society where women were relegated second-class
citizenship, and African Americans not even that. Religion nevertheless
influenced the way that women and Black people understood and ordered their world, and in many respects it empowered them in ways that
ran parallel to the experience of white men.

By 1850, women represented the majority of regular churchgoers and
played an outsize role in voluntary Christian organizations and the religious press. Most church publications regularly published columns
by and for women, and prominent middle-class women like Catharine
Beecher emerged as some of the most prominent arbiters of what proper
Christian households should look like. In a country that regarded the
private home as a sanctuary from the rougher, public world of commerce

and politics, women, and especially mothers, were designated shapers of "tastes, habits, and character," in Beecher's words. The image of the Christian mother pervaded religious publications. Fathers were expected to lead their families in prayer and devotion each day, but mothers taught their children to read the Bible—the "mother's grand textbook." Men still sat at the helm of the major Christian churches and organizations, but women enjoyed broader representation and leadership opportunities than in most other public institutions. Much as a later generation of first-wave feminists would use their presumed dominion over the home to claim a broader role in conversations over education, public health and safety, and labor, Christian women in the mid-nineteenth century embraced the division between the (male) public sphere and the (female) private sphere to claim a role in the religious upbringing of their children and maintenance of proper Christian homes.

The relationship between evangelical Christianity and Black communities in the North and the South—both free and enslaved—was more varied and complicated. In the colonial era, Christianity was slow to take hold. Most enslaved people originated from West Africa, where early contact with Catholic (and Muslim) North Africans and Europeans left a subtle influence on indigenous religious traditions. But no single religion pervaded the first communities of enslaved people, who hailed from distinct nations—Ibo, Akan, Kongo, among others—and who for the most part did not regard themselves as "African" until their forced journey to North America. Most Southern slaveholders in these early decades were ambivalent about converting their enslaved people, given their uncertainty around the religious propriety of holding fellow Christians as property. (By the nineteenth century, few white Southerners continued to voice much worry on this point.) White churches were also on the decline in the late seventeenth and early eighteenth centuries, generally, and lacked the infrastructure to proselytize enslaved Africans and their enslaved descendants. It was during the massive wave of revivals, first in the mid-eighteenth century and later at the turn of the nineteenth century, that large numbers of Black people were converted alongside their white neighbors, choosing to accept Christ as their savior. They joined Baptist and Methodist churches in large numbers and in many cases worshipped alongside their white enslavers and neighbors—albeit segregated, often in the back or balcony of the church. In many Southern churches, they formed the majority of active congregants, sometimes by lopsided numbers.

In the North, many Black Christians—some born into slavery, but an overwhelming majority free by the early nineteenth century—chafed at their separate and unequal status in the growing evangelical churches. In 1794 Black Methodists in Philadelphia, under the leadership of Richard Allen, a formerly enslaved person, left St. George's church in protest over their forced removal from regular pews to a segregated balcony and formed Bethel Church, the first independent Black congregation in the United States. When the local Methodist hierarchy attempted to assert control over the church's building, the congregation—which had raised the money to construct it—sued in the Pennsylvania courts and won. Convinced that there was no place for them within the official Methodist community, in 1816 Bethel's congregants formed a new denomination, the African Methodist Episcopal (AME) Church, and installed Allen as its first bishop. Even as the AME Church took hold in communities across the North, rival Methodist denominations, notably the African Methodist Episcopal Zion Church, emerged alongside it. Black Baptists and Presbyterians also formed independent churches and denominations, asserting their own spiritual authority, as well as financial control and governance of their own congregations. By the eve of the Civil War, these churches operated separate from white-dominated organizations but well within the framework of the evangelical movement. They shared the broader evangelical community's concern for moral uplift and benevolent volunteerism, as well as its fundamental religious tenets. Just as evangelical culture provided women greater room for leadership and engagement than in other public spheres, for Black Northerners, independent churches were perhaps the one institution over which they reliably enjoyed control and claimed full autonomy.

Matters were more complicated in the South, where independent Black churches ministering both to enslaved and free people—and led by Black clergymen—existed, usually in urban areas, though unevenly, given limits and prohibitions that some state governments leveled against them. White Southerners remained divided about the wisdom of converting enslaved and free Black people. Several high-profile uprisings, notably those spearheaded by Denmark Vesey in South Carolina in 1822, and Nat Turner, an enslaved preacher, in Virginia in 1831, involved Black Christian laypeople and preachers and left authorities wary of introducing Black people to religious texts that could just as easily inspire rebellion as encourage obedience. The number of Black evangelical Christians nevertheless swelled in the antebellum period, with most Black Christians attending church alongside their white neighbors and enslavers. The experience was not always fulfilling. One Black Southerner described the attitude of white preachers as: "You slaves will go to heaven if you are good, but don't ever think that you will be close to your mistress and master. No! No there will be a wall between you; but there will be holes in it that will permit you to look out and see your mistress when she passes by. If you want to sit behind this wall, you must do the language of the text 'Obey your masters.'" Another devout person complained, "Church was what they called it but all that the preacher talked about was for us slaves to obey our masters and not to lie and steal. Nothing about Jesus, was ever said and the overseer stood there to see the preacher talked as he wanted him to talk."

To satisfy their religious yearnings outside the control of white authorities, enslaved Christians formed an "invisible church," a forbidden network of informal congregations that met by dark to share in testimony, spirituals, and prayer. Their songs combined the stories of the Bible and the everyday pain of living in bondage.

> One morning I was walking down
> I saw some berries hanging down,
> I pick de berry and I suck de juice,
> Just as sweet as honey in de comb.
> Sometimes I'm up, sometimes I'm down
> Sometimes I'm almost on de groun'.

Whereas mainline evangelical churches emphasized the New Testament over the Old Testament, Southern Black worshippers found particular meaning in stories like the Exodus and forged a rich tapestry of music and prayer around its passages. During the Civil War, white soldiers from the North would encounter formerly enslaved people—civilians and soldiers alike—for the first time in their lives, and the haunting beauty and unfamiliarity of their worship style would leave a deep impression.

North and South, free and enslaved, Black Protestants shared many of the commitments and beliefs of their white coreligionists, with one sharp exception. Most white evangelicals believed in America's providential role in building a more perfect world that would usher in a millennium of peace and, after that, Christ's return. America, in this rendering, was a new Canaan. Black Christians strained to share this understanding of a country that had enslaved them and denied them full citizenship. For Black evangelicals, Christianity was more deeply rooted in the wisdom of the ancient Hebrew prophets who looked dimly upon their fellow man's capacity for justness and warned of the punishment that would befall sinners. David Walker, a leading Black abolitionist and devout AME congregant, captured the prophetic spirit well in his *Appeal to the Coloured Citizens of the World* (1829) when he held that "God rules in the armies of heaven and among the inhabitants of the earth, having his ears continually open to the cries, tears and groans of his oppressed people." In time, "the Lord our God will bring other destructions upon" the wicked—the slaveholders and their enablers— and "not unfrequently will he cause them to rise up one against another, to be split and divided, and to oppress each other, and sometimes to open hostilities with sword in hand. . . . Does the Lord condescend to hear their cries and see their tears in consequence of oppression? Will he let the oppressors rest comfortably and happy always? Will he not cause the very children of the oppressors to rise up against them, and oftimes put them to death? 'God works in many ways his wonders to perform.'" Whether in independent or "invisible" churches, Black Americans embraced Christianity as an empowering, liberationist ideology that promised some future release from bondage and discrimination. America in this rendering was not a new Israel. It was Egypt of old.

IF EVANGELICAL PROTESTANTISM GREW IN TANDEM WITH POPULAR DE-mocracy, its fires burned brightest in parts of the country where the nascent market economy had made its most dramatic encroachments— regions like the "burned-over" counties of western New York State (so-called because the embers of religious enthusiasm burned bright there) or

Ohio's Western Reserve, where canals and, later, railroads created new opportunities for commercial farming and manufacturing and drew Americans from different regions of the country into tighter economic relationships with each other. Foreign visitors to Jacksonian America perceived a connection between its emerging market economy and vibrant religious culture, though they could not always put their finger on just what that connection was. It was clear, however, that Americans were unusually fixated on money and wealth and passionate in their religious commitments, and that these twin enthusiasms often went hand in hand. A visitor from Sweden observed that in cities like Rochester—the scene of Finney's great revival in 1830 and 1831, in the heart of the burned-over district—"we were surprised to notice the great number of *churches* and *banks*—evidence of the greater intensity of both spiritual and material activity here than in older communities." For Francis Grund, an Austrian immigrant to the United States, it seemed intuitive to explain the nature of religious arrangements in business terms. "In America," he observed, "every clergyman may be said to do business on his own account, and under his own firm. He alone is responsible for any deficiency in the discharge of his office, as he is alone entitled to all the credit due to his exertions. He always acts as principal, and is therefore more anxious, and will make greater efforts to obtain popularity, than one who serves for wages. The actual stock in any one of those firms is, of course, less than the immense capital of the Church of England; but the aggregate amount of business transacted by them jointly may nevertheless be greater in the United States."

This phenomenon of upheaval, change, and a desire for order cut across classes. Finney's famous revivals in Rochester reached a mostly professional audience, but the great "Businessman's Revival" of 1857–1858—which swept across cities as diverse as New York, Philadelphia,

Baltimore, Cincinnati, Cleveland, and Chicago—drew not only from the managerial classes, but also from the ranks of workingmen. In Boston, the Old South Church was "thronged with business men," observed one participant, but also by scores of young sailors who cycled through the port city on a regular basis. "I want you to pray for seamen," a ship's captain testified at Old South. "God is bringing that class into the fold of Christ, who are to go forth and spread the tidings of a Saviour's love over the earth." More than most people, seafarers engaged in the emerging world of commercial capitalism and commerce and found resonance in a new religious persuasion that buttressed the lessons that new worldview demanded. In much the same way that political democratization dovetailed with the democratization of American religion, the nation's embrace of the emerging market ethos—with its emphasis of choice, initiative, self-determination, and advancement—reflected and enforced trends in Christian theology and ecclesiastical organization.

In the same way that capitalism and evangelical Christianity reinforced each other, the churches increasingly came to occupy a position that rivaled emerging business and political bureaucracies, with swelling budgets, wide-ranging assets, and extensive operations that employed large numbers of laypeople and clergy. By the eve of the Civil War, aggregate contributions to Protestant churches and affiliated organizations were almost on par with the United States government's annual budget.

It was easy for highbrow critics to write off revivalism as the preserve of backwoods country preachers ministering to (or manipulating the passions of) unlearned people. But not all revivals or evangelical movements were Cane Ridge. Urban professionals, commercial farmers, and members of the emerging middle class enthusiastically embraced evangelicalism, finding the new religious spirit both compatible with the market economy's rules and sensibilities and encouraging of the personal discipline, sobriety, and mutual responsibility necessary to achieve success in a capitalist society. To live in such a changing world could induce uncertainty and unease, even for those who thrived and realized the most success within its rules. Little wonder, then, that evangelists like Finney discovered ways to channel that nervousness into—and to alleviate it through—religious conversion, even as they embraced rather than resisted the trappings and methods of modern society. Finney, who championed "new measures" to win souls, was especially embracing of modern modes of communication and entertainment in planning his highly successful urban revivals. "What do the politicians do?" he asked rhetorically. "They get up meetings, circulate handbills and pamphlets, blaze away in the newspapers, send their ships about the streets on wheels with flags and sailors, send coaches all over town, with handbills, to bring people up to the polls, to gain attention to their cause and elect their candidate . . . The object of our measures is to gain attention and you *must* have something new."

Even as they called for new methods of organizing and for "exciting, powerful preaching" and embraced the modern world, middle-class evangelists like Finney also understood that it was a confusing and disorienting moment for many people living in the throes of a market revolution. Sermons like "The Carnal Mind is Enmity against God" and "The Wages of Sin Is Death" established tension. Exhortations like "if [Christians] were united all over the world the Millennium might be brought about in three months" generated expectation. And devices like the "anxious seat" brought the unrepentant sinner to his or her moment of choice. A literal bench or chair at the front and center of a revival meeting, it was, in Finney's words, a place where "the anxious may come and be addressed particularly and be made the subject of prayers and sometimes conversed with individually." Evangelical reformers sought to smooth the rougher edges of the modern, capitalist society, but they did not resist it. They viewed the United States as the spearhead of the millennial project.

By gathering people into communion with Christ and fellowship with other Christians, they sought to bring order, discipline, and morality to a changing world that most exponents of the new religion eagerly embraced.

By the mid-nineteenth century, evangelical Christian churches that began as centers of antiestablishment fervor matured into pillars of home and community. Tent revivals gave way to formal churches and congregations. Religious books instructed families on how to fashion tidy Christian homes, where a new vogue for Gothic architecture—with stained glass rose windows, vaunted arches, and wooden crosses—gestured at the central role of faith in the family sanctuary. Parlor organs became common in drawing rooms. Women and girls commonly embroidered samplers and pillows with biblical passages and poems. Methodists, who began as a breakaway movement within the Church of England, now controlled a sprawling empire of churches, colleges, and publishing houses, marking the denomination's evolution from backwoods dissenter to middle-class incumbent.

Evangelical Protestantism even formed the background track for the nineteenth century. Methodist, Baptist, and nondenominational hymns—sung in churches and at prayer meetings, and disseminated through sheet music and pocket hymnals—became some of the most popular music in the United States. Millions of Americans could (and did) sing by heart works like "Rescue the Perishing," "Jesus, Keep Me Near the Cross," and "Blessed Assurance." By the eve of the Civil War, the most renowned musical performers in the country were Asa, John, Judson, and Abby Hutchinson—the Hutchinson Family Singers. Brothers and sisters from a devout Baptist home in New Hampshire, the Hutchinsons were deeply involved in evangelical reform movements, most notably abolitionism. Their blend of original songs, many of them sharply antislavery, and religious hymns, and their deep association with evangelical organizations and the antislavery Liberty and Republican Parties, were evidence of both the central role that Protestantism enjoyed in popular American culture and the eventual blurring of the line between church and state that the Civil War would greatly accelerate. In a Protestant nation, a group like the Hutchinsons could do well even as they did good. Their concerts commanded large paying audiences. Over time, they grew rich. In a sense, they embodied evangelicalism's evolution.

What started in the backwoods as a challenge to organized Christianity became, in effect, the new Christian establishment. Evangelical Christianity wove itself inextricably into American civic and private life. Its tenets reinforced and gained reinforcement from the country's noisy democracy and growing embrace of market capitalism. It was against this backdrop that Abraham Lincoln, neither a Christian nor a believer, forged his way into the world.

CHAPTER 3

FLOATING PIECE OF DRIFTWOOD

Settling in Illinois in the spring of 1830, the Lincoln family arrived just in time to endure the famous "Winter of the Deep Snow" that befell central Illinois later that year. The storm began on Christmas Eve, and by the following day, forests and prairies were covered in as much as four feet of snow. At first, the sudden gale brought gaiety to the small towns and trading outposts that dotted Sangamon County, where in a matter of months Abraham Lincoln would put down roots and remain until his election to the presidency. A longtime resident who had been a boy at the time later recalled the informal sleigh parties on Christmas Day: "The rough roomy sleigh, covered with buffalo robes, filled to overflowing with hale, happy companions behind four fiery horses . . . the bells jingle as the merry parting sings out, and they are off, sometimes in deep drifts where they flounder, snow within, snow without, snow everywhere." But in the following days a hard rain covered the snow, just as temperatures plunged to as cold as twelve degrees below zero and remained below freezing for several weeks. More snow soon covered the first icy drifts. It would take months before it all thawed out, grimly revealing the corpses of people who had been caught in the squall and unable to take shelter, and animals that had been buried alive.

The spring thaw swelled the rivers and flooded their adjacent towns. It was in these conditions that Lincoln first set eyes on the village of New Salem in April 1831, as he, cousin John Hanks, and stepbrother John D. Johnston attempted to navigate a flatboat carrying barrels of corn, wheat, and bacon. They had constructed the vessel for Denton Offutt, a local merchant, and pledged to drive it safely to New Orleans, a bustling merchant city where they would sell the cargo before making their way back to Illinois. As floodwaters lodged the boat on a dam just opposite the center of the village, the people of New Salem observed with wonder as Lincoln struggled to save the structure and its freight. "Boots off, hat, coat, and vest off; pants rolled up to his knees and shirt wet with sweat and combing his fuzzie hair with his fingers as he pounded away at the boat," an onlooker remembered years later—the lanky, gaunt boy cut an odd figure. He ingeniously bored a hole on one end of the flatboat, causing river water to rush through and lift the front end of the structure above the dam. Lincoln was later fond of recalling that he was little but a "floating piece of driftwood" when he first came to know New Salem. It was a fitting observation for someone raised on predestinarian faith, with parents who thought little of human agency in this world or the next.

After off-loading the freight in New Orleans, Lincoln and his party journeyed back to Illinois, and Abe paid a brief visit to his parents, stopping over long enough to help Tom build a log cabin, before announcing his intention to cut "entirely adrift from the old life." He left home at age twenty-two, bound for New Salem, where Offutt had proposed to open a general store and make him clerk. He was, as he later described himself, a "friendless, uneducated, penniless boy" alone in the world for the first time. The next six years would prove central in Lincoln's life. One admiring historian later called New Salem his "alma mater." It was there that he became exposed to a broader world of books and ideas; made his first venture at business, when he operated another store, and failed; served as a volunteer officer in the Black Hawk War; ran for the state legislature and lost; ran again and won; possibly fell in love for the first time; and became a lawyer. Lincoln would devote roughly one quarter of his two autobiographical campaign sketches to his brief time in New Salem.

For all its Lincoln lore, New Salem was a modest town that existed for a very short time. Founded in 1829, just two years before Abraham Lincoln drifted by on his flatboat, New Salem seemed to its founders the right place for "our farmers, our mechanics, our merchants and professional men" to build a lasting connection to the emerging market economy. At its high-water mark in the mid-1830s, the village claimed perhaps twenty-five families and roughly as many structures—most of them "log houses and cabins," and a smattering of "brick or framed houses," as a contemporary informed his relatives back east—also a sawmill, tavern, handful of general stores, blacksmith, cooper's shop, and tannery. There was a schoolhouse that doubled as a church, and a cemetery. Nearby hamlets like Clary's Grove supplied a wider population to make the town feel vibrant beyond its size. Though he lived his years there as a roomer and boarder in other people's households, it was certainly a more civilized place than the rough-hewn frontier cabins of Lincoln's youth. Most of the houses were modest, one-story affairs consisting of two or three rooms, but they generally had windows, given New Salem's proximity to a glazier in nearby Springfield.

Still, New Salem was where the future sixteenth president absorbed his earliest ideas about political economy and, equally important, where he first articulated and exchanged his thoughts about religion. In a town of iconoclastic characters, he stood out as a freethinker who was quick to reject orthodox ideas and uncommonly—even inadvisably—loose lipped in his disregard for organized Christianity.

It was the place where he grew up. By 1837, Lincoln, so recently a penniless boy and piece of floating driftwood—now a licensed attorney on the cusp of becoming Whig leader in the state house of representatives—left the town for Springfield. Three years later, New Salem ceased to be. Other river outposts proved better situated to serve as market junctures, and the nascent railroad boom rendered transit by water a largely moot consideration in any event.

⁜

WHEN LINCOLN FIRST ARRIVED THERE, NEW SALEM WAS STILL PART OF Sangamon County, then the most populous county in Illinois, with thirteen thousand residents, roughly 85 percent of whom lived and worked on farms. (It would later be absorbed by Menard County.) Home production was still the norm. Families ate what they grew and made their own soaps, candles, shoes, and clothing. What they could not manufacture at home—coffee, tea, or sugar; tobacco; nails, glass, or lamp oil— they bought from merchants like Denton Offutt, who operated general stores. Payments made by credit or the barter system drew residents into their first interaction with a modern credit economy.

Abe worked as a hired hand on and off through his years in New Salem. Notably, he made no effort to buy land of his own and follow his father, and his father's father, into agriculture. Instead, he moved between one mercantile or white-collar enterprise and another, trying his luck at each, all the while devoting himself doggedly to the business of improving his mind. Nearly all the townspeople whom Herndon tracked down so many decades later recalled his singular reading habits, how he "used to sit up in the late of nights reading & would recommence in the morning when he got up." William Greene, who clerked with Abe at Denton Offutt's short-lived general store and roomed with him for a time in the loft above, remembered that he was an avid consumer of Shakespeare's plays and sonnets, the poetry of Robert Burns and Lord Byron, and American history. Mentor Graham, a local schoolteacher who befriended Lincoln and likely helped him develop his grammar, writing, and mathematical skills, told Herndon that in "New Salem he devoted more time to reading the scripture, books on science and comments on law and to the acquisition of Knowledge of men & things than any man [he] ever knew." He was, according to Graham, "the most studious, diligent strait forward young man in the pursuit of a knowledge of literature" than any of the thousands of students he had taught in the prior and ensuing years. Lincoln also absorbed newspapers—namely, partisan outlets like *The St. Louis Republic* and the *Sangamo Journal*, driving his development into an ardent and outspoken Whig, even as most of his new neighbors retained their affection for, and loyalty to, Andrew Jackson's budding Democratic Party. Though saddled with an inadequate formal education, Lincoln was determined from the start to build a career that required mental acuity rather than physical brawn.

His friends in New Salem remembered Lincoln as shy around women—excepting married women who were older than he, like his friend Jack Armstrong's wife, Hannah, who fed him and "foxed" his trousers—and abstemious in a way that stood out in a rough frontier town. "Salem in those days was a hard place for a temperate Man like Mr. Lincoln was," a friend offered, "and I have often wondered how he could be so extremely popular and not drink and Carouse with them. [He] used to run footraces & jump with the boys and also play ball [but] I am certain he Never Drank any intoxicating liquors[.] He did not in those days even smoke or chew Tobacco." Which is not to say that he was a prude or a scold. Abe became a famous teller of bawdy stories and author of ribald verse and was wont to roughhouse and carouse in good fellowship with other young men, many of them also unmarried and shiftless, who had come to New Salem and its surrounding hamlets in search of better luck or a new start. His friendship with Jack Armstrong, leader of the Clary's Grove Boys—a local gang known for outbursts of drunken violence against people and property—grew out of an impromptu wresting match between the two men that would later become the stuff of Lincoln lore. (Armstrong may or may not have tripped Abe in an unsportsmanlike maneuver. The two nevertheless became fast friends. Decades later, Lincoln left the campaign trail during his bid for the United States Senate in 1858 to serve as defense counsel for Jack's son, who stood trial for murder.) He avoided strong drink and tobacco not out of religious conviction or piety but out of a desire to remain in control of his faculties. He was ambitious. Self-improvement and upward mobility formed his North Star. He had little use for anything that blocked his way.

LINCOLN'S RISE WAS SWIFT, THOUGH TEMPERED BY SETBACKS. IN THE spring and summer of 1832 he volunteered to serve in the Black Hawk War, a brief conflict with local Indian tribes. Though he never saw combat, in testament to his popularity in the village, friends and neighbors elected him captain of their unit. He would later claim that no subsequent success in life "gave him so much satisfaction." Brimming with confidence, Abe stood for the state legislature that fall and lost. He bought a general store with his friend William Barry. It went bust, leaving him with a mound of debt. He was appointed postmaster of New Salem, a position that afforded him access to more newspapers, and assistant surveyor of Sangamon County. In 1834 he was elected to the state legislature, where he served four terms, eventually as the House minority leader. In 1835 his compass and survey equipment were sold at sheriff's auction to satisfy unpaid obligations from his failed commercial enterprise. (A friend bought them and gifted them back.) In between, he likely fell in love with, and was perhaps secretly engaged to, Ann Rutledge, a young woman four years his junior. Her death from typhoid fever in 1835 hit Lincoln hard, though friends and biographers later exaggerated the importance of their relationship beyond proportion. At the urging of John Todd Stuart, a lawyer and fellow legislator who befriended Abe during their service in the Black Hawk War, he studied the law and, in 1836, received his bar license. By the following year he was gone—moved to Springfield, the Sangamon County seat and new state capital, where he continued his legislative service and became Stuart's junior partner.

IN THAT PERIOD OF SELF-REINVENTION, ONE CONSTANT REMAINED: LINcoln determinedly avoided the wave of evangelical enthusiasm that crashed over New Salem and other parts of central Illinois. Most townspeople identified as Hard Shell Baptists, Cumberland Presbyterians, or Methodists, though as was true everywhere in the country, new denominations and movements were on the rise. Each year, his neighbors partook of animated camp meetings at nearby Concord and Rock Creek. "Uncle Jimmy" Short, one of Abe's closest friends—it was Uncle Jimmy who bought back his surveying equipment at the sheriff's auction so that Abe could continue to earn a living—would sit in the front row, engaging call-and-response fashion in the sermon, now and then wagging a finger to object, "Now, brother, that ain't so," if the preacher broke with doctrinal orthodoxy. Peter Cartwright, by then a famous Methodist circuit rider, lived just ten miles from New Salem and frequently spoke at these gatherings. His exhortations would whip the crowd into a frenzy, causing some to be seized with "the jerks." To "get relief," remembered one of Abe's neighbors, some would "rise up a dance, some would try to run away, but could not, some would resist, and on such the jerks were very severe."

Religion saturated local culture, even when the camp meetings were out of season. Residents met for weekly Sunday services at the town schoolhouse or in private homes. Baptists, whose denomination was on the rise, would immerse converts in the Sangamon River. Similar to the Hard Shell Baptists, many evangelical preachers, including Methodists like Cartwright, looked askance at college-educated clergy and proffered a rough and more democratic—more experiential—spiritual awakening. But doctrinal disagreements ran deep. A young, Yale-educated scholar then teaching at Illinois College had no sooner arrived than he encountered a "sea of sectarian rivalries, which was kept in constant agitation." Methodists and Baptists quarreled over whether the "way to heaven [was] by water or dry land," an early historian of New Salem noted. Yet both movements bitterly rejected what Cartwright dismissed as the "high toned doctrines of Calvinism" and the "muddy waters of Campbellism."

Lincoln absented himself conspicuously from the religious doings of New Salem and wider Sangamon County. He did not join some of his rowdier neighbors who menaced the Baptists by throwing logs and even live dogs into the Sangamon River during their immersion rites, but by all accounts he identified with a small, vibrant community of skeptics who preferred Thomas Paine's *Age of Reason* (which he encountered during his New Salem days) to scripture. For Lincoln, the Bible was foundational literature and a commonly shared reference point, but not a divine source of truth. His later friend and political associate, Ward Hill Lamon, would rue that "the fatal misfortune of [Lincoln's] life was the influence of New Salem . . . which enlisted him on the side of unbelief." Whether it was the town's atheists who found Lincoln, or Lincoln who sought them out, by all accounts, the future president appears to have been a full-throated disbeliever—not only among close confidantes in New Salem, but also when on legislative business at the state capitol. He "belonged to no religious sect," recalled Mentor Graham, who firmly believed that Lincoln never had a "change of heart"—even as president ("He would have told me about it," Graham offered. "He couldn't have avoided it.")

Years later, friends remembered that he would privately "ridicule" such Christian doctrines as the Immaculate Conception, virgin birth, and the Trinity, though his "was the language of respect . . . not scoff." He was wont to "pick up the Bible—read a passage—and then Comment on it—show its falsity—and its follies on the ground of *Reason*—would then show its own self-made & self-uttered Contradictions and would in the End—finally ridicule it and as it were Scoff at it." In the wake of Lincoln's death, as a mourning nation apotheosized their slain president, John Todd Stuart even went so far as to say that Lincoln had been an "infidel," "especially when young—Say from 1834 to 1840." He went "further against Christian beliefs—& doctrine & principles than any man I ever heard: he shocked me—don't remember the Exact line of his argument—Suppose it was against the inherent defects so-called of the Bible & on grounds of reason—Lincoln always denied that Jesus was the . . . son of God as understood and maintained by the Christian world."

Some of these memories should be taken with a grain of salt. Recorded after Lincoln's death, they reflect a good deal of prompting on the part of Herndon, who, in light of the public's wont to transform its fallen president into a religious martyr, was explicitly interested in establishing that Lincoln was a nonbeliever. Others, like George Spears, who had been a resident of Clary's Grove in the 1830s, freely admitted, "At that time I had no idea of his ever being President therefore I did not notice his course as close as I should of had." But too many of Herndon's informants remembered Lincoln as a full-throated skeptic. As early as 1837, Lincoln publicly acknowledged, and sought to defuse, rumors that he might be a "deist." Six years later, he privately lamented to a friend that his recent, unsuccessful bid for the Whig congressional nomination suffered a "tax of a considerable per cent. upon my strength throughout the religious community" owing to rumors that "no ch[r]istian ought to go for me, because I belonged to no church, was suspected of being a deist."

Lincoln struck an obvious contrast with his neighbor, the celebrated Methodist circuit rider and Jacksonian Democrat, Peter Cartwright, whose political career intertwined with his in the early years. The two men likely first met in 1830, when Lincoln, still residing with his parents, hired himself out as a farmhand for William Butler in Island Grove. Cartwright, by then a Methodist elder and well-respected political force in central Illinois, was campaigning in an unsuccessful bid for governor. "Lincoln at this time was not prepossessing," Butler would later recount. "He was awkward and very shabbily dressed." As Cartwright "laid down his doctrines"—political and religious alike, for Cartwright perceived little distinction between the two—"in a way which undoubtedly seemed to Lincoln a little too dogmatical," the precocious hired boy "met the great preacher in his arguments, and the extensive acquaintance." Two years later, they would cross swords again as candidates for the state house of representatives. The preacher emerged a winner in the multi-candidate field. Lincoln, making his first bid for office, did not.

In 1834, Cartwright, then closing out his term in the legislature, penned a series of letters calling on young Methodist men to migrate to Illinois to take up teaching posts in the still-nascent common school system. Taking slight at those who would claim that the residents of Sangamon were "without religion, immoral, intemperate, rude, unculti-vated in [their] manners, denying the obligation of the Sabbath for civil or religious purposes, destitute of Evangelical Preachers," Cartwright insisted that the "hundreds of ministers of the Gospel, of the different religious organizations," had erected a strong moral foundation that could only be strengthened by a tighter web between public schools and the church. This casual comingling of the secular and sacred—the sug-gestion that civic health required spiritual, even sectarian, influence—rankled Lincoln, who was likely the author of a scathing rejoinder in the *Beardstown Chronicle*. The article was attributed to another author, though New Salem townspeople remembered Lincoln as the source. Claiming to "know nothing" of religion, the author of the letter turned instead to politics but took care to knock Cartwright for his dual atten-tion to "preaching and electioneering"—for "boasting" during election season "of mustering his militia (alluding to the Methodist Church) and marching and counter-marching them in favor of, or against, this or that candidate. . . . For a church or community to be priest ridden by a man who will take their money and treat them kindly in return is bad enough . . . but to be ridden by one who is continually exposing them to ridicule by making a public boast of his power to hoodwink them, is insufferable."

The two men would meet in open political combat on future occasions, none more fraught than in 1846, when they faced off in a bitter campaign for Congress. By then, New Salem had ceased to exist as a town, its homes left to rot, its residents departed—many of them for nearby Petersburg, others, like Lincoln, to Springfield. Abe was by then a husband, the father of two boys (Robert and Eddie), a lawyer, and a former legislator. He had grown notably more circumspect in his criticism of religion, perhaps out of deference to his wife, Mary Todd Lincoln, who joined a Presbyterian church. More likely, as he grew into respectable adulthood, Lincoln learned to bite his tongue. Cartwright certainly knew that many voters remembered the New Salem days. At the heart of his whispering campaign was the charge that, as a young state legislator, Lincoln had penned a blasphemous essay.

The charge was probably true. Several of Herndon's informants, including Hardin Bale, one of New Salem's earliest residents, easily recalled that sometime around 1834, "Lincoln wrote a work on infidelity, denying the divinity of the Scriptures" and was quickly "persuaded by his friends . . . to burn it." John Hill, whose father, Samuel, was purportedly the friend who persuaded Lincoln to make instant embers of his essay, was too young to remember the occasion firsthand. But he told Herndon that his parents' recounting of the incident was "one of the circumstances from which I date my earliest remembrance. It could not have been on account of Lincoln's position, as at the time I knew no more as to who he was than I did of the Fejee Islands." Hill could not pinpoint the exact moment or year when the incident occurred but was sure that it had been during winter, when the stove in his father's store, where "tradition says it was done," would have been at full roar.

Whether the incident occurred or not, Lincoln felt compelled during his congressional bid, more than ten years after the fact, to address the rumors. In July 1846 he issued a "Handbill Replying to Charges of Infidelity," in which he forcefully denied that he was an "open scoffer at Christianity." (For one so deliberate with language, he sidestepped the question as to whether he might be a private scoffer.) "That I am not a member of any Christian Church, is true," he admitted, "but I have never denied the truth of the Scriptures; and I have never spoken with intentional disrespect of religion in general, or of any denomination of Christians in particular." This claim was, of course, most likely false, though no worse offense than most politicians then or now commit. Lincoln added that he could not personally "be brought to support a man for office, whom [he] knew to be an open enemy of, and scoffer at, religion." Notably, he did not hold that an atheist was unfit for office, simply for being a nonbeliever. He was willing to "leav[e] the higher matter of eternal consequences, between him and his Maker." Instead, he did not "think any man has the right thus to insult the feelings, and injure the morals, of the community in which he may live." He continued, "If, then, I was guilty of such conduct, I should blame no man who should condemn me for it; but I do blame those, whoever they may be, who falsely put such a charge in circulation against me."

Lincoln's circular was tightly worded. He conceded that he did not belong to a church but stopped well short of proclaiming private faith. Instead, he merely—though strenuously, and untruthfully—denied ever having scoffed at religion. He even attempted to align his secular mindset with the fundamentals of Christian theology, acknowledging, "In early life I was inclined to believe in what I understand is called the 'Doctrine of Necessity'—that is, that the human mind is impelled to action, or held in rest by some power, over which the mind itself has no control; and I have sometimes (with one, two or three, but never publicly) tried to maintain this opinion in argument. The habit of arguing thus however, I have, entirely left off for more than five years. And I add here, I have always understood this same opinion to be held by several of the Christian denominations. The foregoing, is the whole truth, briefly stated, in relation to myself, upon this subject."

Lincoln's "Doctrine of Necessity"—the belief that one's personal agency was governed by invisible influences and boundaries, determined in some fashion by divinity or nature—genuinely bore some resemblance to what Henry Ward Beecher termed the "alleviated Calvinism" of his father's, Lyman Beecher's, generation—a form of Arminianized Calvinism that held some scope for individual free will, even as it maintained the traditional concepts of original sin and predestination. In this sense, Lincoln was right to align his earlier thinking with teachings still prevalent in many Presbyterian and Congregationalist churches, though certainly not in the evangelical congregations, most of them Baptist and Methodist, that dominated central Illinois. It was a remnant strain of his parents' predestinarian faith, with the harder edges sanded off.

Lincoln still quietly rejected organized Christianity. He denied the Christian understanding of "the innate depravity of Man, the character & office of the great head of the Church, the atonement, the infallibility of the written revelation, the performance of myricles, the nature & design of present and future rewards & punishments . . . and many other Subjects," a friend recalled. Lincoln was more strongly drawn to the influence of secular literature and philosophy—to Shakespeare, whose plays he devoured; to legal utilitarians, whose works he surely studied in his path to becoming a lawyer; to the writings of Thomas Paine and Robert Chambers, and Constantin François de Chassebœuf, the comte de Volney, political and scientific theorists whose writing influenced his hazy embrace of deism, according to Herndon. Herndon, who became Lincoln's law partner in 1844, remembered that the future president was especially fond of quoting a line from *Hamlet*:

> There's a divinity that shapes our ends,
> Rough-hew them how we will.

Paine, who abhorred the "absurd and impious doctrine of predestination"—"a doctrine destructive of morals, [which] would never have been thought of had it not been for some stupid passages in the Bible, which priestcraft at first, and ignorance since, have imposed upon mankind as revelation"—made a similar claim in *Age of Reason*. He wrote of the "vast machinery of the universe," which "still goes on" whether humans "sleep or wake." "We see our own earth filled with abundance," he continued, "but we forget to consider how much of that abundance is owing to the scientific knowledge the vast machinery of the universe has unfolded."

What distinguished Lincoln's "Doctrine of Necessity" from both his parents' Calvinism and mainline evangelical Christianity was its rejection of a personal or knowing God at the center of all human events. Whether humans were compelled by "some power" (Lincoln's words), a "vast machinery" (Paine), a rough-hewn "divinity" (Shakespeare), or the "mathematical problem" posed by mass human agency (Robert Chambers), that force was mysterious, distant, impersonal, and inscrutable. No amount of Bible study or profession of Christian faith could reveal its nature or intent. It was left to each person to chart his or her own course, fully in the knowledge that one's choices—and likely even the outcomes of those choices—were the sum of a greater design that defied human understanding.

James Keyes, a resident of Springfield who knew him in the 1850s, remembered that Lincoln "believed in a Creator of all things, who had neither beginning nor end, who possessing all power and wisdom, established a principal, in Obedience to which, Worlds move and are upheld, and animel and vegetable life came into existence. A reason he gave for his belief was, that in view of the Order and harmony of all nature which all beheld, it would have been More miraculous to have Come about by chance, than to have been created and arranged by some great thinking power." As to "Christian theory"—whether "Christ is God, or equal to the Creator he said had better be taken for granted"— Lincoln apparently hedged. He could not profess belief, as "evidence of Christs divinity Came to us in somewhat doubtful shape," yet he could not disprove the possibility either. Christian revelation was "perhaps Calculated to do good" by whatever force controlled human events. Another associate concurred that Lincoln "fully believed in a Superintending & overruling Providence, that guides & controls the operations of the world; but Maintained that Law and Order, & not their violation of suspension; are the appointed means by which this providence is exercised."

Joseph Gillespie, a friend and political associate whom Lincoln first met during the Black Hawk War, remembered the future president as "*theoretically* a predestinarian." In other words, Lincoln believed in some natural order of things, without formally embracing a Christian church. Jesse Fell, who had known the future president since late 1834, and who helped engineer his nomination for president a quarter century later, found popular accounts of the slain leader's religiosity "utterly at variance with his Known sentiments." "True," Fell allowed, "he may have changed or modified those views, after his removal from among us"—after he left Springfield for the White House—"though this is hardly reconcilable with the history of the man." Conceding that "Mr. Lincoln Seldom communicated to any one his views on the subject," Fell still confidently maintained that "whilst he held many opinions in common with the great mass of Christian believers, *he did not* believe in what are regarded as the orthodox or evangelical view of Christianity."

❖

BETWEEN HIS FIRST ARRIVAL IN NEW SALEM IN 1831, AND HIS ELECTION to Congress in 1846, Lincoln rejected Christianity, for all intents and purposes. But he was not devoid of belief. Lincoln left some clues about his moral worldview in an address to the Young Men's Lyceum of Springfield, delivered in 1838, a year after he relocated to the state's new capital city. "Passion has helped us," he told his audience of upwardly mobile professionals and tradesmen, "but can do so no more. It will in future be our enemy. Reason, cold, calculating, unimpassioned reason, must furnish all the materials for our future support and defence." A Whig in politics, Lincoln advocated market competition, state financing for infrastructure and education, and a dispassionate, fact-driven political and social discourse that seemed to many Whigs the antithesis of Andrew Jackson's Democratic Party, with its disregard for law and order, stirring of public emotions, and reliance on coercion (against Indians, African Americans, political opponents). He delivered the address less than three months after a proslavery horde in Alton, Illinois—eighty miles south of Sangamon County, in the state's southern and Southern-aligned region—lynched the Presbyterian minister and abolitionist editor Elijah P. Lovejoy, throwing his printing press into the river to punctuate the act. Lincoln did not mention the incident directly, though his speech was an implicit repudiation of mob violence. When he cautioned his townspeople to favor reason over passion, he might also have had revivals in mind, with their excitations and appeals to emotion over reason—the way they caused men and women to jerk and faint when overcome by the spirit. Lincoln called on citizens to make "reverence for the laws . . . the *political religion* of the nation; and let the old and the young, the rich and the poor, the grave and the gay, of all sexes and tongues, and colors and conditions, sacrifice unceasingly upon its altars." Ultimately, American "political institutions" did more to advance "the ends of civil and religious liberty, than any of which the history of former times tells us."

Notably, Lincoln closed his remarks by quoting Matthew 16:18, with a wish that "intelligence, sound morality and, in particular, a reverence for the constitution and laws" might support the "fabric of freedom," for "as has been said of the only greater institution, *'the gates of hell shall not prevail against it.'*"

Beyond a handful of public and private protestations that he was not a scoffer, this was the nearest Lincoln came in the New Salem and Springfield days to professing a public viewpoint on religion, and an early example of his later tendency to draw liberally on biblical citations in his speeches, knowing that his audiences were familiar with and could relate to these passages. Firm in his conviction that "cold, calculating, unimpassioned reason" should be the lodestar of all things, yet vaguely of the belief that an undiscernible force—natural or spiritual, he seemed neither to know nor care—governed human affairs from a distance, he affirmed the imperative behind religious freedom and learned to speak with discretion, if even at all, where sectarian matters were concerned. He stood deliberately aloof from the evangelical backdrop of his age, even when other men on the make might have found it easier to join a church, offer a token nod to commitment, and feign belief. For Lincoln, intelligence, sound morality, and a reverence for civil laws were the foundation of a good society. The Bible was simply a useful reference point for his audience.

He hoped, in the words of his New Salem friend Elizabeth Abell, that even if he were "a Christian not in the common term," it would suffice that he "was always doing good the same today and tomorrow," and that his neighbors would accept him into their fellowship on his own, peculiar terms.

CHAPTER 4

THE EVANGELICAL
UNITED FRONT

For many of Abraham Lincoln's countrypeople, faith and patriotism ran from the same spring. A French visitor in 1824 remarked that expressions of religious commitment resembled "a sentiment as much as their love of liberty resembles a creed. Among them a political orator never closes a preparatory address without invoking or returning thanks to the Almighty; as a minister, when he ascends the pulpit, always begins by reminding his audience of their duties as citizens and the happiness they enjoy in living under wise institutions. It may be said that this mixture of political morality and theology extends through all the actions of the Americans, a tincture of gravity and profound conviction." Alexis de Tocqueville, whose travel journals left an indelible impression of America in the Jacksonian era, made a similar observation in his private diary after observing a Protestant minister deliver the invocation at an Independence Day event in Albany, New York. "[It] is characteristic of this country," he remarked, "where they never do anything without the assistance of religion."

The porous boundary between the secular and the sacred made sense within the eschatological worldview that many evangelical Christians shared. For the vast majority of Protestants whose faith was premillennial, Christ's return would necessarily be preceded by a thousand-year age of peace, and the United States—a virgin land (so the thinking went; Americans in the nineteenth century easily wrote Indians out of the continent's history)—represented a new Canaan where that destiny would be fulfilled. Protestant sermons frequently described the young nation as "God's New Israel," a people invested with biblical significance—"a Union of purpose [and] feeling," as President John Tyler told an audience in 1843. Several years later, the editors of a typical evangelical publication affirmed that a "grand feature of our times is that *all is Progress*." Christianity and American democracy ran on parallel paths, "inward and upward," and together would hasten the "grand consummation of prophecy in a civilized, an enlightened, and a sanctified world"—the "spiritual kingdom which God has ordained shall triumph and endure. . . . Let it be a future of Holiness." If Christians did their part, a clergyman promised, the "strong towers of sin shall fall, the glory of the Lord shall be displayed, and the millennial glory shall dawn on the earth." American churches, a British traveler in the United States believed, would soon effect "the transformation of society into the kingdom of Christ."

To speed the Second Coming, evangelical reformers devoted themselves broadly to two tasks: winning souls, and ensuring that God's New Israel was righteous and free of sin. In a growing, industrializing, increasingly diverse and urban country, it was a tall order. The year Lincoln was born, the United States had only forty-six "urban" places, defined as towns or cities with over two thousand five hundred people. By the eve of his election to the presidency in 1860, there were almost four hundred urban centers, including cities like New York and Philadelphia, each of which claimed over a half million residents. Where canals and rail-roads cut through the land, and where market centers sprouted up, new social problems emerged to challenge the evangelical mission: drunken-ness, prostitution, Sabbath breaking, crime. Such problems were not unique to urban America, but towns and cities allowed people a certain anonymity and concentration that seemed to magnify transgression. In response to these challenges, Christian activists created a vast network of reform societies—a "Benevolent Empire" of loosely connected causes and organizations that aspired to make America a Christian nation in both word and deed.

Some organizations focused on introducing the wayward and lost to Christianity through sacred texts. The American Bible Society, founded in 1816, endeavored to furnish citizens with the one tool they needed to achieve "moral cultivation." Simply owning a Bible and studying scrip-ture would inevitably exert a "restraining effect" on the newly itinerant and urbanized young men and women flooding towns and cities and would more generally "strengthen the fabric of civil society." Funded by wealthy merchants and real estate developers in New York City, the society embraced modern tools of commercial reproduction to issue and disseminate roughly six million Protestant Bibles—more than one for every four residents of the United States—by 1849. "We cannot manu-facture missionaries," a spokesperson for the organization conceded, "but we can manufacture Bibles." The American Sunday School Union, founded in 1824, sought to furnish religious instruction, books, and pamphlets to the thousands who "come in from the country in pursuit of trades and employment, who are thrown into promiscuous associa-tion in boarding-houses, over whom there is no sort of supervision what-ever except during the working hours of the day." Such urban newcomers were highly susceptible to vice. "The excitements and allurements of their

new situation and the connection they instantly form with the thought-
less if not with the licentious, soon break up their good habits, unless
there is something at hand in the form of a Sunday School, Bible class,
or family influence to restrain and guide them." For its sheer prodigiousness, no benevolent society could beat the American Tract Society,
which turned out as many as six million broadsides and pamphlets
annually. These efforts were a new phenomenon, aided by the rise of
faster and cheaper printing presses and a general vogue for volunteerism
in the antebellum period.

Distributing Bibles and religious tracts or holding worship classes for
wayward youth were reasonably anodyne undertakings as far as religious
reform went. But the closed, Puritan communities of seventeenth-century
New England had long since yielded to a diverse nation in which there
were no established churches to impose their values on individuals and
communities. Agitating for various political and legal reforms—an end
to postal delivery on Sundays, prohibitions against shopkeeping and
commerce on the Sabbath, limits on the production and sale of alcohol—
often proved controversial. In some quarters, clergymen asserted new
liberty to preach on social and political topics that were arguably not
within the purview of the churches. "No class has such opportunities
for influence, such means of power" as the nation's twenty-eight thousand Protestant preachers, wrote an essayist in *The Atlantic Monthly* in
1858. "Sunday morning all the land is still . . . Even in this great Babel
of Commerce, one day in seven is given up to the minister." Not everyone agreed. Non-evangelicals, particularly the nation's growing Catholic population, resented the overtones of social control that Protestant
reformers sought to impose on the entire country. Even some evangelicals bristled at the politicization of the pulpit, preferring that churches
attend to the business of saving souls rather than meddling in politics.

"There can be no doubt that the tendency at the present day is to magnify the political, the social, the secular, or what may be called the worldly-humanitarian aspects [of] professedly religious movements," wrote one such critic. Where the real business at hand should have been winning more converts for Christ, it was "almost as common to hear about the regeneration of the *race* as the salvation of souls." What would truly speed the coming of Christ was the winning of hearts, not the creation of a "politico-religious age."

Arthur and Lewis Tappan surely disagreed. The two brothers, raised in a strict Calvinist household, were the very model of their age: self-made businessmen who built their fortune in commerce, devout lay leaders, funders and organizers of diverse Christian causes ranging from Sunday schools and Bible societies to tract organizations and abolition. Each night at the close of business, they shuttered the doors to their mercantile agency in New York and made haste to religious meetings that lasted for hours. Rejecting their parents' faith, they believed, in Lewis's words, that individuals could, "from careful attention to the means of grace and from special influences of the Holy Spirit," be redeemed. Some associates believed that the brothers' almost manic commitment to religion and reform was a manifestation of spiritual anxiety. They had "gradually and almost imperceptibly quitted Calvinism for Arminianism," a friend remarked, "therefore they feel less confident of being amongst the elect, and take more pains to work out their own salvation, not only by religious observance, but by deeds of beneficence and mercy." Even coreligionists like Lyman Beecher believed that the brothers sometimes went overboard, as when they supported an independent stage coach company that would not transport travelers on Sunday. In their zeal, they gave Sabbatarianism a bad name. But there was little doubting their commitment. The American Education Society. The American

Tract Society (of which Arthur was a cofounder). The American Bible Society. The American Home Missionary Society. The American Society for Meliorating the Condition of the Jews (which assisted only Jews who converted to Christianity). And especially, and above all, abolitionism, a cause for which Arthur and Lewis made notable financial and personal sacrifices. They were generous donors, to be sure. But they also put themselves on the line in more immediate ways. It was Arthur who scoured the wharves of Brooklyn to find someone who could serve as an interpreter for the enslaved people who famously rebelled and commandeered the slaver *Amistad*, and sued for their freedom upon entry to the United States. The Tappans helped fund their defense, visited them in prison, and sat beside them in the courtroom. Leading Southerners, many of them devout evangelical Christians, despised the brothers and sponsored a boycott of their mercantile agency, a retributive measure that exacted a steep economic toll on the Tappans' business, which was a primary mover of staples like cotton. In New York, their hometown, a mob ransacked their offices, destroying inventory as well as promissory notes, all but ruining their agency. None of these actions cooled their ardor.

Political and social reformers like the Tappan brothers comprised a small minority of evangelical Christians, but the vast majority of reformers were ardent Christians. Their prominent place in the churches and their outsize social influence made it easy to associate evangelisms with all manner of reform, as well as with the Whig Party, whose leaders styled themselves as the "Christian party"—focused on the moral, spiritual, and physical improvement of the nation. Unsurprisingly, many Democrats, including Democrats who belonged to and worshipped in evangelical congregations, came to view reformers with a skeptical and even critical eye. All the more so in the 1850s, as many of the nation's leading Christian reformers embraced a range of causes that, for the time, seemed both narrow-minded and bigoted, as well as socially coercive or simply eccentric—in the words of Lincoln's nemesis, Senator Stephen Douglas of Illinois, "an allied army, composed of [nativist] Know Nothings, Abolitionists, Free Soilers, Maine Liquor Law men, woman's rights men, Antirenters, Anti-Masons, and all the isms that have been sloughed off from all the honest parties in the country." George Fitzhugh, a prominent Southern polemicist before the war, echoed Douglas when he denounced the "Bloomers and Women's Rights men," the "Millerites, and Spiritual Rappers, and Shakers, and Widow Wakemanites, and Agrarians, and Grahamites, and a thousand other superstitious and infidel isms." In New York, critics of evangelical reformers mocked Arthur Tappan as "St. Arthur de Fanaticus." Of course, most leading evangelical reformers did not embrace all of the isms to which Douglas and Fitzhugh pointed as emblems of social and religious fanaticism. But they embraced one: the abolition or restriction of slavery. And that seemed the most dangerous ism of all—in the North and the South alike.

TWO THINGS WERE TRUE AT THE SAME TIME: MOST EVANGELICAL CHRISTIANS were not abolitionists, but the vast majority of abolitionists were evangelical Christians, motivated by the same spirit of perfectionism and holiness that stirred them to participate in a broad field of other social reform movements. Unsurprisingly, abolitionism thrived in "burned-over" districts where canals and, later, railroads introduced market values, including the promotion of stable nuclear families, sober and industrious workers, and adherence to Christian values and teachings. These areas tended to be settled first and predominantly by New Englanders, who fostered a long-standing antipathy toward slavery. In Washtenaw, Michigan; Oswego, New York; Ashtubula, Ohio; Pittsfield, Massachusetts;

Dover, New Hampshire; Ohio's Western Reserve; and northern Indiana and Illinois, abolitionists, who were a small and largely despised minority in the North, planted some of their deepest roots. Gerrit Smith, a devout Christian, philanthropist, and abolitionist from western New York State who served a single term in Congress, urged his neighbors to oppose slavery in their own "self-defense," lest the South should "prepare the way for reducing northern laborers into a herd of slaves."

To oppose slavery was not the same as embracing abolition. The vast majority of antislavery Northerners regarded the peculiar institution as a drag on the country. They worried that slavery was inimical to economic and social progress and that it encouraged antidemocratic tendencies on the part of the white majority. Some antislavery Americans genuinely found the institution distasteful, but just as many harbored profoundly racist sentiments and opposed slavery because they did not wish to coexist with Black people. For the most part, antislavery Northerners supported restrictions on slavery, rather than its wholesale elimination. They wanted to see the institution contained to Southern states, where it already existed, and believed that if it were so contained, it would gradually crumble under the weight of economic and political reality. Many antislavery proponents favored colonization schemes that would resettle formerly enslaved people in Africa. They could not anticipate a day when white and Black people would coexist equally in the United States.

Abolitionists were cut from a different cloth. Most were committed to what in 1831 William Lloyd Garrison, the abolitionist editor and founder of the American Anti-Slavery Society (AASS), coined "immediate abolition." They meant precisely what they said: in opposition to the "pernicious doctrine of gradual abolition," they demanded an instant end to slavery everywhere it existed. Some abolitionists, though hardly all, also advocated legal equality for formerly enslaved people. Though a minority movement and almost entirely nonexistent in the South, abolitionism nevertheless was not a negligible force. By 1838 the AASS numbered 250,000 members across 1,300 local chapters, and 400,000 Americans signed antislavery petitions to Congress. Profoundly religious, most abolitionists regarded slaveholding as sinful and could no more tolerate its perpetuation than they could abide intemperance or Sabbath breaking. Theodore Weld, a disciple of Charles Finney and a prominent abolitionist leader, considered the fight against slavery first among equals in the pantheon of Christian reform. It "not only *overshadows* all others but . . . absorbs them into itself. Revivals, moral Reform etc. will remain stationary until the temple is cleansed." Another leading abolitionist, James Birney, denounced gradualism and colonialization as "an opiate to the consciences" of those who "feel deeply and keenly the sin of slavery." It degraded humankind and slowed the work of preparing for the millennium.

Until the 1840s, most abolitionists favored a campaign of moral suasion and deliberately withdrew from all direct political engagement. They believed that the antislavery cause, much like the work of filling church pews, was one of personal conversion, and that a political system that tolerated and supported slavery was inherently sinful. Later, in the 1840s, a sizeable number of abolitionists embraced electoral politics and broke away from the AASS, favoring a "vote as you pray" approach to combating slavery. But in the early years, abolitionists focused their efforts on winning the hearts and souls of slaveholders, printing over one million pieces of literature—much of it informed by Christian principles—for Southern readers. They also flooded Congress with religious petitions. Unsurprisingly, their appeals fell on deaf ears. In South Carolina and elsewhere, mobs broke into post offices and simply destroyed the pamphlets and circulars. Congress demurred when President Andrew Jackson advocated a ban on the distribution of abolitionist newspapers and literature by mail, but in practice, local postmasters and proslavery agitators prevented such material from reaching its destination. In Congress, the House of Representatives, at the behest of Southern members and their Northern enablers, enacted a gag rule that banned the introduction of antislavery petitions during debate. These actions were harbingers of a protracted and often violent reaction against abolitionists everywhere—and not only in the South. In Utica, New York, the city's leading merchants and lawyers whipped up a mob of day laborers to break up a religious antislavery convention. In Boston, workingmen dragged the visiting British abolitionist George Thompson through the streets. Henry Stanton, an abolitionist lecturer, estimated that he faced down more than seventy mobs across Ohio. They fared better than Elijah P. Lovejoy, whom proslavery men lynched in 1837 in Alton, Illinois, a southern-facing city on the Missouri border. "We did not anticipate that, in order to protect southern slavery, the free states would voluntarily trample under foot all order, law and government, or brand the advocates of universal liberty as incendiaries," Garrison observed. Given the hostility with which they were met, it was little wonder that most religious abolitionists maintained a distance from organized politics until such separation no longer seemed a viable strategy.

Some abolitionist sympathizers did, however, find their way to politics. Joshua Giddings, who for eleven terms in Congress represented the Western Reserve, a classic burned-over district in northeast Ohio, was typical of evangelical Christians who brought their religious conviction to bear in the political sphere. Born and raised a Congregationalist, Giddings, who was a successful, self-taught lawyer prior to his election to the House of Representatives, experienced a spiritual awakening in 1837 that brought him closer to the new religion and to its reform spirit. Theodore Weld later claimed to have converted him to the abolitionist cause, though it is more likely that Giddings, who had long been involved in Christian causes like temperance and Bible study, came to the movement on his own. He resigned from the local colonization society and fervently advocated abolition. As a Whig congressman, Giddings emerged as the most strident antislavery voice in the House. Flatly violating the gag rule, he repeatedly attempted to introduce antislavery petitions into the record. Southerners and their Northern sympathizers responded by issuing an official censure. In response, Giddings resigned from Congress, returned home, and by an overwhelming margin won the special election to fill his vacant seat. There was little mistaking the convergence of his religious commitment and his opposition to slavery. Slaveholding was sinful, and in the parlance of evangelical Christianity, sinners enjoyed free will to renounce their crimes. "No real distinction can be drawn between the infidelity which denies the responsibility of human action," he declared, in clear reference to evangelical faith in the individual's responsibility to repent and redeem himself, "and that political conservatism which maintains a traffic in human flesh."

Another Ohioan, Salmon P. Chase, similarly came to the antislavery cause through the lens of religion. Raised a devout Episcopalian (not in his time an evangelical denomination), Chase was a lifelong churchgoer whose typical Sundays, even as a young man, involved private prayer and reflection, "thanksgiving for past mercies, and supplications for needed aids and blessings, to the great All-Giver." He bookmarked his weekdays with Bible study at four thirty in the morning and devotions from eight to ten o'clock in the evening. Lyman Beecher, the leading light of alleviated Calvinism, officiated his second wedding. (Chase was widowed three times and harbored grave concerns about his wives' acceptance of

Christ and their fate in the afterworld.) After moving to Cincinnati, he became active in the Young Men's Temperance Society, the American Sunday School Union, and other Christian reform groups. He also became increasingly radical on the question of slavery, a position that grew out of his Christian faith. In a series of pathbreaking legal cases, Chase represented both abolitionists seeking legal enforcement of their right to free speech and fugitives seeking to convince the Ohio state courts that, once on free soil, they ceased to be enslaved people. He initially did so with hesitancy, as he "had just begun to acquire a pretty good practice for a young man and among the gentlemen to be sued were several of my personal friends." But Chase's antislavery ardor prevailed. He held that slaveholding was sinful, and pioneered the innovative legal position that the Constitution did not recognize slavery outside the narrow borders where it was specifically permitted. Freedom was national, he maintained, and slavery a local condition. It was an argument that later became foundational in the political antislavery movement. Over his long career, including his tenure as Lincoln's Treasury secretary, Chase rankled many peers with his seemingly bottomless ambition and high self-regard. He was, according to one contemporary, "possessed by the desire to be President even to the extent of honestly believing that he owed it to the country and the country owed it to him." But he was earnest in his religious commitments and opposition to slavery. He described the struggle against slavery as "more a moral and religious movement" than a political enterprise.

SOUTHERNERS AND THEIR NORTHERN APOLOGISTS OFTEN LAMBASTED Christian reformers as eccentric extremists on a wide variety of social questions, but particularly on the subject of slavery. In reality, the churches

enjoyed a tense and paradoxical relationship with the peculiar institution. Most abolitionists were evangelical Christians whose moral opposition to slavery flowed from deeply felt religious commitment—but
most evangelicals in the years preceding the Civil War were not abolitionists, many were antagonistic toward abolitionism, and most were
deeply antagonistic toward African Americans. Charles K. Whipple, an
abolitionist from Massachusetts, was fundamentally correct when, on
the eve of the Civil War, he characterized the antislavery movement as
"thoroughly and emphatically a religious enterprise," but it was equally
true that by the 1850s, many abolitionists had soured on organized Christianity. They bitterly resented the churches' uneasy accommodation of
slavery and tolerance of slaveholders in their ranks, and they bristled at
the false comparison between slaveholding and abolitionism. An activist from Newbury, Massachusetts, best encapsulated this point of view
when he publicly withdrew from his congregation. "I am deeply and
sorrowfully impressed with the belief that by your opposition to the
Anti-Slavery enterprise, and by your silence in regard to the wrongs of
the slave and the guilt of the slaveholder, you, as a church, are doing more
to make our holy religion the scorn and execration of mankind than all
that Jew, or Heathen, or Infidel, ever did or can do," he wrote. "I cannot
regard you as a Christian church; and I DO HEREBY RENOUNCE YOU AS A
CHRISTIAN CHURCH."

If many abolitionists were disgusted by their churches, it was because
they initially held high expectations of religious leaders and institutions.
Religious abolitionists who experienced their own moral awakenings
had, according to Whipple, "attributed the silence of the clergy respect-
ing slavery to the same source with their own former quiescence, partly
thoughtlessness, partly ignorance of the essential character and actual
workings of the system, and partly preoccupation with subjects nearer

home." They assumed that, when confronted with the spiritual imperative of dismantling the slave system, church leaders would rush to the
abolitionist cause. When that embrace of the antislavery position failed
to materialize, friction naturally emerged between religious abolitionists and the major evangelical denominations.

Religious abolitionists were not wrong in assuming discordance between slavery and Christianity. Several tenets of evangelical faith made
any accommodation of slaveholding untenable. Perfectionism—and, for
Methodists particularly, the concept of entire sanctification—required
that Christians live upright and morally just lives even amid corruption
and sin. Millennialism—the belief that Christ would return only after
a thousand-year era of peace—was both common to evangelical faith
and a key underpinning of the evangelical front's social reform agenda.
As long as slavery—that greatest of sins—stood intact, the clock remained stuck. Finally, the conviction that all humans were born with
free will was fundamentally in conflict with slavery, whose victims were
denied bodily or spiritual autonomy. In short, religious abolitionists
drew from their own theological tradition when they identified slavery
as a "sin per se" and denounced the "moral cowardice" of churchgoers
who did not join in the holy cause of abolition. An antislavery convention in northern Illinois in 1851 captured the tension between abolitionism and organized Christianity when it resolved that "slavery is a sin
[and] should be immediately repented of, and abolished . . . churches
which array themselves against the cause of emancipation, or which
maintain a studied indifference, give evidence in this respect of ceasing
to be true churches of Christ . . . all churches should labor earnestly,
consistently with their convictions of duty and their ideas of church
government and organization, for the entire expulsion of slaveholders
from their communion."

On paper, most of the major evangelical denominations formally opposed the "buying and selling of men, women, and children," in the words of the Methodist *Book of Discipline*, which from the church's very inception as an independent religious body took an unequivocal stance against slavery. The Presbyterian General Assembly echoed this sentiment in 1818 when it held "the voluntary enslaving of one part of the human race by another, as a gross violation of the most precious and sacred rights of human nature, as utterly inconsistent with the law of God." Baptists, representing the largest denomination in the antebellum period, were a decentralized movement, but many local bodies similarly condemned slaveholding. None of these positions aligned the churches with the immediate abolitionism that William Lloyd Garrison and his allies championed, but they placed the nation's largest evangelical bodies squarely in the moderate antislavery camp—on paper, at least.

Conviction soon ran up against the practical need to placate slaveholders in the South and border states, as well as Southern transplants to the Midwest. Competing fiercely for new adherents, the major evangelical churches were loath to alienate current or prospective members. It was one matter to oppose slavery in official church documents and organs. It was another to sanction slaveholders or exclude them from Christian fellowship—a step that many churchgoers considered both counterintuitive to the project of saving souls and filling pews on Sunday and more likely to alienate than persuade. Thus in 1836 the Presbyterian General Assembly rejected a resolution to censure slaveholders, reasoning that such a measure "would tend to distract and divide" Christians of good faith. The same year, the Methodist General Conference similarly voted down a proposal to sanction slaveholding church members and even took the additional step of formally denouncing two abolitionist ministers for agitating against slavery at the conference. As Jesse Peck, a Methodist minister and unofficial church historian later wrote, "We thought and felt that everything must bow to the one great sentiment of confraternity." These accommodations were not uncontroversial. Many outspoken Presbyterian, Methodist, and Baptist abolitionists, lay and clergy alike, sharply criticized the "inroads the spirit of Slavery has made on the Church of Christ." But in the main, the churches attempted to take a compromise position, opposing slavery in theory but declining to enforce discipline on clergy or parishioners who were themselves implicated in its maintenance.

Southern Christians, for their part, could and did locate ample evidence of Biblical support for slavery.

> Genesis 9:25: "And he said, Cursed be Canaan; a servant of servants shall he be unto his brethren."

> Deuteronomy 21:10–11: "When thou goest forth to war against thine enemies, and the Lord thy God hath delivered them into thine hands, and thou hast taken them captive . . ."

> Leviticus 25:44: "Both thy bondmen, and thy bondmaids . . . shall be of the heathen that are round about you."

> Colossians 3:22: "Servants, obey in all things your masters according to the flesh . . ."

> 1 Peter 2:18–19: "Servants, be subject to your masters with all fear. . . . For this is thankworthy . . ."

But within the Northern evangelical churches, their arguments generally fell flat. Jesus's annulment of Old Testament laws conveniently rendered most such biblical justifications of slavery moot, even if the New

Testament was not without its own endorsements of servitude. Christian perfectionism provided a more urgent and overarching imperative to create a fellowship of humankind that necessarily precluded holding property in human beings. The Presbyterian minister and abolitionist George Bourne laid the matter bare when he wrote that "every man who holds Slaves and who pretends to be a Christian or a Republican is either an incurable Idiot who cannot distinguish good from evil, or an obdurate sinner who resolutely defies every social, moral, and divine requisition." He maintained that "one rational creature cannot become the property of another, is totally repugnant to the rule of equity, the rights of nature, and the existence of civil society."

Most leading churchmen condemned both slaveholding (though not usually slaveholders) and abolitionism as two sides of the same bad coin. Rejecting the abolitionists' insistence that slaveholding was sinful in all circumstances, they made allowances for church members who came into possession of bondmen through inheritance or other nondeliberate legal outcomes, and urged that such persons recognize that "their slaves, though legal property, are morally and actually men," deserving of fundamental material support and good treatment. Edward Beecher, Lyman's son and a prominent evangelical clergyman in his own right, preached that slaveholding was an "organic sin," but that slaveholders were not necessarily sinners by natural extension. Rather, American society, which legally sanctioned chattel slavery, was primarily culpable for the institution's wickedness.

Such prevarication was sharply at odds with a religious ethos that emphasized human agency, a point that many abolitionists noted, often out of anger or disgust. Slaveholders were sentient human beings invested with free will. No one compelled them to keep their enslaved people. Writing for *The Emancipator*, an abolitionist newspaper founded by

Arthur Tappan, Elihu Burritt, a prominent activist, wondered how moderates could square the logic of "organic sin" with their interest in social reforms meant to redress the economic and social sins associated with the modern market economy. If slaveholders were not individually culpable for the crime done to enslaved people, could anyone be held to account for the injustices committed by corporations, governments, or other institutions? The idea of organic sin "teaches that private consciences are not held responsible for incorporated or organized sins," Burritt remarked, "although said consciences may be stockholders and directors in the hugest system of iniquity." Meeting in Chicago in 1851, the Christian Anti-Slavery Convention flatly rebuked Beecher, finding that "it is not 'God's method of procedure' to allow national and organic, any more than individual sins in the church, and so long as this course is pursued in the missions of the Protestant Church, the Gospel can never have free course, and 'the latter-day glory' can never dawn upon the world."

Abolitionists took particular offense to the double standard that many religious leaders applied. While absolving slaveholders of individual culpability for their sins, in the same breath, moderate church leaders often condemned abolitionists for exciting "the worst passions, in the Reformer himself, in the slaveholders, in the slave, and in the whole community." By this logic, "ultraisms" compromised the fellowship of Christ, but slaveholding did not. Rather than chastise, banish, or censure slaveholders, opponents of slavery should "speak to them as friends—as those influenced by the high principles of the gospel of Christ; and with a regard to *their* highest good, as well as to the good of the suffering slaves." This attitude, pervasive in the first half of the nineteenth century, struck abolitionists as the height of hypocrisy.

Religious abolitionists grappled with the logic of their "no fellowship with slaveholders" standard. If the churches would not expel slave-holders, should real Christians establish their own churches? Some did. A variety of "come-outer" sects broke away from the established evangelical churches in the 1830s and 1840s, believing, in the words of a convention that convened in 1851 in Putnam County, Illinois, that "the complete divorce of the church and of missions from national sins will form a new and glorious era in her history—the precursor of Millennial blessedness." Prominent abolitionists including James Birney, who ran for president in 1840 and 1844 as the nominee of the Liberty Party—a small, single-issue party dedicated to abolition—William Lloyd Garrison, and William Goodell, the author of *Come-Outerism: The Duty of Secession from a Corrupt Church*, openly encouraged Christians to leave their churches and make fellowship with like-minded opponents of slavery. The very term was steeped in biblical meaning that most churchgoers would have recognized, the book of Revelation 18:

> And he cried mightily with a strong voice, saying, Babylon the great is fallen, is fallen, and is become the habitation of devils, and the hold of every foul spirit, and a cage of every unclean and hateful bird. . . .
>
> And I heard another voice from heaven, saying, Come out of her, my people, that ye be not partakers of her sins, and that ye receive not of her plagues.

Reflecting this spirit, the Massachusetts Anti-Slavery Society resolved in 1843 that the "Church or minister that refuses to treat the sin of slaveholding, which is the sum of other sins, its perpetrators and abettors, near and remote, direct and indirect, as they do all other sins and sinners, is not a Church of Christ, or minister of the gospel; and that it is the duty of all true abolitionists to withdraw all support or countenance from such ministers and Churches."

Come-outers nevertheless represented a minuscule fraction of organized Christianity. In the end, breaking fellowship with their coreligionists was a step too far for all but a small number of deeply committed activists. Some churches were closer to the antislavery cause than others. Congregationalists generally refused membership to slaveholders, considering "slavery as it exists in our country . . . a heinous sin" and finding that "slaveholders ought not to be admitted to our Pulpits and communion tables." Yet despite its outsize influence on American religious and intellectual life, the Congregationalist church was a much smaller cousin to the other evangelical denominations, and few slaveholders likely contemplated membership in any event, given the church's New England origins, strength in burned-over areas of the upper Midwest, and strong aversion to slavery.

Not coincidentally, immediate abolition planted its deepest roots among New England migrants to burned-over districts in the West, where the market economy also produced an uptick in church membership, revival activities, and reform movements generally. Such was the case in Ohio's Western Reserve (home to Joshua Giddings), northern Indiana, eastern Michigan, and upstate New York, where religious fervor and abolitionism grew in tandem, even if the churches themselves did not necessarily embrace the antislavery movement in full. In these regions, new canals and land routes—and, later, railroads—connected new migrants to distant markets and broke with the protomarket values that young Abraham Lincoln learned as a child in backwoods Indiana. As towns like Washtenaw, Michigan, and Ashtabula, Ohio, emerged into important market centers, they gave rise to evangelical churches, and to religious reform. Abolitionism, though it remained a minority movement inside and outside of the churches, was one piece of that puzzle.

Despite their tension with organized Christianity, most abolitionists believed that their movement was a firmly religious calling. Their disillusionment was not with Christianity, but rather with the failure of churches to live and realize the force of Christian conviction and obligation. "The Anti-Slavery Society is avowedly a *Christian* Society," wrote William Jay, corresponding secretary for the American Anti-Slavery Society. "On this fact rests our hope of divine assistance & on this alone rests our confidence in each other. I do not trust any coadjutor who [does] not act with us from Christian principles. . . . I do not depend on any man as an abolitionist who does not act from a sense of religious obligation."

In the North, church membership or affiliation was not merely coincidental with antislavery commitment. It was a driving force. Theodore Weld recruited and organized the Seventy, a squad of antislavery speakers whose ranks drew predominantly from ordained clergy and seminary students, and which focused its efforts on church audiences and religious conventions. Some radical abolitionists like Stephen S. Foster and Parker Pillsbury riled the faithful by targeting church audiences, often interrupting Congregationalist services to deliver impromptu sermons denouncing the connivance of churches in propagating slavery. More commonly, religious antislavery advocates plied the same campaign of moral suasion that activists also brought to bear in a host of moral reform movements, from temperance to Sabbatarianism. Despite the activists' frustration with organized religious authorities, the churches remained the best hope for immediate abolitionism, a point that Weld made somewhat earnestly—and naively—when he predicted in 1834 that "scores of clergymen in the slaveholding states . . . *are really with us.*" "The whole system of slavery will fall to pieces with a rapidity that will astonish," another religious abolitionist believed.

Perhaps no episode better laid bare the tension within organized Christianity than the student rebellion in 1834 at Lane Seminary, a Presbyterian college located in present-day Cincinnati. With backing from wealthy East Coast patrons, the institution was an incubator for evangelical activity in the West. The Tappan brothers had recruited none other than Lyman Beecher to serve as the seminary's president. It was a solid brick in the wall of the evangelical united front. But the arrival of Theodore Weld, at Arthur Tappan's behest, sparked two weeks of "protracted sessions" of prayer and reflection on the question of immediate abolitionism. The students eagerly embraced Weld's position and undertook a direct action program in Cincinnati's Black community. Some of the seminarians even took sabbaticals from their studies to teach at a local Black school. The community's response was predictably irate, leading the Lane trustees to call for a halt to antislavery and civil rights activity. Beecher, a moderate who opposed slavery but was hardly an abolitionist, was stuck in the middle. Ultimately, Weld persuaded forty students—henceforth known as the "Lane Rebels"—to withdraw from the school and form a new college in Oberlin, a town outside Cleveland, in the more hospitable environs of northern Ohio. With seed money from the Tappans, Oberlin College was the first racially integrated institution of higher learning in the United States, open to men *and* women of all races. Weld was offered, but turned down, a faculty position, preferring to continue his efforts at proselytizing the local community in the name of the church and abolitionism.

❖

FOR BLACK EVANGELICALS, THE TENSION BETWEEN CHRISTIANITY AND slavery was especially pronounced. As in the broader movement, evangelical Black churches furnished the leadership and shock troops of abolitionism within the African American community. Leading Methodist and Baptist clergyman—including Samuel Cornish, Henry Highland Garnet, Theodore S. Wright, and Samuel Ringgold Ward—used their pulpits to thunder forth against slavery and to call out the hypocrisy of churches that professed to be Christian but welcomed slaveholders in their fellowship. For Black evangelicals, the message of Christian perfectionism carried less resonance than Old Testament stories of God's retributive justice against the wicked—both wicked individuals and nations. This interpretive emphasis also made Garrisonian abolitionism, which insisted on pacifism and disengagement from politics and political parties, a less attractive reform movement.

Frederick Douglass, the fugitive turned abolitionist writer and organizer, was representative of Black evangelicals who influenced the transformation of the broader abolitionist movement. An autodidact who learned to read by parsing copies of the Bible, the Methodist hymnal, and *The Columbian Orator*—a religious and political reader that Abraham Lincoln also used to advance his own literacy, at roughly the same time—Douglass was a devout churchgoer who wove biblical themes and imagery into his writings. Like other Black evangelicals, he frequently invoked the prophetic tradition of the Old Testament and patterned his lectures after Puritan jeremiads, with their warnings of societal decline in the face of iniquity. "Ah sinful nation," he quoted Isaiah 1, "hear the word of the Lord, ye rulers of Sodom; give ear unto the law of our God, ye people of Gomorrah . . . your hands are full of blood."

From his earliest memories of emotive Methodist camp meetings on Maryland's Eastern Shore during his childhood in slavery, to his experience as a lay preacher in New Bedford, Massachusetts, in the early years following his escape from bondage, Douglass easily toggled between religious and secular condemnations of both slavery and slaveholders, not just for the crime against Black persons but for the violence that the institution visited upon the church. "In America Bibles and slaveholders go hand in hand," he intoned. "The church and the slave prison stand together, and while you hear the chanting of psalms in one, you hear the clanking of chains in the other. The man who wields the cowhide during the week used to . . . show me the way of life on the Sabbath." Like many activists, ranging from Christian abolitionists to antislavery politicians like William Seward, Douglass affirmed the preeminence of a "higher law" over the laws of man. "Some things are settled, and settled forever—" he insisted, "not by the laws of man, but by the laws of God . . . liberty and slavery cannot dwell in the United States in peaceful relations." In the wake of the Supreme Court's decision in the Dred Scott case in 1857, in which the justices ruled that United States citizens had a right to bring their property, including slaves, into federal territories, he held that the "Supreme Court of the United States is not the only power in the world, but the Supreme Court of the Almighty is greater." Say what they might, the justices could "not change the essential nature of things, making evil good, and good evil."

While white and Black antislavery activists shared common faith in a higher law, many Black abolitionists rejected the movement's pacifistic faith. Though initially aligned with the Garrisonian wing of the abolitionist movement, Douglass grew increasingly skeptical that moral suasion alone could destroy North American slavery. Breaking with the Garrisonians, he embraced political engagement (first through the Liberty Party and, later, the Republicans) and violent conflict. He welcomed armed resistance to the Fugitive Slave Act of 1850, encouraging free Black Americans and their white sympathizers to "greet" slave catchers "with a hospitality befitting the place and occasion." (More specifically, they should "be murdered in your streets.") Because of, and not despite, his religious conviction that slaveholding was sinful, Douglass urged that there must be "blows to take as well as blows to give." He was a "peace man," he insisted, but white men who willingly acted as "bloodhounds," hunting down human beings to return them to slavery, had "no right to live." "I do believe that two or three dead slaveholders will make this law a dead letter." In a speech entitled "Is It Right and Wise to Kill a Kidnapper?" Douglass conceded that perhaps it was not strategically smart, given the disbalance of power, but he affirmed that it "is in all cases, a crime to deprive a human being of life" and not a sin to kill those who would. "For a *white* man to defend his friend unto blood is praiseworthy," Douglass wrote in 1854, "but for a *Black* man to do the same thing is crime. It was glorious for Patrick Henry to say, '*Give me liberty or give me death!*' It was glorious for Americans to drench the soil, and crimson the sea with blood, *to escape the payment of three-penny tax upon tea*; but it is a crime to shoot down a monster in defense of the liberty of a Black man and to save him from bondage."

By the mid-1850s, Douglass was well on record in predicting that slavery, "that perpetual contemner of God's laws, and disturber of the nation's peace," would meet with a bloody end. Its "peaceful annihilation is almost hopeless," he wrote. "The recoil, when it comes, will be in exact proportion to the wrongs inflicted; terrible as it will be, we accept and hope for it. The slaveholder has been tried and sentenced, his execution only waits the finish to the training of his executioners. He is training his own executioners." This theoretical embrace of violent opposition to slavery brought Douglass into association with John Brown, another religious zealot in the cause of freedom. In the wake of Brown's failed attempt to initiate an uprising of enslaved people in Virginia, Douglass, who had not been involved in planning the incursion but knew enough to be held culpable, fled temporarily to Canada.

Douglass was not alone. Samuel Ringgold Ward, a leading Congregationalist minister and abolitionist who, like Douglass, had been born into slavery in Maryland but escaped in his youth to freedom, followed the same road. Active in the Liberty Party and Free Soil Party, he preached the "right and duty of the oppressed to destroy their oppressors." Far from proscribing violence, "God's Holy Writ," as Ward described it, demanded that Christians affirmatively defy the Fugitive Slave Act—with deadly force, if necessary, just "as you are not to lie, steal and murder." Other Black abolitionists agreed. Some, like Henry Highland Garnet, favored an armed insurrection of enslaved people. Others, like Martin Delany, a physician, abolitionist, and active congregant of the African Methodist Episcopal Church, urged African Americans to abandon the United States for Africa. The nation, he believed, was irredeemable.

Excepting those on the fringe, including a group of religious abolitionists who, alongside Douglass, helped raise funds for John Brown's doomed uprising, most white evangelicals—even those of unimpeachable antislavery credentials—continued to forswear coercion and violence before the Civil War. In their response to Brown's arrest and execution by federal authorities, they made their pacifism abundantly clear. Though he sympathized with the old man's antislavery zeal, William Crane, a Methodist leader in Michigan, doubted that "these violent massacres were calculated to benefit the slave or reform the slaveholder." Another prominent evangelical, George Bethune, thought it was "madness . . . to precipitate changes by violence which the progress of the Gospel will bring about peacefully." Henry Ward Beecher agreed that "mad and feeble schemes" deserved no quarter in Christian circles, while Eden B. Foster, an outspoken critic of slavery, affirmed, "I am living under the same constitution with the Slave States. . . . That constitution does not allow me to incite slave rebellion." Instead, "argument, love, and persuasion are all the weapons that we, as individuals, can employ."

Black abolitionists influenced the direction of the broader movement, which by the late 1850s moved markedly away from its legacy of political disengagement and pacifism. Equally important, their belief in retributive justice presaged the direction many religious Northerners would follow during the 1860s, as they came to view warfare as a legitimate and even divinely ordained enforcement of God's will.

DESPITE THE RELUCTANCE OF MAJOR DENOMINATIONS TO CONFRONT THE issue, slavery inevitably opened a rift between Northern and Southern churches. The first lightning bolt struck in 1837, when the Presbyterian church formally split between its New School and Old School factions. Technically the divide was over matters of theology and biblical exegesis, with New School churches and synods adopting a highly Arminianized or "alleviated" form of Calvinism, "new measures" of winning converts, and an ecumenical approach to working with other evangelical churches. Old School traditionalists, by contrast, retained a traditional interpretation of the Westminster standards. While most of the nation's New School Presbyterians, numbering roughly 100,000 communicants across 1,200 churches, lived in Northern states, the Old

School, with roughly 127,000 members and 1,763 churches, was not strictly a Southern religious movement. It enjoyed pockets of strength in Pennsylvania and New Jersey. Contemporaries nevertheless believed that the controversy over slavery was firmly behind the rupture. A year before the formal divorce, delegates to the General Assembly held separate caucuses—one in the North, one in the South. John Witherspoon, attending from South Carolina, reported a rumor that 150 abolitionists had taken to the convention floor. "I can scarcely believe this, and yet I am convinced they be very many . . . I say, Sir, let the *South look well to her interests.*" Another delegate observed that "it is the prevalent opinion among southerners that we are to be unchurched by a considerable majority. If so, we can retire south of *Mason's and Dixon's* line and . . . dwell in peace and harmony." The *Cincinnati Journal and Luminary*, a religious publication that closely followed the Presbyterian schism, concluded that the "question is not between the new and the old school—is not in relation to doctrinal errors; but it is *slavery and anti-slavery*. It is not the [Westminster] *standards* which were to be protected, but the *system of slavery.*"

Discord over slavery soon spread to the other major denominations. In 1844 the General Conference of the Methodist Episcopal Church convened in New York for its annual meeting. A year earlier, dozens of Northern congregations representing roughly six thousand members broke with their parent church over its toleration of slavery, forming the come-outer Wesleyan Methodist Church. Recognizing the possibility of further defections, church officials hoped to gesture at their opposition to slavery without fully antagonizing Southern coreligionists. The test came when the conference confronted the case of James O. Andrew, a bishop from Georgia who "became connected with slavery" when his first wife died, leaving him in possession of two enslaved people whom she owned. The matter was compounded when Andrew's second wife inherited several enslaved people from her late husband. Bishop Andrew signed legal documents forswearing a property relationship to his second wife's enslaved people and offered to resign his post, but some of his more ardent, antislavery peers would have nothing of it, hoping to force the issue at the General Conference. By a vote of 110 to 68, the assembly deemed that Andrew's "connection" with slavery would "greatly embarrass the exercise of his office . . . if not in some places entirely prevent it" and found that he should step aside "so long as this impediment remains." In response, Southern Methodists withdrew from the church and formed their own denomination, the Methodist Episcopal Church, South. Leaders on both sides negotiated an equitable distribution of assets and went their separate ways. Peter Cartwright, the Methodist minister and politician who would run unsuccessfully against Lincoln for Congress two years later, was present at the conference. "I knew, if the Southern preachers failed to carry the point they had fixed, namely, the tolerance of slaveholding in episcopacy, that they would fly the track, and set up for themselves," he later recalled. "And I the more deeply regretted it because any abomination sanctioned by the priesthood, would take a firmer hold on the country, and that this very circumstance would the longer perpetuate the evil of slavery, and perhaps would be the entering wedge to the dissolution of our glorious Union; and perhaps the downfall of this great republic."

Baptists experienced a similar schism, one that resulted in a permanent split between the movement's northern and southern congregations. Meeting in New York in 1840, leaders of the American Baptist Anti-Slavery Convention warned that "we cannot and we dare not recognize you as consistent brethren in Christ . . . and we cannot at the Lord's table, cordially take that as a brother's hand, which plies the scourge on

woman's naked flesh,—which thrusts a gag in the mouth of a man,—
which rivets fetters on the innocent,—and which shuts the Bible from
human eyes." Southern Baptists, ever sensitive to the moral judgment
of non-slaveholders, took umbrage at "aspersions upon their character"
and, despite hand-wringing over the political consequences of disunion
within the church, made good on their threat to cut off ties with their
Northern churchmen. In 1845 they withdrew and formed the Southern
Baptist Convention.

The split in some ways freed Northern Baptists from the necessity of
placating their Southern brothers and sisters. The late 1840s saw many
Northern congregations and Baptist organizations pass resolutions ex-
cluding slaveholders from their fellowship and denouncing as sinners
those who held enslaved people. Such activity was more prevalent in
New England and northern parts of the Midwest. Border states and the
lower Midwest remained Southern in origin and more closely tied to the
institution of slavery.

Though the major churches normally paid little more than lip service to the antislavery cause, Southern churchgoers recoiled at even the
slightest tolerance of abolitionism within the ranks. The same anti-
majoritarian instincts that informed their drive to prohibit the postal
service from delivering antislavery newspapers and tracts, and which led
the Southern bloc in Congress to insist on a gag rule against the presen-
tation of antislavery petitions in the House of Representatives, led Southern Christians to break ties with their Northern brothers and sisters
over the slightest provocation. "The division of the Methodist Church
will demonstrate . . . that Southern forbearance has its limits," wrote a
slaveholder for the *Southern Christian Advocate*, "and that a vigorous
and united resistance will be made at all costs, to the spread of the
pseudo-religious phrenzy called abolitionism." Matthew Simpson, the

president of Indiana Asbury University and a future leader of the Methodist Episcopal Church, recalled hearing a Southern coreligionist unleash his ire on "Northern Abolitionists" and the entire "Northern church" for their "ignorance of the Bible." (In response to such fulminations, Peter Cartwright denounced Southern separatism as "APOSTACY FROM THE GOOD AND RIGHT WAY OF METHODISM.") Tempers ran at least as hot on the other side. The Old School Presbyterian leader James Henley Thornwell, known as the "Calhoun of the southern church," was incensed by the suggestion that slavery was a sin. "If Slavery indeed be consistent with the Bible," he wrote—and Thornwell was sure that it was—it naturally stood to reason that abolitionists bore "tremendous" responsibility for the split. It was they, after all, who "in obedience to blind impulses and visionary theories, pull down the fairest fabric of government the world has ever seen, rend the body of Christ in sunder, and dethrone the Saviour in His own Kingdom. . . . Are our country, our Bible, our interests on earth and our hopes for heaven to be sacrificed on the altars of a fierce fanaticism?"

The withdrawal of Southern coreligionists from the major evangelical churches polarized the denominations on a regional basis and weakened the rationale for tempering antislavery activity in Northern churches, though in the southern Midwest and border states, religious leaders had to walk a fine line. But events in the 1850s—from the passage of the Fugitive Slave Act of 1850 to the Kansas-Nebraska Act of 1854, which effectively abrogated the Missouri Compromise and opened the western territories to slavery—radicalized Northern Christians in a way that few abolitionists could have predicted. Northern evangelicals recoiled especially at the fugitive law, which denied accused runaways their right to a jury trial and stipulated harsh fines and prison sentences for people who refused to cooperate with or aid federal agents in the capture of accused fugitives. Religious newspapers, which in some states, like New York, comprised as much as 25 percent of all periodicals in circulation, devoted increasing space to high-profile cases, including that of Ellen and William Craft, a Black couple from Georgia whom Theodore Parker and other Boston abolitionists smuggled into Canada, and Shadrach Minkins, a runaway from Norfolk, Virginia, whom an abolitionist citizen militia spirited away from federal authorities. "We heard a shout from across the courthouse," remembered Richard Henry Dana Jr., a lawyer whose office window in Boston overlooked the federal building, "continued into a yell of triumph, and in an instant after down the steps came two negroes bearing the prisoner between them with his clothes half torn off, and so stupefied by his sudden rescue and the violence of the dragging off that he sat almost dumb, and I thought had fainted . . . It was all done in an instant, too quick to be believed." Abel Stevens, editor of *Zion's Herald*, a Methodist weekly based in Boston, spoke for an increasing number of Northern religious leaders who were incensed that the law would make Northerners into "kidnappers for the South." The Constitution might sanction slavery, he conceded, but the religious obligation to "obey God" stood in stark conflict with the law's requirement that Christians make themselves complicit in its execution. Matthew Simpson struck a more cautious tone, reflecting a widespread unease about blurring the line between secular politics and religion. But like many moderates, he found himself unable to bite his tongue on the Fugitive Slave Act and could not imagine that a "frank and kind expression against acknowledged evils" could offend "rational minds."

By the mid-1850s, even the most cautious or conservative lay and religious leaders found their voice. Responding to Democratic criticisms of political sermons delivered by antislavery clergy, the editor of a Baptist newspaper asserted the clergy's "right" and "duty, as ministers, charged to 'declare the whole counsel of God,' in certain circumstances to weigh schemes of public policy in the balance of the sanctuary." Meaning, spiritual leaders must sometimes weigh in on public questions, when those questions concerned matters of moral and religious imperative—like slavery. Though by definition a highly decentralized denomination, Baptist churches and religious organizations experienced an uptick in antislavery petitions. Some congregations in the lower Midwest that resisted or criticized these activities saw increasing numbers of defections to come-outer Baptist congregations. A special committee appointed by the New England Conference of Methodist Ministers declared the Fugitive Slave Act "as anti-scriptural as it is unconstitutional . . . as wicked as it is anti-scriptural, and . . . as disgraceful as it is wicked," while in Utica, New York, a Methodist congregation denounced the law as a crime against God and vowed to resist and impede it by "any just means."

As slavery increasingly consumed national politics, it came to occupy a prominent place in Sunday sermons, Christian periodicals, and evangelical organizations. Some churches worried that if they continued to dither—if they muted their opposition to slavery—they might lose congregants. Among New School Presbyterians, heavy defections to come-outer congregations or to Congregationalist churches that had long staked out an unforgiving position on slavery created an impetus to engage more stridently in the antislavery cause. Among Northern Methodists, a long-standing policy of suppressing debate over slavery gave way by the late 1850s to a rising tide of antislavery activism within the church, as leading denominational abolitionists including Gilbert Haven, William Hosmer, John Twombly, and Hiram Mattison successfully persuaded their coreligionists to adopt a "no fellowship with slaveholders" policy in their individual congregations. Antislavery sentiment increasingly predominated Methodist churches in New England, the burned-over districts of western New York, and the upper Midwest. By the 1850s antislavery clerics like Haven, who affirmed not only the injustice of slavery but also the "absolute oneness of the race of man, in Adam, Noah, and Christ," enjoyed increased sway in a more radicalized Methodist church. "In Christ, not in the Constitution, must we put our trust," he told congregants in a sermon entitled "The Higher Law"—likely a knowing reference to New York senator William Seward's speech of the same title several months earlier. "On his law we should meditate, not on that which nails him, scourged and bleeding, to that fatal cross." Haven would serve as an army chaplain during the Civil War and, later, a popular Methodist bishop. "The march of events in the political, the religious, the social world, all show that He is soon to appear who will unloose these heavy burdens and let the oppressed go free, and break every yoke," he confided to a friend in later years. That someone of Haven's deep antislavery and egalitarian commitment could thrive within the Methodist establishment confirmed the church's increasingly strident opposition to slavery in the lead-up to the war.

Religious antislavery activists remained a minority within their churches and throughout the North until the mid-1850s, but events would soon drive slavery to the forefront of national politics. In Illinois, controversy over the Kansas-Nebraska Act would also stir Abraham Lincoln from a five-year political slumber and bring him more closely into alignment with his state's growing evangelical churches.

CHAPTER 5

VOTE AS YOU PRAY

Abraham Lincoln's brief stint in Congress had been unmemorable, and even unsuccessful: so stridently had he opposed President James Polk's war in Mexico—a popular war in which the United States acquired vast southern and western territories—that many of his constituents soured on the Whig Party and sent a Democrat to Washington to replace him. He did not technically lose his reelection bid, as the local Whig organization operated according to a rotation system by which each officeholder served one term. But the party's loss in 1848 was in no small respect a repudiation of his congressional service. After a failed attempt to secure a federal appointment from incoming president Zachary Taylor, the now ex-congressman returned to Springfield and retired from public life. "From 1849 to 1854, both inclusive, [I] practiced law more assiduously than ever before," he told a newspaperman in 1859. "Always a whig in politics, and generally on the whig electoral tickets, making active canvasses. I was losing interest in politics, when the repeal of the Missouri Compromise aroused me again. What I have done since then is pretty well known." This was something of an understatement.

The Kansas-Nebraska Act of 1854, which inspired Lincoln's return to political life, formally organized the Kansas and Nebraska Territories in preparation for the construction of a midwestern link to a planned transcontinental railroad. At the insistence of Southern Democrats who had conditioned their support of the bill on a provision that it would open the new territories to slavery, Senator Stephen Douglas, Lincoln's longtime political antagonist and now chairman of the Committee on Territories, inserted a "popular sovereignty" clause in the bill that enabled residents of Kansas and Nebraska to decide for themselves whether to permit slavery. The territories were part of the Louisiana Purchase and therefore fell under the terms of the Missouri Compromise of 1820, which had prohibited slavery north of the 36'30" parallel. Effectively, Douglas and his Democratic colleagues shattered a long-standing agreement between the North and the South and reignited the slavery question into American politics.

Lincoln was not alone in his political reawakening. The Kansas-Nebraska Act had inspired "a deep-seated, intense, and ineradicable hatred" of slavery, the editor of *The New York Times* wrote. It was not just that the ruling Democratic Party had repealed the Missouri Compromise. It also seemed intent on flouting any law or tradition that stood in the way of slavery's extension into the territories. William Pitt Fessenden, a Whig senator from Maine, spoke for many Northerners when he called the Kansas-Nebraska Act "a terrible outrage. . . . The more I look at it, the more enraged I become. It needs but little to make me an out & out abolitionist."

The introduction of the Kansas-Nebraska Act snapped the cords that bound many Northern voters to the two political parties, and in-

troduced a period of extreme volatility and excitement. For all intents
and purposes, the Whig Party—which for reasons unrelated to the
slavery issue had been in a state of slow decline—ceased to exist, while
throughout the North, Democrats suffered massive defections by antislavery voters and officeholders. At hundreds of political meetings around
the country, antislavery activists abandoned their political bases for
new "fusion" tickets uniting antislavery "Conscience" Whigs and "Anti-
Nebraska" Democrats, who opposed the Whigs on most policy questions but thought slavery was a dangerous social and political system. In
some states, these fusion tickets were called Anti-Nebraska, Democrat-
Republican, or Free Soil. In Ripon, Wisconsin, on February 28, 1854, several dozen residents of the surrounding county converged on the town's
simple, one-room, wood-frame schoolhouse to forge a new political party.
They called themselves Republicans, and the name soon stuck.

Republicans were disgusted not simply by the imposition of "popular
sovereignty" in territories that by the terms of the now-defunct Missouri
Compromise should have been free. They also watched as Democrats
perverted the very idea of free elections and democratic process. "Border ruffians," led by Missouri's Democratic senator David Atchison,
moved in and out of the Kansas Territory with impunity, stuffing ballot
boxes, visiting violence on Free State settlers, and attempting to tilt the
scales in favor of slavery. "You know how to protect your own interests,"
Atchison declared. "Your rifles will free you from such neighbors. . . .
You will go there, if necessary, with the bayonet and with blood." He
promised, "If we win, we can carry slavery to the Pacific Ocean." Although antislavery voters probably made up a healthy majority of the
population, proslavery forces stole a series of territorial elections, leading the Free Soilers to establish a shadow government in Lawrence,
Kansas.

Though he was slow to reconcile with the demise of the Whig Party and a late convert to the Republican cause, Lincoln soon emerged as the acknowledged leader of the political antislavery movement in Illinois. His unsuccessful Senate campaign against Stephen Douglas in 1858 transformed him into a figure of national prominence in the Republican Party. Lincoln's evolution into a fiery, single-issue politician was all the more remarkable given how complete that transformation was. As a young member of the state legislature, he had been, in most respects, a fiercely partisan attack dog, partial to slash-and-burn rhetoric on the hustings, but with scant legislative accomplishment to his name. Few of his contemporaries regarded him as much more than a workaday politician. His one term in Congress was hardly more notable. Yet after five years on the sidelines, and having waited until the very end of the 1854 campaign season before engaging in the debate over the Kansas-Nebraska Act, he emerged as a man on fire—a very different sort of politician from the one he had formerly been. He became consumed by the moral injustice of slavery and seemingly disinterested in every other public topic.

This was not a matter of opportunism. Lincoln was reluctant and late in abandoning the Whig Party for the Republican coalition. But his disgust over slavery was genuine, profound, and long held. It increased in the immediate aftermath of the Kansas-Nebraska Act and led him to assume a far more public and strident position against slavery than in his years as a state legislator and congressman. A close friend, Joseph Gillespie, remembered that it was "about the only public question on which he would become excited." In language that closely echoed the evangelical jeremiads of Christian abolitionists, Lincoln told Gillespie that "slavery was a great & crying injustice, an enormous national crime and that we could not expect to escape judgement for it." Leonard Swett, another close confidante from the Springfield days, would later tell William Herndon that Lincoln's "whole life was a calculation of the law of forces, and ultimate results. The world to him was a question of cause and effect. He believed the results to which certain causes tended, would surely follow; he did not believe that those causes could be materially hastened, or impeded. His whole political history, especially since the agitation of the Slavery question, has been based upon this theory. He believed from the first . . . that the agitation of Slavery would produce its overthrow."

In a long and uncharacteristically acid letter that he penned in 1855 to his former roommate and best friend, Joshua Speed, Lincoln laid bare his hatred of the institution. He and Speed had been closely associated for almost two decades. They had shared a room in Springfield for several years, knew each other's wives and families, and counseled each other through troubled courtships. Speed was a Kentuckian who professed opposition to slavery, though in fact he owned enslaved people. In May, he had written Lincoln, warning that the political firestorm surrounding the Kansas-Nebraska Act portended a dissolution of the Union. By then a leading voice in the Anti-Nebraska movement, Lincoln sat on the letter for three months before responding. His response was scathing. "You know I dislike slavery," he wrote, "and you fully admit the abstract wrong of it. So far there is no cause of difference. But you say that sooner than yield your legal right to the slave . . . you would see the union dissolved. I am not aware that *any one* is bidding you yield that right, very certainly *I* am not. I leave that matter entirely to yourself. I also acknowledge *your* rights and *my* obligations under the constitution, in regard to your slaves. I confess I hate to see the poor creatures hunted down; and caught, and carried back to their stripes and unrewarded toils; but I bite my lips and keep quiet." Though in this case, he did not bite his lips or keep quiet. In a tirade several pages long, Lincoln denounced the Kansas-Nebraska Act as "not . . . a law, but a violence from the beginning." He was unsparing in his criticism of Speed, his dearest friend, who like many border state slaveholders professed a distaste for slavery while continuing to hold human beings in bondage. "You say that if Kansas fairly votes herself a free state, as a Christian you will rather rejoice in it," Lincoln wrote. "All decent slave-holders *talk* that way; and I do not doubt their candor—But they never *vote* that way. Although in a private letter, or conversation, you will express your preference that Kansas shall be free, you would vote for no man for Congress who would say the same thing publicly. . . . The Slave-breeders and slave-traders, are a small, odious and detested class, among you; and yet in politics, they dictate the course of all of you, and are as completely your masters, as you are masters of your own negroes." It was a remarkably intemperate letter for someone who, in different times, claimed to be "rather inclined to silence . . . and whether that be wise or not, it is at least more unusual now-a-days to find a man who can hold his tongue than to find one who cannot."

Like other antislavery leaders, Lincoln deplored human bondage while retaining the prejudices of his generation. In his antislavery speeches between 1854 and 1858, when he challenged Douglas for the United States Senate, he vociferously denied charges that he believed in social equality between Black and white Americans—a crude political necessity, given southern Illinois's cultural kinship with the slaveholding South, though probably a position in which he genuinely held. But he also articulated a strong moral stance, insisting the "profound central truth" that "slavery is wrong and ought to be dealt with as a wrong." He denounced human bondage as "morally and politically" unjust, "an unqualified evil," a "moral, social, and political wrong." As always, Lincoln chose his words carefully, playing to the prejudices of moderate Republicans and swing voters who feared that white, yeomen farmers—independent landholders working small homesteads who embodied the Jeffersonian ideal—could never compete on a level playing field with plantation owners who employed a vast army of Black laborers. One leading antislavery politician best articulated this position when he denied any "squeamish . . . sensitiveness" or "morbid sympathy for the slave." Instead, he lamented that "the negro race already occupy enough of this fair continent . . . I would preserve for free white labor a fair country . . . where the sons of toil, of my own race and own color, can live without the disgrace which association with negro slavery brings upon free labor." Lincoln gestured at these concerns. "The whole nation is interested that the best use shall be made of these territories," he wrote. "We want them for the homes of free white people. This they cannot be, to any considerable extent, if slavery shall be planted within them." But he implored voters to consider that "if the negro is a man, is it not to that extent, a total destruction of self-government to say that he too shall not govern himself? When the white man governs himself that is self-government; but when he governs himself, and also governs another man, that is more than self-government—that is despotism. If the negro is a man, why then my ancient faith teaches me that 'all men are created equal'; and that there can be no moral right in connection with one man's making a slave of another."

The term "faith" was operative. In stipulating that slavery was a "moral, social, and political wrong," Lincoln covered the full spectrum of antislavery conviction. He spoke to voters who opposed slavery for its injurious impact on the nation's economy and political culture *and* to those who were offended by its violation of religious or humanistic principles. But the "faith" that informed his position was not religious.

It was decidedly secular. "My faith in the proposition that each man should do precisely as he pleases with all which is exclusively his own, lies at the foundation of the sense of justice that is in me," he proclaimed. "No man is good enough to govern another man *without that other's consent.*"

Lincoln's secular argument against slavery situated him well within the mainstream of the Illinois Republican Party but notably apart from some of the Anti-Nebraska coalition's most prominent spokesmen and leaders. In their influential circular, "Appeal of the Independent Democrats," leading antislavery politicians, including Senators Salmon P. Chase and Charles Sumner, and Congressmen Joshua Giddings and Edward Wade, identified the fight against the Kansas-Nebraska Act as a religious imperative. "We implore Christians and Christian ministers to interpose," they wrote. "Their divine religion requires them to behold in every man a brother, and to labor for the advancement and regeneration of the human race." In a sharp break with their prior moderation and silence on the slavery question, many religious leaders now engaged in the battle, using their pulpits to call congregants to cause against the spread of slavery. In New England, 350 clergymen implored their representatives to oppose the bill "in the name of Almighty God." An organized group of ministers in Chicago petitioned their elected officials, prompting Douglas—who called the city home—to condemn political preachers who would "desecrate the pulpit, and prostitute the sacred desk to the miserable and corrupting influence of party politics." That Douglas felt it necessary to protest clergy who invoked "the name of the Almighty upon a political question" likely spoke to the intensity of Northern evangelical mobilization against his Kansas-Nebraska bill. Normally unflappable, and certainly willing to take a risk on reopening parts of the West to slavery—a measure that he acknowledged would

VOTE AS YOU PRAY

"raise a hell of a storm"—Douglas now worried that Anti-Nebraska clergymen would coalesce "the whole religious community into their schemes of political aggrandizement" and spearhead the creation of "a great political sectional party for Abolition."

Douglas exaggerated the importance of clergymen in the formation of the Republican Party, though the party was in fact a sectional anti-slavery (though hardly abolitionist) political organization. But he did not overstate the anger with which many evangelical leaders received word of the Kansas-Nebraska Act. "Clergymen and college professors, who, in by-gone days of technical abolitionism, stood conservative, now stand up and solemnly protest," reported the *Presbyterian of the West*. Protestant ministers denounced the new law as "a great national crime," "a measure fraught not only with political evil, but dishonorable, un-just, wicked, ungodly; contrary to the laws of God," "an act of perfidy." Some viewed it as a "providential retribution to the north" for its com-plicity over many decades in propping up an ungodly institution. Charles Beecher warned that instead of "a favored land with Bibles, preachers, temples, schools, arts, science, industry, and all that marks a great, a pious, a prosperous and happy people," Kansas under the Slave Power's thumb would degenerate into a "dungeon-brothel."

Given their perception of the stakes at hand, religious antislavery activists became more accepting of violence as a political instrument, particularly in Kansas. Like Black evangelical leaders who arrived at the same conclusion years earlier, a new generation of leaders welcomed an eye-for-an-eye approach to keeping the territories free. Subsidized by a group of Massachusetts businessmen and religious abolitionists, the New England Emigrant Aid Company offered material assistance to Northern homesteaders. It also furnished them with rifles (known pop-ularly as "Beecher's Bibles") and ammunition to help settlers stave off attacks by border ruffians who pillaged Free State property and rigged territorial elections. By 1857 the tide had turned so profoundly that when Henry Clarke Wright urged the Massachusetts Anti-Slavery Society to furnish material support for armed insurrections by enslaved people, even Wendell Phillips, heretofore a pacifist, rose to agree. "I want to accustom Massachusetts to the idea of insurrection," he said, "to the idea that every slave has the right to seize his freedom on the spot." It was this embrace of retributive justice and support for violent liberation that led figures like Thomas Wentworth Higginson (a Unitarian minister), Gerrit Smith (a wealthy reformer and founder of a nonsectarian church in upstate New York), Theodore Parker (also a Unitarian clergyman), and Frederick Douglass to furnish John Brown with funds for his failed attempt to organize an uprising of enslaved people. Brown, a religious zealot who came to believe that he was God's instrument in the service of emancipation, was widely scorned as a fanatic when in 1859 he was hanged for murder, incitement of an enslaved people's rebellion, and "treason" against the state of Virginia. Within a few short years, his belief in a divine imperative to erase slavery through force would become a common theme in mainline Christian churches.

Not all religious opponents of slavery embraced violence in the lead-up to the Civil War, but most channeled their spiritual fervor into a new enthusiasm for politics. Central to the new Republican Party was a phalanx of committed Christian antislavery advocates, many of whom had come to political consciousness through the now-defunct Liberty Party. Though never more than a small portion of the Anti-Nebraska coalition, which drew primarily from the ranks of Free Soil Democrats and Conscience Whigs, former Liberty Party partisans nevertheless comprised some of the most unswerving and religiously devout members of the new political organization. Many, like a Liberty Party convention that met in Hamilton, New York, some ten years earlier, had already resolved to make slavery a single-issue litmus test. "Those who admit the sinfulness of slavery . . . and yet vote for oppression, or for those who are connected with pro-slavery parties, are guilty of the most gross inconsistency," they declared, "and are undeserving the name Christian patriots, and unworthy to be recognized as the true friends of downtrodden humanity." In states like Vermont, Maine, and Connecticut, the Liberty Party was so thoroughly recognized as a vehicle of evangelical reform that party meetings often overlapped with interdenominational Christian antislavery conventions. Prominent Liberty Party leaders like Salmon P. Chase of Ohio and Owen Lovejoy of Illinois (the brother of the abolitionist martyr Elijah Lovejoy) were deeply involved in Christian reform movements and soon melded easily into leadership positions in the new Republican Party.

Many—if not most—Republicans regarded slavery primarily as an economic or political evil. They drew a sharp contrast between the North, with its prosperous mix of agriculture and industry, emergent public school system, and vast network of rail and water transportation, and the South, which they viewed as a depressed, undeveloped backwater. Slavery, they feared, formed a drag on the nation's economy and culture. It disincentivized work and industry among white people, and it created a brutal but inefficient labor regime among enslaved people, who, lacking any possibility of upward mobility—let alone freedom— had no real motivation to work harder or smarter. On a sojourn to Virginia, Senator William Seward of New York saw "exhausted soil, old and decaying towns, wretchedly-neglected roads, and, in every respect, an absence of enterprise and improvement. . . . Such has been the effect of slavery." They also argued that slavery promoted a violent and antidemocratic political culture that, if permitted to spread westward, would inevitably infect the rest of the country. Joshua Giddings, whose anti-slavery beliefs were fundamentally religious in character, nevertheless complained of the "self-important airs" and "over-bearing manners" of his Southern colleagues in Congress. Where Northern representatives were "diffident, taciturn, and *forbearing*," Southerners, because they held unchecked dominion over their enslaved people, lacked the core character traits necessary to sustain a democratic system of government.

In the party's early days, most Republicans were probably closer in sentiment to Seward than to Chase or Lovejoy (or, for that matter, Giddings). But Christian activists furnished the coalition with some of its most talented leaders and most ardent antislavery activists. They were long committed to the proposition: "Vote as you pray. You must do it, or be recreant to your country, recreant to your religion, recreant to your God." Regarding slavery as a "sin against God and a crime against man," they viewed politics and religion as inseparable undertakings and formed an evangelical religious base within the Republican Party that would, in the coming decade, grow into its most motivated and sizeable constituency.

FOR HIS PART, LINCOLN STUDIOUSLY AVOIDED MIXING RELIGION AND POLI-tics. As late as 1858, when he and Douglas crisscrossed the state in a series of seven debates, he held to a strictly secular indictment of slavery. There is no doubt that Lincoln considered slavery a moral offense. He said as much on the hustings and marveled at Douglas's unprincipled refusal to condemn or support the institution. His opponent, he quipped, earned "the high distinction . . . of never having said that slavery is either right or wrong. Almost everybody else says one or the other, but the Judge never does." But his reference points were the nation's founding documents and a Whiggish belief in the precepts of a free labor economy—not the Bible, nor the embracing idea of Christian fellowship, nor the conviction that slaveholding was a sin. "I hold that . . . there is no reason in the world why the negro is not entitled to all the rights enumerated in the Declaration of Independence," he told audiences, "*the right of life, liberty, and the pursuit of happiness.* I hold that he is as much entitled to these as the white man. I agree with Judge Douglas that he is not my equal in many respects, certainly not in color— perhaps not in intellectual and moral endowments; *but in the right to eat the bread without the leave of anybody else which his own hand earns, he is my equal and the equal of Judge Douglas, and the equal of every other man.*" It was a radical assertion of Black people's right to personal and economic liberty, but it was nowhere approaching racial egalitarianism and notably devoid of Christian sentiment.

If either candidate invoked religion, it was more often Douglas, who spoke with pride of white citizens' role in "spreading civilization and Christianity where before there was nothing but savage barbarism." Douglas repeatedly attempted to associate Lincoln with radical Christian abolitionists who "tell the people of Kentucky that they have no consciences, that they are living in a state of iniquity, and that they are cherishing an institution to their bosoms in violation of the law of God," offering the biblical retort: "judge not lest ye shall be judged." Lincoln, for his part, studiously avoided engaging in a religious culture war. In contrast to later years, when he frequently invoked the name of God, the Almighty, or the Lord, Lincoln only passingly grounded his antislavery argument in scripture. "The Savior, I suppose, did not expect that any human creature could be perfect as the Father in Heaven," he told an audience in Chicago, "but He said: 'As your Father in Heaven is perfect, be ye also perfect.' He set that up as a standard, and he who did most towards reaching that standard, attained the highest degree of moral perfection. So I say in relation to the principle that all men are created equal, let it be as nearly reached as we can. If we cannot give freedom to every creature, let us do nothing that will impose slavery upon any other creature."

More commonly, Lincoln warned that the controversy over slavery was disruptive to religion, as well as other foundations of civil society. "Does it not enter into the churches and rend them asunder?" he asked. "What divided the great Methodist Church into two parts, North and South? What has raised this constant disturbance in every Presbyterian General Assembly that meets? What disturbed the Unitarian Church in this very city two years ago? What has jarred and shaken the great American Tract Society recently, not yet splitting it, but sure to divide it in the end? Is it not this same mighty, deep-seated power that somehow operates on the minds of men, exciting and stirring them up in every avenue of society—in politics, in religion, in literature, in morals, in all the manifold relations of life?" Slavery, he told an audience in Alton, Illinois—where over twenty years earlier, an angry mob had lynched Elijah Lovejoy—created a rift in the Christian fellowship. Notably, however, he did not claim that it violated Christian doctrine or sentiment.

"You must not say anything about it in the free States, because it is not here," he observed on another occasion. "You must not say anything about it in the slave States, because it is there. You must not say anything about it in the pulpit, because that is religion and has nothing to do with it." It was a subtle acknowledgment that churches had every right to take up a topic of urgent moral consequence, but still a mostly secular objection to the stifling role that proslavery forces played in political and civic discourse.

✦

THERE IS LITTLE EVIDENCE TO SUGGEST THAT LINCOLN'S VIEWS ON RE-
ligion had evolved significantly by 1860. Christopher Brown, a young
lawyer who was at his side the moment Lincoln learned that the Republican National Convention in Chicago had nominated him for the presidency, "never heard Lincoln say anything about his religious views—or
religion in any aspect."

It was true that the Lincolns rented a pew at Springfield's First Presbyterian Church and that the candidate sometimes attended services
with his wife. But it was Mary—a born and raised Presbyterian who had
for some years attended Episcopalian worship—who formally joined the
congregation, after meeting its dynamic, Scottish-born minister, Reverend James Smith. Her husband was not a church member. Smith later
claimed that the death of the couple's three-year-old son, Eddie, in 1850,
brought Lincoln closer to Christianity. The minister had written a book,
The Christian Defence, and asserted that in their discussions about its
contents, he had converted the future president. During Lincoln's final
years in Springfield, Smith claimed that the future president "placed
himself and family under my pastoral Care, and when at home he was
a regular attendant upon my ministry." No one else remembered it that
way. Lincoln's oldest son, Robert, dismissed with Smith's claim to have
"'converted' my father from 'Unitarian' to 'Trinitarian' belief," as did
John Stuart, Lincoln's first law partner (and Mary's cousin). "Lincoln
always denied that Jesus was the Christ of God," he remembered, "denied that Jesus was the son of God as understood and maintained by the
Christian world." Smith did try to convert him, Stuart conceded, but
"Couldn't do it." More likely than not, Smith's memory was clouded in

equal measures by the passage of time, a harmless inclination toward self-aggrandizement, and a popular yearning in the years immediately after Lincoln's assassination to apotheosize the slain president.

It is nevertheless true that Lincoln's speeches increasingly sounded the language of Christian moralism and that the candidate (and, later, president-elect) was more attentive than in earlier years to the religious sensibilities of his audiences. "The good old maxims of the Bible are applicable, and truly applicable to human affairs," he told listeners in Cincinnati in 1859, "and in this as in other things, we may say here that he who is not for us is against us; he who gathereth not with us scattereth."

In February 1860, Lincoln arrived in New York, where he had been invited to address Henry Ward Beecher's congregation at Plymouth Church in Brooklyn. It was a rare opportunity to reach two critical constituencies: the nation's evangelical united front, in which Beecher (indeed, the entire Beecher family) and his congregation were central actors, and the city's Republican Party establishment, which would be influential in the following year's presidential nominating process. The candidate devoted weeks of labor to his text, only to learn upon arriving in New York that the speech had been moved from Plymouth Church to Cooper Union's Greta Hall in Manhattan, and from under the auspices of Beecher's congregation to the Young Men's Central Republican Union. Lincoln scurried to revise his address, rendering it more secular, in light of the switch in venue and sponsorship. The original document does not survive, but even stripped of its religious scaffolding, the speech that Lincoln ultimately delivered subtly appealed to many Republican voters, including those in the hall, whose politics were inspired by deep evangelical conviction. "LET US HAVE FAITH THAT RIGHT MAKES RIGHT," the candidate said in closing, "AND IN THAT FAITH, LET US, TO THE END,

DARE TO DO OUR DUTY AS WE UNDERSTAND IT." It was a line that he repeated in speeches to Republican audiences throughout New England
in the following weeks.

Above all, Lincoln was acutely sensitive to the growing political importance of evangelical churches and philanthropies, which by 1860 were
unqualifiedly the largest and best organized pillars of American civil
society. As mainline Northern churches increasingly adopted a more
strident antislavery stance, their voters provided a solid electoral foundation for the Republican Party. By no stretch of the imagination did all
evangelical voters align with the Republicans. *Most* American Christians
were evangelicals, and by extension, many evangelicals supported the
Democratic Party and its position on slavery. But it was increasingly the
case that evangelical Christians were steadily shifting to the Republicans, while older, devotional denominations (Episcopalians, Catholics)
tended to cast their ballots for Democrats. Lincoln understood this dynamic, as did party leaders throughout the North. In Lincoln's home
state, Methodist, Baptist, Presbyterian, and Congregationalist lay and
religious leaders increasingly claimed the political antislavery movement as a religious imperative.

Little wonder that the Republican Party vocally asserted itself as the
only legitimate Christian party in 1860. At the national convention,
Caleb Smith, a former congressman from Indiana, told delegates: "We
stand upon a rock, and the gates of hell shall not prevail against it."
Partisan newspapers identified Lincoln's candidacy as "worthy of the
holy cause" and warned that "Democratic Jacobins" were locked in a
battle with "civilization and Christianity," with the very "moral sentiment of the nation." It was a contest between "the pulpit, the church,
the academy," on one side, and pure evil on the other. At a monster election rally in Springfield that fall, the Republican faithful drew with ease

on the language of millennial expectation when they prayed: "May God speed the right." It proved impossible, as well as inexpedient, to separate the candidate from the cause. Official biographies took pains to identify the standard-bearer as a "regular attendant upon religious worship, and though not a communicant, a pew-holder and liberal supporter of the Presbyterian church in Springfield, to which Mrs. Lincoln belongs." If not a formal member of any church, Lincoln "always held up the doctrines of the Bible, and the truths and examples of the Christian religion." In Albany, the *Evening Journal* boasted that a survey of Sunday schoolteachers found overwhelming support for Lincoln and the Republican ticket.

It was not just Republicans who perceived a political realignment of evangelical Christians. When Democrats like Stephen Douglas carped about the politicization of Protestant churches—in Springfield, church bells tolled throughout the city upon word of Lincoln's nomination, leading a local Democratic newspaper to whine that "Black republicanism has ever recognized pulpits and church bells as party adjuncts, but yesterday's performance run the thing a little beyond the line of decency"—they begrudgingly acknowledged what people on both sides of the political divide believed. Not all evangelicals were Republicans, but the most ardent Republicans were undeniably evangelical, driven by sincere religious commitment, increasingly in control of their congregations, and eager to place their faith in the forefront of the political debate. It rankled Democrats that their rivals piously claimed hold on being "the *decency, moral* and *Christian party*," as though Democrats were indecent, immoral, and un-Christian. Republicans were rather a "religious sect" with a "holy zeal for one idea" (abolition, allegedly; in reality, opposition to slavery's extension). They were "fanatical Sabbatarians" and imperious social reformers with a frenzied addiction to isms. If the party did not have "slavery for a hobby, it would be vexing us about some other questions of morals or of social arrangement." But slavery was the issue of the day, and it drove leading Democrats to distraction that their churches had lined in opposition to it.

Usually wise to where the political winds blew, Lincoln appreciated the importance of religion to his base. He was hardly naive. In his hometown of Springfield, which stood on the border between southern and northern Illinois—and which he narrowly lost in 1860—most clergymen lined up against him, leading him to complain privately that the city was home to "twenty-three ministers of different denominations," all but three of whom supported the Democratic ticket, and a "great many prominent members of the churches, a very large majority of whom are against me." But statewide and in the main, the leading Protestant churches—particularly the Methodists—who enjoyed a three-to-one numerical advantage over Baptists in Illinois, warmed to his candidacy. He, in turn, made a concerted effort to show kinship with their faith.

In an emotional farewell address to his neighbors, Lincoln acknowledged the gravity of the task before him. "Without the assistance of that Divine Being, who ever attended him," he said, "I cannot succeed. With that assistance I cannot fail. Trusting in Him, who can go with me, and remain with you and be every where for good, let us confidently hope that all will yet be well. To His care commending you, as I hope in your prayers you will commend me, I bid you an affectionate farewell." It was, at the time, his most embracing acknowledgment of his constituents' Christian faith, and a theme to which he would return over the following ten days, through seven states and nineteen hundred miles, as he delivered at least one hundred planned and impromptu speeches while making his way toward Washington, DC, to be inaugurated as the nation's sixteenth president. In a deliberate nod to the Christian sensibilities of his audiences, he paid uncharacteristic homage to "the Providence of God," "that God who has never forsaken this people," "the Divine Power, without whose aid we can do nothing," "Divine Providence," "that Supreme Being, who has never forsaken this favored land," "the Maker of the Universe," the "Almighty," the "Almighty God."

This was an altogether different Abraham Lincoln. Different from the "floating piece of driftwood" who landed on the banks of the San-gamon River in 1831, eager to escape his parents' stern religiosity and narrow scope of ambition. Different from the iconoclast and blasphemer who regaled his siblings and cousins with mocking imitations of church sermons, and who openly questioned the divinity of Christ before learn-ing, out of political expediency, to bite his tongue. Different, too, from the cool, single-minded antislavery politician who summoned every ar-gument *except* the Christian argument to excoriate the Slave Power. He was now the leader of a nation cloaked in sincere Christian faith, chosen to marshal his countrymen to a higher purpose. He may not have shared this faith, but he knew that many of them did.

On February 21, in Trenton, he told the New Jersey Senate, "I shall be most happy indeed if I shall be a humble instrument in the hands of the Almighty, and of this, his almost chosen people." It was a line crafted largely for the benefit of the assembled legislators and newspaper readers. But it would not be long before Lincoln, too, believed it.

PART

II

CHAPTER 6

AND THE WAR CAME

Having achieved the great prize he had long coveted, Lincoln found the presidency a series of never-ending trials. By the time he arrived in Washington, DC, to assume the oath of office, seven Southern states had already seceded from the Union. The first two years of the war, beginning with the Confederate attack on Fort Sumter on April 12, and followed by the secession of four more upper-South states, delivered a string of disappointing setbacks and defeats—at Bull Run in Virginia, Wilson's Creek in Missouri, and Bull Run in Virginia *again*. Even Union victories, like those at Shiloh and Antietam, were often conditional and came at a terrible cost of lives and fortunes. By the close of 1861, Lincoln was near despondent. "The people are impatient; [Secretary of Treasury Salmon] Chase has no money and he tells me he can raise no more; the General of the Army has typhoid fever. The bottom is out of the tub. What shall I do?"

Even as he faced the necessity of raising, provisioning, and training an army, half a million strong by late 1861, the president faced near insurrection in border states like Maryland, where he was forced to declare martial law and arrest one third of the legislature to avoid a vote of secession. Kentucky, where Lincoln was born, declared itself neutral and initially refused to aid the Union's war effort. Though the vast majority of Missourians were Unionists, marauding bands of pro-Confederate bushwhackers—including William Quantrill, George Todd, and Frank and Jesse James—terrorized citizens and engaged in gory guerilla battles with pro-Union militias.

There were early victories in the West, where in 1862 soldiers under the command of Ulysses S. Grant wrested Fort Donelson from Confederate hands after a tense three-day battle, thereby delivering control of the Cumberland River, cordoning off Confederate access to the key border state of Kentucky, and enabling the Union to occupy the western half of Tennessee. Later that fall, the Union army dislodged Confederate forces from Corinth, a railroad junction in Mississippi that connected east-west and south-north trunk lines. The western campaign had been a success.

But the intensity of the fighting and full extent of the carnage at Shiloh came as a shock to the Northern public. Early on, it became clear to most Northerners that this would not be the swift, bloodless, thirty-day war many had anticipated. It would be a long-drawn-out struggle to choke the Confederacy from the Eastern Seaboard and the Mississippi, in the face of stiff resistance from a population that had no intention of losing its war for independence. For Lincoln, those first two years in the Executive Mansion were marked by countless political and military setbacks, and constant infighting among his fractious cabinet members, several of whom believed they, not he, should have won the presidency. He faced unrelenting criticism from Republicans who felt he was bungling the war and from Democrats who wanted to sue for peace and let the

South go. With every rout, Lincoln grew more despondent. After the Battle of Chancellorsville in 1863, a terrible defeat that left more than eleven thousand Yankees and ten thousand rebels either dead or wounded—where, in the words of a Union soldier from Massachusetts, "many of my comrades fell on Sabbath morn"—Lincoln was inconsolable. "My God! My God!" he reportedly cried. "What will the country say?"

The presidency proved quite unlike the prize he had cherished and chased for the better part of his adult life.

❖

MANY RELIGIOUS LEADERS INITIALLY RESPONDED TO THE COMING OF war, and to the Union's struggle to find its footing, with an outpouring of contrition. "The judgements of God are upon us," a Presbyterian minister told his congregation. For their materialism and hubris, and for falling away from God, the Union was made to suffer. In a widely circulated sermon delivered in the immediate aftermath of the rout at Bull Run, Horace Bushnell identified the nation's fall from grace as the immediate cause of God's certain displeasure. The Union was "a man-made compact," devised by men like Thomas Jefferson who were fundamentally "atheistic," and who viewed the new nation as "a mere human composition." Having built a "government without moral ideas," Americans neglected Paul's teaching in Romans 13:1, "Let every soul be subject unto the higher powers. For there is no power but of God: the powers that be are ordained of God." Americans, Bushnell argued, had lost sight of a fundamental truth, that God "dominates in all history, building all societies into forms of order and law." Because of their indulgence and avarice, the people invited God's punishment and could not expect deliverance until they fully repented and got right with their Lord. This was a common theme in early wartime sermons. The Methodist minister

Thomas Stockton, who served as chaplain of the US House of Representatives, also invoked Romans 13 in explaining the Union's stunning loss at Bull Run. The original Puritan settlers operated under God's directive to "found the State and found the Church, on the Bible; to make their State a Bible-State and their Church a Bible-Church." Instead, their grandchildren forsook Paul's command to subject government to "the higher powers" and invited God's wrath. "The *first* sovereignty in our land is the sovereignty of the Bible," Stockton intoned, followed at a great distance by the "sovereignty of the State." Only when Congress recognized this fact and viewed itself as a fundamentally "sacred ministerial office" would the Union war effort rebound.

While they may have viewed the Union's troubles as God's rebuke of a nation that had fallen from grace and become too much enthralled by material and secular concerns, evangelical leaders nevertheless affirmed in the early days of the conflict that the war was both a holy undertaking and potentially a regenerative mission. William Barrows, a minister in Reading, Massachusetts, preached an early war sermon, "Our War and Our Religion: And Their Harmony," in which he implored his congregation to get comfortable with the violence that war demanded. God was "as glorious when he takes vengeance as when he shows mercy," Barrows insisted, "when he burns Sodom as when he builds Jerusalem. Sinai reflects his excellency as much as Calvary." The war, in fact, might bring Americans closer to the Bible they had forsaken. "Times and seasons are profound interpreters of Scripture," the preacher continued, "and the hurrying and expository events of the present providences in our land are issuing monthly and almost daily volumes of commentaries" on God's word. "So the exigencies of the hour may help us discover a meaning in the sterner and imprecatory parts of God's word that an expounding in times of peace would never furnish us." Another clergyman put the matter in sharper relief. "Our cause is sacred," he declared. "How can we doubt it, when we know that it has been consecrated by a holy baptism of fire and blood."

The Bible was not without its own stories of nations rent by civil war, and for some religious leaders, its example portended nothing but disaster if the North and the South could not arrive at a peaceful reunification. In the aftermath of King David's death, the united kingdoms of Israel and Judah broke apart in internecine warfare. John Cotton Smith, an Episcopalian minister and rector of New York City's Church of the Ascension, reminded his congregants early in the war that ruin came to both kingdoms. "This melancholy history of the rending asunder and the subsequent ruin of a mighty kingdom has a solemn warning for the people of this land," he insisted. "God grant that it may not be too late to avert a like ruin from ourselves!"

But this was a minority position, especially in the evangelical churches. For many churchmen, the war opened the door to a much-welcomed reformation of the American experiment, an experiment that was marred by the Constitution's sanction of slavery. "For the continuance of this Union we are exhorted to pray," Lester Williams, a minister in Holden, Massachusetts, sermonized. "Can we do it? Can we in conscience? Let us see. . . . The Union if it exists, must be made to bear slavery on its shoulders, and so become a bond of iniquity. Shall we be called upon to pray for *such* a Union? I don't believe God can regard with complacency such a prayer. It is too repulsive to Christian faith to think it. I could as soon pray that Satan might be prospered and his kingdom come."

Frederick Douglass, who from the war's first moments prophesied that only the emancipation and arming of enslaved people would bring an end to the conflict, preached that "Men have their choice in this world. They can be angels, or they may be demons." Drawing on John the Apostle's "apocalyptic vision," he concluded that Americans were engaged in "the eternal conflict between right and wrong, good and evil, liberty and slavery, truth and falsehood, the glorious light of love, and the appalling darkness of human selfishness and sin." Slaveholders, he maintained, had already made their decision. They would "rather reign in hell than serve in heaven." White Northerners now had to make theirs. "Not a slave should be left a slave in the returning footprints of the American army gone to put down this slaveholding rebellion. Sound policy, not less than humanity, demands the instant liberation of every slave in the rebel states."

Just a few months earlier, such a position would likely have met with uncomfortable silence in most Northern evangelical churches, but the onset of war emboldened many preachers and lay leaders to stake out a more radical posture. When John C. Frémont, the 1856 Republican presidential nominee and now a general in the army, placed Missouri under martial law and announced the immediate emancipation of all enslaved people owned by Confederate sympathizers, Lincoln asked him to withdraw his directive. He worried that the order would cause border states to bolt the Union. When the general refused, the president canceled the order himself. "I think to lose Kentucky is nearly the same as to lose the whole game," he said. "Kentucky gone, we cannot hold Missouri, nor, as I think, Maryland. These all against us, and the job on our hands is too large for us." Church leaders and activists howled angrily at Lincoln's decision. The Illinois Conference of the Methodist Episcopal Church unanimously passed a resolution in Frémont's favor. From Kalamazoo, Michigan, the president of the County Sunday School Society wrote to the president that his "order has sent much pain through Christian hearts" and urged him "in the fear of God and love of your country" to let Frémont's directive stand. An interdenominational meeting in Coldwater, Michigan, passed a resolution similarly calling on Lincoln to reverse course. "Leave the consequence to God after you have performed your duty," they decreed. Rank-and-file church members deluged the Executive Mansion with mail, urging the president to "pursue the right, looking to God to reward the right," and warning that he had "risked the retribution of Egypt of old."

From southern Illinois, a place Lincoln knew all too well, a minister implored the president to stand by Frémont, whose order would have liberated only those enslaved people owned by Confederate sympathizers. "For God's sake, for humanity's sake, for our nation's sake," the clergyman implored, Lincoln must uphold his general. "The only people supporting the president's order in southern Illinois" were the "foulmouthed men who cried negro preachers to us poor Republicans in the campaign of 1860." One of Lincoln's former neighbors from Springfield reinforced this point, informing the president that he had just attended the state fair and found that "99 of every 100 said Amen" to Frémont's order. "It is a fearful thing to contend against God." From Chicago, John Scripps, who had authored one of Lincoln's campaign biographies, viewed Frémont's missive as a chance to "wipe out forever that execrable institution" and told the president that his reversal was "repugnant to the twenty millions of loyal people." From dozens of local Baptist, Methodist, and Congregationalist conventions and meetings, and from individual clergymen across the North, came the same message—in "God's name and in the name of justice and humanity," it was righteous that the institution of slavery be considered collateral damage in the war for Union.

The following year, in May 1862, and to the considerable frustration of antislavery stalwarts in his own party, Lincoln overturned a similar

order issued by General David Hunter that would have freed every enslaved person across vast swaths of the southern Atlantic coast. Slavery
was crumbling fast. Lincoln knew it and encouraged it. But as before,
he walked a fine line. He could not afford to alienate citizens of the four
loyal border states where slavery remained legal—Maryland, Delaware,
Kentucky, Missouri. He also recognized that public opinion outside the
border states was shifting in a more radical direction. The year 1862
would see the president sign legislation banning slavery in Washington,
DC, and the western territories. Even as he disavowed abolition as a
primary objective, Lincoln privately beseeched border state representatives to emancipate their enslaved people under generous terms, before
the tide of war swept away the whole system under no terms at all. "You
can not if you would, be blind to the signs of the times," he warned.
Still, he could not abide General Hunter's order. "I wanted him to *do*
it," Lincoln explained to a friend, "not say it."

And so it went for the first year and a half of the war. As the Union's
war effort stalled and sputtered, church leaders grew more frustrated
with the administration's refusal to strike a blow at slavery. "Why should
we pour out our blood" in order to save the Union as it was, allowing
four million people to remain "in unrighteous bondage to the enemies
of our country," fumed a Congregationalist clergyman from Illinois. By
1862 the major religious journals, including the *Congregational Journal, Zion's Herald and Wesleyan Journal, The Presbyterian Quarterly
Review*, and the *Christian Advocate and Journal*, came out strongly in
favor of abolition, reflecting a sea change in public opinion that would
scarcely have been imaginable a short time before.

It is possible, if not likely, that church leaders in many parts of the
country were well ahead of their flocks on the question of emancipation.

Not every part of the North was the Western Reserve or rural New England, where antislavery fires burned bright. "Whenever you preach abolitionism you give me the greatest pain," a Presbyterian churchgoer from Ohio informed his minister. Sermons that cast the war as a struggle to blot out slavery were "unpatriotic in the extreme." In some Protestant churches—namely Old School Presbyterian and Episcopalian—and in Catholic churches and some Jewish congregations, lay and religious leaders tended to avoid direct mention of slavery and emancipation in the early years of the war. They shared with their evangelical counterparts an intense outpouring of patriotism but cast their support for the war as a matter of patriotism and civic duty, not a struggle to regenerate a sinful nation.

By contrast, Black Christians took deep offense at the president's reluctance to embrace abolition as a war measure and aim. Henry Mc-Neal Turner, a bishop of the African Methodist Episcopal Church, wrote scathingly of the "very singular correspondence existing between the war in the United States and the Egyptian plagues." By Turner's account, it was "Abraham Lincoln and not Jeff Davis" who played the part of Pharoah in this modern telling of the story. It was Lincoln who rescinded Frémont's abolition order, and Lincoln who repeated the same offense a year later. "And however willing to comply with a dispensation of liberation, nature's God calls from heaven, echoed to by five million of mystic Israelites (abject slaves), in peals of vivid vengeance, *let my people go*. Moses and Aaron, in the garb of threats for the nations' heart-blood, stand by the mystic Pharoah with a demand endorsed by the purposed of their God, for their redemption; but being refused, a series of plagues begins." Turner listed the plagues, beginning with the fall of Fort Sumter and stretching through "the extermination of a Maryland regiment, the capturing of thousands of prisoners by Stonewall Jackson, the running of General Banks, and the perpetration of other cruelties too horrible, too brutal, too infernal to mention." Despite all this, "the presidential Pharoah hardened his heart." In a separate article, Turner rated the war a divinely ordained stalemate. "The whole affair appears to be nothing more nor less than a national scourge. To-day we are gaining great victories, tomorrow we are being taken prisoners. To-day we are before Richmond, tomorrow the rebels are before Washington." Citing a sermon by another clergyman, Turner concluded that God "'intended to punish the whole as due to its unnumbered crimes,' for the contest has been attended with a circumvolution of retreats and re-retreats ever since it commenced." In his belief that the Union's war losses were the modern-day equivalent of the plagues that God visited on the Egyptians, he expressed an increasingly popular view among clerical leaders. James Liggett, a minister from Kansas, interpreted the Union's loss at Bull Run as a result of Lincoln's misguided attempt to "preserve the national life and slavery too, if he can." The crushing defeat was God's way of "thunder[ing] in [Lincoln's] ears . . . 'You cannot.'"

Days before Lincoln signaled his intent to emancipate Southern enslaved people by executive order, an interdenominational convention of white Protestant ministers meeting in Chicago issued an appeal, calling the war "divine retribution for national sin, in which our crime has justly shaped our punishment." It was "almost atheism to deny . . . that there can be no deliverance from Divine judgments till slavery ceases in the land. We cannot expect God to save a nation that clings to its sin. . . . As Christian patriots we dare not conceal the truth that these judgments mean what the divine judgments meant in Egypt. They are God's stern command—'Let my people go!'" The clergy implored Lincoln "to proclaim, *without delay*, NATIONAL EMANCIPATION."

✦

INEVITABLY, HOUSES OF WORSHIP BECAME FOCAL POINTS OF AN EMERG-
ing civic religion that celebrated the nation's Christian and democratic
spirit. As early as the immediate aftermath of Fort Sumter, flags and
patriotic songs became commonplace alongside religious hymns and
prayer. Even as some ministers met each setback with wailful jeremiads
beckoning to the Puritan tradition, interpreting Union losses as God's
answer to the nation's many sins, many others expressed confidence
that America's providential mission remained intact, and that the Union's
cause was righteous. "The ideas of Church and State, Religion and Politics, have been practically separated so long that people specially delighted with any manifestation of the Church's sympathy with the State,"
observed George Templeton Strong, a New York businessman and
diarist.

Moving beyond their function as a "private soul-saving society," in
Strong's words, the religious communities now engaged fully and freely
in the political life of the nation. A Methodist minister spoke generally
for his vocation, writing, "from pure motives I have ignored politics."
He continued, "Since I became a minister of Christ, my only business
has been to save souls." Most organizations aligned with the evangelical
united front had trained their sights on personal salvation and regeneration: furnishing individuals with Bibles, educating individuals in
Sunday schools, helping individuals forswear the demon drink or vice.
Before the late 1850s, Sabbatarianism was arguably the only religious
reform movement that engaged directly in political lobbying. The war
shattered this precedent, as the churches "found something to pray for,"
as the *Springfield Republican* observed. Congregants now demanded
that their ministers speak to the momentous events overtaking the nation,

and most ministers readily obliged. For every cautious clergyman who held that patriotism was "both natural and right, but when it attempts to supplant prayer and worship, it needs to be restrained," there were two who declared the conflict a "religious war. There is no middle ground."

Clergymen learned to navigate seamlessly between biblical and secular themes, as in 1862 when George W. Gardner, minister of the First Baptist Church in Charlestown, Massachusetts, likened the Civil War to "the imprecations of David upon the enemies of Israel," and walked his congregation through the historic times in which *they* lived: "the massing of forces about the threatened capital" in the spring of 1861; "the blockade, the manufacture of arms and ammunitions of war; then the reverses at Big Bethel, Manassas, and Ball's Bluff; then the anxious waiting and seeming inactivity . . . The successes at Henry and Donelson, and more recently the evacuation of the strong hold of Manassas; the utter discomfiture of rebellion in Missouri, Kentucky, and Tennessee; the victories at Pea Ridge, at Winchester." The Bible—particularly the Old Testament—increasingly offered a lens through which ordinary Americans in the North (as well as the South) observed and assessed the unimaginable drama in which each citizen now played a part.

Speaking to a group of departing soldiers in 1862, a Congregationalist minister in New Hampshire noted that "the position you occupy is one of exceeding interest." Thinking back on recent events, he proposed that "two years ago, thousands of men in this country would have shuddered at the idea of being personally engaged in war." Now, farm boys and factory workers were "called to hasten the rescue of that beloved flag from the foul hands of traitors" and to protect "the sacred institutions of our land—the sanctuaries, the schools, the homes, the loved ones—parents, wives and children" that they left behind. Theirs was a holy mission, and one that Protestant leaders largely supported and sustained. In the early days of the conflict, it was still unclear just what that would mean for those fighting the war, and for American Christianity itself.

CHAPTER 7

LOSING WILLIE

By early 1862, the strain on Abraham Lincoln had grown intolerable. The war effort was stalled, with mounting casualties and losses, an army seemingly stuck in the mud, and precious few opportunities for victory on the horizon. The Northern public was restive. And then personal tragedy hit. In early February, the Lincolns' young boys, Willie and Tad, fell gravely ill. The White House drew its water from the Potomac River; with tens of thousands of soldiers camped along its banks, and their latrines in a constant state of overflow, contamination was inevitable. Infected by typhoid, the older boy, Willie, aged twelve, suffered weeks of excruciating cramps, diarrhea, and spasms before falling into a coma. The Lincolns watched helplessly as Willie slipped away. Late in the afternoon on Thursday, February 20, the president walked into the office of his secretary John Nicolay. "'Well, Nicolay,' said he choking with emotion, 'my boy is gone—he is actually gone!' and bursting into tears, turned and went into his own office."

In the months that followed, the president and First Lady dealt with their anguish in different ways. The president locked himself in his son's bedroom every Thursday and on occasion visited his grave alone. "He was too good for this earth," Lincoln said of Willie mournfully, "but then we loved him so." A passing acquaintance later remembered that Lincoln had once asked him, "Did you ever dream of a lost friend and feel that you were having a direct communion with that friend & yet a consciousness that it was not a reality. . . . I dream of my boy Willey." Lincoln was "utterly overcome" as he remembered his son. "His great frame shook & Bowing down on the table he wept as only such a man in the breaking down of a great sorrow could weep."

Mary was too grief-stricken to attend Willie's funeral or burial, though at the time, it was not altogether unusual for women to absent themselves from public rites. For the rest of her days in the White House, she never again stepped foot in the Green Room, where Willie's body had been laid out for mourning. Mary later turned to mediums in a desperate effort to speak with her son from beyond the grave. Historians would subsequently cite her grasping effort to reunite with Willie as evidence of Mary's mental instability and unfitness, but millions of Americans in the 1860s embraced or at least dabbled in Spiritualism, an occult movement founded by two sisters, Margaret and Catherine Fox, who in 1848 perceived strange sounds in their home in Hydesville, New York, and became convinced that certain people—mediums—were capable of interacting with souls in the afterlife.

Spiritualism was neither mainstream nor fringe. Neither was it unique to the United States. Queen Victoria was said to have consulted spiritualists who enabled her to communicate with her late husband, Prince Albert. But in a decade that saw unspeakable battlefield carnage and mass casualties, it was hardly unusual that many Americans at least considered the possibility that death was not a forever goodbye, and that they turned to Spiritualism in the hope of communing with loved ones who had passed. Navy secretary Gideon Welles, Senator Ira Harris of New York, and Henrietta Bennett, wife of the prominent Democratic newspaper publisher James Gordon Bennett, explored the movement after their children died. Other prominent communicants included William Lloyd Garrison; the novelist James Fenimore Cooper; Senator Benjamin Wade, a leading Radical Republican; and Joshua Giddings (who had, many years earlier, been Wade's law partner). Americans consumed spiritualist literature en masse—from Elizabeth Stuart Phelps's fictional trilogy on the topic to Robert Dale Owen's *Footfalls on the Boundary of Another World* (1859) and, a few years after the war, *The Debatable Land between This World and the Next* (1872). It was an age, the British novelist Sir Arthur Conan Doyle later asserted, when "thousands of spirit photographs"—modified to superimpose the ghostlike image of the deceased behind the living—offered solace to grieving parents and spouses who surely knew that the pictures were doctored for effect, but who nevertheless took comfort in the idea that they might be able to maintain contact with the departed.

Mary's enemies, of whom there were many, ridiculed her efforts. It was a cruel denial of a mother's profound grief. "Our home is very beautiful," she confided to a friend. "The grounds are very enchanting, the world still smiles and pays homage and we are left desolate—the world has lost its charm." Mary worked with Nettie Colburn, a spiritualist and medium who staged as many as eight séances in the White House, one of which the president attended, whether out of his own hope and bereavement, or to provide emotional support to his wife. Either way, Lincoln was unconvinced. But Mary became certain that Colburn had unlocked a door to communication with the dead. "Willie lives," she wrote her sister. "He comes to me every night and stands at the foot of the bed with the same sweet adorable smile he always had. . . . Little Eddie"—the Lincolns' second son, who died in 1850—"is sometimes with him." Colburn would later claim that Abraham Lincoln told her that she had a "very singular gift; but that it is a gift of God, there is no doubt." This account seems unlikely, though it was possible the president merely uttered a few kind words to his wife's visitor. Slightly more plausible was her memory of lecturing Lincoln on the importance of emancipation. Many spiritualists were also ardent opponents of slavery, and it is possible that she did in fact warn him that until enslaved people were made free, the Union would not win the war. This argument, which would have been radical just a year before, was more commonplace by mid-1862.

IN THEIR PERSONAL STRUGGLE TO ACCEPT, OR MAKE SENSE OF, WILLIE'S passing, Abraham and Mary Todd Lincoln joined millions of Americans for whom death assumed immediate urgency and uncertain meaning. The Civil War ultimately took the lives of approximately 750,000 Americans, North and South. It was the first modern war, fought with technology that made combat more deadly than anything that preceded it. The new instruments of battle, from rifles and minié balls that were accurate at a range of three hundred yards, to breech-loading guns that enabled soldiers to reload and fire in a matter of seconds, transformed the scale of human suffering, as did the diseases that ran rampant in Union and Confederate camps. At least one in sixteen white men in the North died of sickness or in battle, visiting mass grief upon families in every community and every congregation. At the Battle of Shiloh alone, in April 1862, more soldiers were killed or wounded than in all American wars preceding the Civil War combined. Even as he grieved for Willie, Lincoln understood that he bore a heavy responsibility for asking the nation to tolerate so awful a burden.

In a nation of devout evangelical Christians, it was not only the scale and pervasiveness of death, but the way in which it transpired, that strained traditional understandings of the liminal space between this world and the next. In the nineteenth century, most people died at home, with family nearby. During the war, Northern soldiers died hundreds or thousands of miles from home, often buried in mass graves on Southern battlefields or, if more fortunate, in an army hospital. The mothers and fathers, sisters and brothers, and wives and children of fallen soldiers were denied their opportunity to say goodbye and to confirm that their fallen soldiers left the world in a state of grace. It was a lonely death, and soldiers knew it, as did their families. A man from Georgia surely captured the sentiment of officers and enlisted men on both sides of the conflict when he lamented that his brother, who died in battle in Virginia, "always did desire . . . to die at home." Or a woman from South Carolina who mourned that it was "much more painful" when a loved one passed as "a stranger in a strange land." Gravediggers discovered a dead Union soldier, killed at Gettysburg, with a photograph of his three children "tightly clasped in his hands." In his dying moment he was alone, but not nameless. "Death is so common," Elisha Hunt Rhodes, a Union soldier from Rhode Island, recorded in his diary. "It is not like death at home."

Christians sincerely believed that heaven awaited those who welcomed Christ into their hearts. But how could one be sure if a fallen soldier was saved? Because they were not with their sons, brothers, or husbands when they passed, family members devoted intense concern to the spiritual condition of their lost loved ones. Sarah Dooley, whose son, Atellus, died in Baton Rouge in 1864, could not help but wonder if her boy "appeared willing to die" in the hours before he fell, and if he thought of his family in his last moments on earth. But she was confident, and took solace in the knowledge, that he "reflect[ed] and prepare[d] to meet his God." Another mother was comforted by the assurance that "unseen . . . angels watched" over the body of her deceased son, George, and "escorted his soul" to heaven. Edward Meyer was relieved to know that after his son was killed at South Mountain, the Bible he held was open to 2 Kings 22:19–20: "Because thine heart was tender, and thou hast humbled thyself before the Lord. . . . I will gather thee unto thy fathers, and thou shalt be gathered into thy grave in peace." The verse was "so strikingly true" of his son's "character, course & ending" that it was surely "sent providentially for our consolation." "I have no doubt but Lycurgus has gone to heaven," Jane Remley said of her boy. "I have always believed him to be a devoted christian."

For believers, the conviction that their loved ones passed repentant and redeemed, even if far from home and without the comfort of family, offered some measure of consolation. They assured each other that "God has taken him to himself," and that it must surely be a "comfort . . . to know he died a happy Christian rejoicing in the Savior." Even Oliver Wendell Holmes Jr., an avowed skeptic, understood the prevalent concern over the spiritual condition of soldiers. As he lay wounded and dying after Ball's Bluff, Holmes pondered whether he was "en route for Hell" and briefly considered a "deathbed recantation" of his beliefs. He ultimately decided that doing so would be a "cowardly giving way to fear." (Holmes survived his wounds and would later become a prominent jurist and Supreme Court justice.)

Every community absorbed the pain of loss. The pioneering author Rebecca Harding Davis described a wrenching scene at a small railroad depot in Pennsylvania. "Nobody was in sight but a poor thin country girl in a faded calico gown and sunbonnet, waiting," she detailed. "A child was playing beside her. When we stopped, the men took out from a freight car a rough unplaned pine box and laid it down, baring their heads for a moment. Then the train steamed away. She sat down on the ground and put her arms around the box and leaned her head on it. The child went on playing." The young woman whom Harding observed might have counted herself among the lucky ones, as more often than not, husbands and brothers were buried in mass graves or soldiers' cemeteries far from home.

As they hoped and prayed that their lost loved ones were ascendant, American Protestants subtly refined their ideas about heaven. Prior to the mid-nineteenth century, they widely understood heaven as a subliminal place where earthly cares and concerns gave way to eternal salvation and worship of God. Concepts like pain, sickness, worry, or dying—or friendship, love, and family—ceased to exist. It was the very opposite of earth, with its worldly worries and concerns. In the decades just prior to the Civil War, Americans began to recast their conception of heaven as a replica of the life they enjoyed on earth, and they anticipated a reunion with loved ones who preceded them on their journey. Influenced by the theologian Emanuel Swedenborg's work *Heaven and Hell*, published in 1758, Protestant authorities came to the notion that, in death, people inhabited an afterlife so similar to that which they inhabited in life that they often did not even realize their own passing. Swedenborgianism— the religious movement associated with its founder—did not take hold in the United States, but its ideas about eternity and the afterlife resonated with religious Americans, so much so that Ralph Waldo Emerson declared that "this age is Swedenborg's." An ascetic, deeply theological, and abstract understanding of heaven gradually yielded to a belief in a hereafter that resembled life on earth.

This idea proved especially powerful during the war, as people came to envision heaven as an eternal version of their Victorian families and homes, rather than a more ethereal eternity of communion with God. The two concepts were not necessarily in contradiction. Northern Protestants took heart knowing that a fallen soldier would now be "with his savior," that he would meet with the peace "that awaits the christian in heaven where he shall see the redeemer face to face and enjoy his presants forever." At the same time, they hoped that "God grant that we may meet again . . . in this world," as Lizzie Bowler wrote her soldier husband, "and above all prepare us both for the future world that we may not be separated there." Lizzie Griffith of Chicago echoed the popular hope that loved ones who "have gone first . . . are only waiting for us on the other shore." For devout Christians like Amanda Hudelson of Indiana, "heaven look[s] much brighter to me, and more interest I have to live so as to gain that bright shore to meet my dear father and mother there." In a country where newspapers in every city and town posted weekly accounts of the dead and grievously wounded, people took comfort from the faith that they would meet again in a place devoid of life's trials. This was not only true of families that lost sons or husbands in battle. It relieved the burden on believers who contended with the prevalence of disease, infant death, and childhood mortality—people like the Lincolns, who had now lost two sons. "I never had so tender a yearning for *heaven* until I had a *link* to . . . what had been *earthly*," wrote the mother of a boy who died in infancy during the war. "I can realize there is a *heaven* much more since I have friends . . . there."

Popular interest in the topic of heaven flourished in the 1860s, as families and communities touched by death sought assurance that their loved ones were waiting expectantly for them in the next life. In addition to roughly one hundred books on heaven published in the decade following the war, hundreds of sermons (also published and sold for public consumption) and newspaper and magazine articles pondered the afterlife. Poems like "Hereafter" and "Up to the Hills," and books like *Heaven Our Home*, which offered a "new source of consolation," added to the Protestant public's growing conviction that those who were saved would live eternally and reunite with their families. A popular song verse captured this spirit well when it described heaven as a place that would "turn our mourning into joy." "Shall we know each other, shall we know each other, shall we know each other there?" another ballad asked. "Ye shall join the loved and lost ones / In the land of perfect day . . . 'We shall know each other there.'" One of the most widely read novels of the decade, Elizabeth Stuart Phelps's *The Gates Ajar*, published in 1868, told the familiar tale of a young woman who receives a telegram informing her that her brother was killed in the war. In her grief, she comes gradually to understand that he is not really gone, but with God, in a place that looks and feels much like home. He is watching over her and anticipating the day of their reunion.

In context, Mary Todd Lincoln's embrace of Spiritualism was of a kind with the more popular shift in ideas about the afterlife. American Protestants in the 1860s hoped fervently that the mass death the country imposed on its young men might not represent a final parting. John Sweet, a Baptist minister in Massachusetts, and by no means a spiritualist, spoke to the convergence of these ideas when he memorialized a fallen Union soldier as one of "the speaking dead," with a "life and character that still moves and acts among us." "They whom we call dead have voices for us," he promised, and "speak to us by the lives they have lived."

✦

WEEKS AFTER LINCOLN'S ASSASSINATION IN 1865, JOHN NICOLAY, THE slain president's trusted White House secretary and, in later years, biographer, assured William Herndon, "Mr. Lincoln did not, to my knowledge, in any way change his religious ideas, opinions or beliefs from the time he left Springfield to the day of his death. I do not know just what they were, never having heard him explain them in detail; but I am very sure he gave no outward indication of his mind having undergone any changes in that regard while here." Herndon, who was determined to push back against the religious hagiography already forming around his former law partner, delighted in this news. "Mr. Lincoln loved Nicolay," he noted, "trusted him. Nicolay was a close observer, and he would have discovered Lincoln's change, if any. Lincoln would have told him of the change." But uncharacteristically, Nicolay seems to have missed a subtle but clear transformation.

Though Lincoln issued several proclamations of thanksgiving and penance during the war, by 1863 these documents conveyed a markedly biblical tone and providential message. His call for a "day for National prayer and humiliation" in March 1863 affirmed, in language he would never have invoked before the war, that it was "the duty of nations as well as of men . . . to confess their sins and transgressions, in humble sorrow, yet with assured hope that genuine repentance will lead to mercy and pardon; and to recognize the sublime truth, announced in the Holy Scriptures and proven by all history, that those nations only are blessed whose God is the Lord." This appeal could very well have reflected Lincoln's keen sense of audience—a nation of evangelical Christians who believed in their ability to achieve redemption through repentance and faith, many of whom were anxious to know that soldiers who died as

Christians would be saved. But as the burden of the war fell ever more heavily on his shoulders, he may also have come to perceive and justify his role as a central actor in a historical drama, driven by a divine, though invisible, force. "We have been the recipients of the choicest bounties of Heaven," he wrote, in language closely mirroring the classic Puritan jeremiads that Frederick Douglass and other Black Christians favored. "But we have forgotten God. We have forgotten the gracious hand which preserved us in peace. . . . Intoxicated with unbroken success, we have become too self-sufficient to feel the necessity of redeeming and preserving grace, too proud to pray to the God that made us! It behooves us then, to humble ourselves before the offended Power, to confess our national sins, and to pray for clemency and forgiveness."

Lincoln once again called for a day of thanksgiving in August 1863, this time to celebrate the fall of Vicksburg to Ulysses S. Grant's forces, and the Union victory at Gettysburg the month before. Acknowledging that "these victories have been accorded not without sacrifices of life, limb, health and liberty incurred by brave, loyal and patriotic citizens," and that "domestic affliction . . . follows in the train of these fearful bereavements," Lincoln called on citizens to "recognize and confess the presence of the Almighty Father and the power of His Hand equally in these triumphs and in these sorrows." God could determine winners and losers but also "subdue the anger, which has produced, and so long sustained a needless and cruel rebellion." It could "change the hearts of the insurgents" and "lead the whole nation, through the paths of repentance and submission to the Divine Will, back to the perfect enjoyment of Union and fraternal peace."

The proclamation was one of Lincoln's first, and possibly only, invocations of "the influence of His Holy Spirit" at the center of historical events. The language was subtle but unmistakable to Christians who recognized the president's reference to Trinitarian theology. Now that Lincoln had spoken to Christ's place in human affairs, Charles McIlvaine, an evangelical Episcopalian bishop, believed all that remained unsaid was "a distinct acknowledgement of Christ as the Savior of Sinner." Others focused less on the theological subtleties of the message but took strength from its marriage of civil and religious authority. Elizabeth Duncan was a resident of Jacksonville, Illinois, who volunteered with sick and wounded soldiers, offering them "maps of scripture" so that men "who never read God's word at home . . . are delighted by the truths" within them. She took pride in laboring in "God's vineyard" and was "delighted with Lincoln's idea of Thanksgiving." Duncan believed "we ought to give God the glory for which he alone has been our help in this hour of need."

These public utterances signaled a sharp break with Lincoln's earlier tendency to resort to "reason, cold, calculating, unimpassioned reason," in communicating with the political public, but in more private settings, the president had already begun to invoke spiritual language in his official deliberations. Always a shrewd student of popular opinion, he understood that an already religious nation had rallied to the Union cause and ascribed to it considerable religious meaning. His rhetorical pivot was surely calibrated in some part for his audience, as when he addressed a Presbyterian synod in Baltimore in October 1863 and claimed to have been "early brought" in his presidency "to a living reflection that nothing in my power whatever, in others to rely upon, would succeed without the direct assistance of the Almighty, but all must fail." "I have often wished that I was a more devout man than I am," he continued. "Nevertheless, amid the greatest difficulties of my Administration, when I could not see any other resort, I would place my whole reliance in God, knowing that all would go well, and that He would decide for the right."

The president hardly exaggerated when he observed that "the religious people of the country" had extended him "the most unanimous support." But his invocation of religion was not just the stuff of political design. When a crowd serenaded him at the Executive Mansion earlier that year, in July, Lincoln twice offered praise of "Almighty God," a spontaneous display of spirituality that would have been unthinkable just a few years earlier.

Just prior to the Union's costly win at Antietam in September 1862, Lincoln—who had drafted a preliminary Emancipation Proclamation but agreed to hold it until the next Union victory, lest it seem a measure born of desperation—informed his cabinet that he would regard the battle's outcome as an indication of Divine will on the momentous issue of presidential emancipation. In its aftermath, he determined that "God had decided this question in favor of the slaves." At the time, Gideon Welles, secretary of the navy, thought that the president had "submitted the disposal of matters when the way was not clear to his mind what he should do" to God. Even the final draft of the Emancipation Proclamation, which was in most respects a dry, legalistic document, included an appeal to God. Lincoln deliberately framed the order as a war measure, not a moral blow against slavery. He needed political cover: conservative Republicans and War Democrats might accept emancipation as a means to weaken the Confederacy, but not as a war aim. He also needed legal cover: he had no authority to expropriate the property of citizens, unless he did so in his capacity as commander in chief, in the service of putting down an armed rebellion. Still, at the urging of his treasury secretary, Salmon P. Chase, he closed: "Upon this act, sincerely believed to be an act of justice, warranted by the Constitution, upon military necessity, I invoke the considerate judgment of mankind, and the gracious favor of Almighty God."

If Nicolay, who would likely have been in the room for the cabinet meeting, took little note of Lincoln's gradual invocation of religious themes in his public interactions, and of his growing inclination to look for divine meaning behind the outcome of political and military events, others did. Orville Browning, a Republican whom the governor of Illinois appointed to the United States Senate after Stephen Douglas's death, later told Nicolay that he counseled Lincoln in late 1861—several months before Willie's death—that "we can't hope for the blessing of God on the efforts of our armies, until we strike a decisive blow against slavery. This is the great curse of our land, and we must make an effort to remove it before we can hope to receive the help of the Almighty." Lincoln, he claimed, was unsure. "Browning, suppose God is against us in our view of the subject of slavery in this country, and our method of dealing with it?" Browning recalled that it was "the first time that he was thinking deeply of what a higher power than man sought to bring about by the great events then transpiring." This question of providence—of a divine force either guiding events or establishing the parameters within which humans operated—was one that Lincoln increasingly pondered as the war dragged on.

Others also perceived a change in these years. Mary, who was in a better position than most to offer an intimate understanding of her husband's evolution, told Herndon that for the better part of their marriage, "Mr. Lincoln had no hope & no faith in the usual acceptation of those words; he never joined a Church." While she felt that Lincoln had always been spiritual in some indeterminate sense, it was only "when Willie died" that he began to turn to religion as a way to make sense of the tragedy that befell his family and the larger tragedy that enveloped the nation he had been chosen to lead. "He felt religious More than Ever about the time he went to Gettysburg," she remembered, referring to his visit to Pennsylvania in November 1863 to attend the formal dedication of the Union cemetery. Though he was "not a technical Christian [he] read the bible a good deal about 1864."

Others observed the same spiritual development. Since his youth, even in his days as a confirmed nonbeliever, Lincoln often turned to the Bible for literary inspiration. Now he seemed to read scripture with extra care. His close friend Joshua Speed noted that when he "first knew Mr. L[incoln] he was skeptical as to the great truths of the Christian Religion. I think that after he was elected President, he sought to become a believer—and to make the Bible a preceptor to his faith and a guide for his conduct." Orville Browning remembered that by the middle of the war, Lincoln "was reading the bible a good deal." On a military ferry to Norfolk, bystanders observed the president "reading a dog-eared *pocket* copy of the New Testament all by himself." On Sundays, he became a frequent communicant at the New York Avenue Presbyterian Church—notably, an Old School congregation that still adhered in principle fashion to the predestinarian faith on which he was raised. "I have often wished that I was a more devout man than I am," he confessed to a delegation of Presbyterian visitors—the frank acknowledgment of a president who believed that the war was divinely ordained, but who could still not reconcile himself to conventional (in Mary's words, technical) Christianity.

Francis Carpenter observed the same subtle transformation. An artist who lived in the White House for six months in 1864 while painting a portrait of the president, he believed that "during the last four years of [Lincoln's] life he passed through what few men could have experienced without growth and change." He told Herndon that "if you could have resumed your old intercourse with him at the end of his four years you would have found his religious sentiments more fixed, possibly more christian for 'deism' is not Christianity." When Noyes Miner, a Baptist minister and former neighbor from Springfield, paid a visit to the Executive Mansion, Lincoln shared his growing belief that it had "pleased Almighty God to put me in my present position, and looking up to him for divine guidance, I must work out my destiny as best I can." Miner recognized in the president a man grappling to understand his role in a national tragedy, and struggling to understand what God wanted of him. The clergyman, who had known Lincoln as a nonbeliever, now believed that "if Mr. Lincoln was not a christian he was acting like one."

Lincoln's brief remarks at Gettysburg, at a time when Mary remembered that he "felt more religious than ever," revealed a president turning to the Bible for words that might make meaning of the carnage over which he presided. In the opening lines of his speech, he dated the nation's founding to 1776, not 1789—a subtle but important nod to antislavery radicals, many of whom had long held the Declaration of Independence as America's true founding document, and not the Constitution, with its two-thirds compromise and recognition of the international slave trade. *How* he said it was almost as remarkable as what he said. "Four score and seven years ago, our fathers brought forth on this continent a new nation" might seem a florid way to say "eighty-seven years ago, our nation was born," but to devout Christians, it was a familiar linguistic construction, similar to "threescore years and ten" (Psalm 90:10)—"an hundred and fourscore days" (Esther 1:4)—or "brought forth a man child, who was to rule all nations" (Revelation 12:5). When he continued, "We can not dedicate—we can not consecrate—we can not hallow this ground," he knowingly chose three purposeful verbs that appeared frequently in the King James Bible.

"We here highly resolve," Lincoln closed, "that these dead shall not have died in vain—that this nation, under God, shall have a new birth of freedom—and that government of the people, by the people, for the people, shall not perish from the earth." Here, Lincoln indicated a shift in the war's meaning, from a battle to preserve the Union as it was, to a war that, should the Union win, would result in the death of slavery.

In beckoning a new purpose behind the war, the president invoked language designed to appeal to a nation of devout Christians. The idea of "new birth" was deeply steeped in evangelical theology—a knowing reference to the sinner's regeneration upon accepting Christ in his or her heart. The phrase "shall not perish from this earth" appears verbatim, two times, in the King James Bible, and a third time nearly verbatim ("His remembrance shall perish from the earth" [Job 18:17]). This idea surely resonated with devout Protestants who had grown accustomed to hearing their ministers frame the death of loved ones as a necessary step toward national regeneration.

"We all have faith that the giant curse is to be removed from the land," one clergyman said. "But, friends, this is but the beginning of the good that will come. . . . The imagination cannot begin to depict the glories of the new Era which will open upon Christendom." Horace Bushnell urged that "without shedding of blood there is no grace prepared." Or in the words of Byron Sunderland, minister of the First Presbyterian Church in Washington, "We cannot any longer trifle before God. These are days of sacrifice—the days of heroic suffering—the days of many and most noble martyrdoms." More pointedly, a clergyman in Boston likened the fallen soldiers to Christ. "These are the great resurrection days of American character," he told his congregants, "and there is no resurrection without a grave."

At Gettysburg, the president channeled popular religious conviction to ascribe meaning to the war, just as he turned to religion, however quietly and privately, to make sense of the personal responsibility he bore for hundreds of thousands of deaths. But his spirituality moved against the currents of his countrymen. As it became more common for Protestant clergy and lay leaders to conceive of the war as a holy writ, Lincoln grew convinced that God's will was imperceptible to humankind, and that his own freedom of action was limited and ordained. In effect, he inched closer to his parents' religious fatalism—the very fatalism he had rejected in his youth.

His message at Gettysburg, if subtle, was not lost on Southerners and their sympathizers. In its immediate aftermath, an Ohio Democrat denounced the speech as a "mawkish harangue "in favor of emancipation. (Lincoln did not once mention enslaved people or Black Americans in his address.) *The Chicago Times*, a fierce enemy of the administration, complained, "Lincoln did most foully traduce the motives of the men who were slain at Gettysburg." They had not perished to give the nation a "new birth of freedom." Instead, "they gave their lives to maintain the old government, and the old constitution and Union." By late 1863, a majority of Northern Christians strongly disagreed.

CHAPTER 8

THE WILL OF GOD PREVAILS

In September 1862, half a year after Willie's death, and just weeks before he issued the preliminary Emancipation Proclamation, Lincoln wrestled with the enormous dilemma of whether to shift course and change the stakes of the conflict. Democrats and many conservative Republicans fought to preserve the "Union as it was" and the "Constitution as it is"—with all the states restored to their former relationship to each other, and with slavery intact. To make emancipation an objective or outcome of the war would jeopardize the support of the border states and lower Midwest. But pressure was equally intense from antislavery advocates, including many evangelical Christians. Enslaved people, and slavery, contributed materially to the South's economic and military effort. To do battle with the Confederacy without raising the stakes— without forcing them to bet on the very future of their economy and social system—was anathema to many radical and moderate Republicans.

And then there were the moral stakes. Every Sunday, ministers across the North assured their congregants that the Union was engaged in a holy and divinely ordained cause. Lincoln, for his part, was never sure. As he deliberated on the wisdom and justice of emancipation by presidential decree, and as he contemplated his role in the nation's ordeal, he committed private thoughts to paper. The war was going badly. After a crushing rout at the second battle of Bull Run, Lincoln was, according to Attorney General Edward Bates, "wrung by the bitterest anguish—said he felt almost ready to hang himself." In this private document, which his secretaries found after his death, the president struggled to understand what God expected of him and of the nation.

"The will of God prevails," Lincoln began. "In great contests each party claims to act in accordance with the will of God. Both *may* be, and one *must* be wrong. God can not be *for*, and *against* the same thing at the same time. In the present civil war it is quite possible that God's purpose is something different from the purpose of either party—and yet the human instrumentalities, working just as they do, are of the best adaptation to effect His purpose." The former religious skeptic was not writing for an audience. His ruminations were private and demonstrated a profound, if grasping, turn to faith. "I am almost ready to say this is probably true," he continued, "that God wills this contest, and wills that it shall not end yet. By his mere quiet power, on the minds of the now contestants, He could have either *saved* or *destroyed* the Union without a human contest. Yet the contest began. And having begun He could give the final victory to either side any day. Yet the contest proceeds."

Like many of his religious supporters, Lincoln believed that God had willed the Civil War, and, in time, the president would echo popular jeremiads that cast the suffering imposed on the nation as divine retribution for the sin of slavery. Such thinking became increasingly common, as when M. R. Watkinson, a clergyman from Pennsylvania, told

Salmon P. Chase that he "felt our national shame in disowning God as not the least of our present national disasters." Or in the words of William W. Patton, a Congregationalist minister in Chicago, the war was a "just rebuke from God, of the tolerance of slavery by our fathers after the revolution, & of the numerous concessions made to it from that period to the present." It was this belief in the spiritual connection between battlefield events and divine intent that led Congress to add the phrase "In God We Trust" to federal currency. The words contained both spiritual and political meaning, as abolitionists had for some years invoked the phrase in verse and song ("Let the far West repeat the strain / The East and the North—and South disdain / On Freedom's soil to forge a chain! / 'In God We Trust'"). Lincoln also felt the heavy burden of responsibility for the war, a burden that religious leaders frequently reinforced in their letters to the president and in their personal meetings with him. "It is your high mission under God to save us," a Congregationalist minister from New Hampshire told him. "God has raised [you] up for such a time as this." John Locke Scripps, Lincoln's campaign biographer and a devout Methodist, believed that the president had "voluntarily accepted the highest responsibilities which any one not endowed with the Godhead could assume."

Where he parted ways with most religious Americans, however, was in their certainty that God favored the North. Lincoln knew that God could "not be *for*, and *against* the same thing at the same," but he grappled with the question of which side God had chosen. Was it the North, and if so, why the steady string of losses and casualties? Were these losses punishment for the country's founding sin, slavery? When a delegation of lay and religious leaders from Chicago's Protestant churches called on the president at the Executive Mansion, certain, like many religious Americans, that God was on the Union's side and also on the antislavery side, Lincoln, who was already contemplating the Emancipation Proclamation, responded testily that too many people from every corner were "equally certain that they represent the Divine will." The president was impatient with his visitors. "I hope it will not be irreverent for me to say that if it is probable that God would reveal his will to others, on a point so connected with my duty, it might be supposed he would reveal it directly to me for . . . it is my earnest desire to know the will of Providence in this matter. *And if I can learn what it is I will do it!*"

Most of his countrymen did not share these doubts. They grew firmer with each passing year in the certainty that the war was, as Joseph Medill, the editor of the staunchly Republican *Chicago Tribune*, affirmed, "in its profoundest aspect, a religious contest. It grows out of the conflict between the Christian law of love and the barbarism of slavery . . . all the social influences which are opposed to Christianity are the last allies of slavery in its efforts to overthrow the Government. . . . This is a war for Christian civilization, for God's pure truth and man's universal brotherhood, against ignorance, depravity, and slavery allied." Studies of wartime Cincinnati, Ohio, and Pennsylvania found that clergy "transferred the war into a moral venture, a blending of Christian and national loyalty," and that "the ministers of the gospel probably rallied more completely to the support of the government than any large, influential class." Individual denominations often blurred the line between the sacred and the secular in their own fashions. A Presbyterian synod likened the Confederacy to Satan's attempted usurpation of the throne of God. At Methodist meetings, flags were often on prominent display—many Methodist churches also flew them on flagstaffs beside the crosses on their rooftops—and congregants were frequently encouraged to swear mass loyalty oaths. Behind this convergence of religion and patriotism was a decades-old tendency of evangelical Christians to think of the United States as a providential land—a new Canaan that God favored above other countries. Citing Romans 13:1, which taught that "the powers that be are ordained of God," and that it was Christian duty to obey the laws, ministers framed the act of secession and rebellion itself as a sinful affront not just to Congress, or to Abraham Lincoln, but to God himself.

The *Western Christian Advocate*, which styled itself the "official organ of the Methodist Episcopalian Church," implored readers to consider "which is God's side" (the question was rhetorical) and to recognize that "the interests of Christ's kingdom" and "the progress of the race" demanded not only support for the war effort but full-throated allegiance to Abraham Lincoln and the Republican Party. By 1864 a minister in Ohio went so far as to warn congregants that a Democratic victory in the presidential election would "displease the God of heaven." Such thinking was deeply rooted in a tradition that identified the United States as part of a providential plan to speed the arrival of the millennium. During the war, from thousands of pulpits and dozens of church periodicals, the identification of the struggle as "a religious war," in the words of a devout Presbyterian, assumed new urgency. Henry Clay Fish, a prominent Baptist clergyman, summoned the image of a new world made by the war: "The bondman everywhere a freeman; the degraded white man everywhere educated and ennobled . . . local jealousies and animosities at an end . . . a school house and church in every district; the people talking the highest type of civilization—intelligent, God-fearing, liberty-loving, self-governed, and bound together in one tender and beautiful brotherhood."

It was a grand vision of Christian democracy, and one many religious

Northerners felt was worth fighting, and even dying, for. That formulation often blurred the distinction between religion and politics, and
the sacred and the profane. It invested in the nation's leaders and soldiers a holy writ. Thus, when a clergyman from Illinois told Lincoln
that he perceived "the hand of God . . . in [his] election," he gave voice
to a growing tendency to see the president and his army as instruments
of a higher power. A minister in Michigan addressed troops from his
state, assuring them that, like the ancient Israelites, whom God chose
and who often did battle in his name, the Union's "cause was always just
and the necessity [of war] inevitable." The Stars and Stripes, another
clergyman affirmed, was a "*sacred* flag" that "God gave . . . to the Republic for a holy purpose." The war was, by the estimation of William
Goodrich, the pastor of the First Presbyterian Church in Cleveland,
"the consecration of ourselves to our country's service . . . the noblest
duty we can render to our Redeemer and our God."

If most Northern evangelical churches were united and impassioned
in their displays of patriotism, and in their belief that the Union's cause
was holy, the Methodist Episcopal Church went the extra mile. "Methodism is loyalty" became the church's unofficial watchword during the
war. "The cause of the country is the cause of God," a minister intoned,
reflecting the denomination's broader commitment. When attendees at
the New York East Conference in 1863 took a loyalty oath, en masse,
administered jointly by a federal judge and an army general, they placed
on full display the convergence of secular and religious enthusiasm.
Salmon Chase, a devout Episcopalian, "thanked God that the Methodist church . . . knew only one sentiment, that of devotion to . . . our
country." Methodist leaders encouraged the faithful to see a powerful
confluence between loyalty to God and country, bidding them to remember, in the words of the Southern Illinois Conference, that "it is an

enormous sin against God and humanity for any person to oppose the Constitutional Government of the United States."

Lincoln, for his part, never shared in this certainty that the Union's cause was God's cause. Speaking the familiar language of the Puritan jeremiad, he deemed the conflict a "terrible visitation" from God and bade Americans to reflect "in sorrowful remembrance of our own faults and crimes as a nation and as individuals, to humble ourselves before Him, and to pray for His mercy,—to pray that we may be spared further punishment, though most justly deserved." In another prayer day proclamation, he wrote that the "cry of the Nation will be heard on high, and answered with blessings, no less than the pardon of our national sins, and the restoration of our now divided and suffering Country, to its former happy condition of unity and peace." These were not the utterances of a president who believed that God was on the Union's side, or that the Union was necessarily on God's side. By contrast, Jefferson Davis, president of the Confederacy, urged his citizens to join in prayerful worship to God so that "He may set naught the efforts of our enemies, and humble them to confusion and shame." He hoped that "the Lord of Hosts will be with our armies, and fight for us against our enemies." Davis, if not certain that God favored the Confederacy, certainly hoped it might be so, and that the Almighty would crush his enemy.

In his belief that "God's purpose is something different from the purpose of either party," Lincoln parted ways with many Northern political leaders who maintained, as did Orville Browning, that "God is entering into judgement" with the South, and that the Union's war effort was "as holy . . . as ever engaged men's feelings." Edwin Stanton, who served as secretary of war after 1862, "believing that our national destiny is as immediately in the hands of the Most High as ever was that the Children of Israel," felt "not only undismayed, but full of hope."

Clergymen and lay leaders, too, increasingly trumpeted God's favor for the Union and, as the war dragged on, blurred the line between the secular and the holy. "Christians must carry their religion into politics," wrote a Presbyterian editor, "if they would save their country from the wrath of heaven." Antislavery ministers like W. G. Johnson of Geneseo, Illinois, assured their congregants that God "has seen the affliction of his oppressed people in the South . . . and will send deliverance."

One sure indication that many clergymen infused their sermons with political themes, often claiming God's favor for both the Union and the Republican Party, were the frequent cries and protestations from Democrats and other anti-abolitionist Christians who felt unwelcomed and besieged in their own congregations. John Reynolds, a Democrat who served as governor of Illinois in the 1830s, denounced the conflict as a "*quasi* religious war" and bemoaned the blasphemous violation of "religion by preaching politics and singing hypocritical psalms."

Democratic newspapers, like *The York Gazette* in Pennsylvania, fulminated against "political priests" who stoked anti-Southern passions and promoted endless war against the South. Farther west, *The Indianapolis Star* railed against the administration's "Puritan abolition game" to "protract the war till the period of another Presidential election is passed, to be decided not by the people, but by the army." In the days just after the national fast day that Lincoln proclaimed in August 1863, *The Hancock Courier* in Ohio railed against a Presbyterian minister who, the editors claimed, had delivered a "violent partisan harangue" during an interdenominational fast service at the local Methodist church. The paper begrudgingly admitted that the congregants welcomed the sermon with cheers and applause. Opponents of "political preaching" hardly exaggerated the increased politicization of the pulpit. In Fort

Wayne, Indiana, a Presbyterian minister declared the war a holy cause to stamp out slavery. In Iowa City, a Methodist minister likened slaveholders to the ancient Egyptians, promising that God would deliver "only *wrath*" against the South for the sin of slaveholding and disunion. A former army chaplain and Methodist clergyman, J. W. T. McMullen, delivered his fiery "War Sermon" at his church in Lafayette, Indiana, where he promised to purge his congregation of Copperheads (the derogatory term for anti-war Democrats), declared his congregation a "loyal church," and affirmed that "the rebel confederacy must go to hell and be damned." In Indiana, a churchgoer recalled hearing a long "political harangue" in the form of a sermon—complete with a "hot abolition prayer"—that made her "tired nearly to death." In some cases, anti-war Democrats—or those who were offended by the incursion of politics into the sanctuary—simply patterned themselves after the come-outers of the antebellum period, leaving their churches altogether and establishing new congregations. That development suited John Chapin, a Presbyterian minister in Plymouth, Indiana, just fine. He considered the departure of the "Copperhead element" a benefit to his church.

Though they were outspoken and visible, anti-war Democrats were a minority in the North as well as in the leading Northern churches. When, early in the war, a pastor at a church in New York offered prayers for both the Union and the Confederacy, his congregants angrily demanded and secured his resignation. In Brooklyn, a Presbyterian clergyman landed in a bitter and prolonged dispute with congregants when he refused their demands that the American flag be flown over the church. They were the outliers. John C. Gregg, a Methodist minister and Union army chaplain, spoke for the majority when he affirmed that "politics frequently runs unto religion," as it had at least from the time that "Jesus preached against those who sat in Moses' seat and governed Judea." The Boston Methodist Preachers' Meeting, a local standing committee, frequently considered whether it was "under existing circumstances the duty of ministers to preach on the subject of the present war." Most of those in attendance agreed that it was. In 1862 the New-York Conference adopted resolutions supporting not only the government's war effort but also taxation to support it. In Newark, New Jersey, the following year, a speaker rose to complain that some "people say that the ministers have turned politicians; it is not so. If preaching loyalty to the Government be politics, then we can afford to be called politicians and, if need be, abolitionists. In this great struggle the spirit of war is the spirit of gospel." How could one reach any other conclusion if he or she believed, as did a Presbyterian minister from Pittsburgh, that the conflict was a struggle between God and Satan—"far above the petty interests of politics and parties. It is a war of principalities and powers, and the rulers of the darkness in this world, and spiritual wickedness in high places, no less than a war of flesh and blood."

In some ways, the critics were right. The collapsed wall between secular and sacred was in fact a new phenomenon that represented a radical departure from an earlier consensus that Christians should attend to winning converts, saving souls, and helping sinners achieve new birth and regeneration. Devout men and women might pursue a broad moral reform agenda, but before the war, they generally agreed to leave politics to the politicians. But American evangelicals also shared a long-held conviction that the success of the United States government, the modern world's first democratic republic, was deeply connected to the millennial project—or as one antebellum clergyman explained it, the march toward a "millennium of republicanism." A decade before the war began, a Methodist women's magazine cheerfully anticipated new means of "extending civilization, republicanism, and Christianity over the earth. . . . Our government will be the grand center of this mighty influence." Where Christianity and democracy flourished, "wrong and injustice [will] be forever banished," "men 'shall beat their swords into plough shares . . .'" and "then shall come to pass the millennium." These were heady expectations, but they established an intellectual and spiritual framework that allowed many Christians to view political events through a spiritual lens, and to support the politicization of the pulpit in years of unparalleled danger for the Union.

If not every Northern churchgoer felt comfortable with the new formulation, more likely did than not. When, during a Christian religious meeting, Methodist bishop Matthew Simpson held aloft a torn battle flag belonging to the Seventy-Third Ohio, congregants burst into spontaneous hoots and cheers. It was a "humiliating reflection on Christianity," lamented one critic. But it was a clear reflection of the certainty, shared by millions of evangelicals, that God was on the Union's side, just as assuredly as the Union was on God's side.

AS HE GREW MORE RELIGIOUS, LINCOLN DID NOT SHARE IN HIS COUNTRY-men's conviction that a more personal God would reward the Union and punish the Confederacy. God remained, for him, a more abstract and unknowable force. That did not make him any less a believer. Try as he might over his lifetime to snap free of his father's faith and fatalism, during the war, Lincoln traveled a road back to a subtle form of predestinarianism, even as most evangelical Protestants continued to walk away from it. He likely did not believe that people were born among the elect or not, but he believed God had a plan that men and women were powerless to alter. "I am of the opinion that there was a slight tinge of fatalism in Mr. Lincoln's composition which would or might have led him to believe somewhat in destiny," a friend, Joseph Gillespie, later wrote. "Mr. Lincoln once told me that he could not avoid believing in predestination although he considered it a very unprofitable field of speculation because it was hard to reconcile that belief with responsibility for one's act." Lincoln was "a fatalist," offered one of his former law clerks, Henry Clay Whitney, who remained close to him during his presidency. He was fond of quoting Shakespeare's *Hamlet*, in which the title character tells Horatio, "There's a divinity that shapes our ends, / Rough-hew them how we will."

Mary Todd Lincoln, who migrated from the Episcopalian to the Presbyterian church during her days in Springfield and Washington, DC, would later observe that her husband believed that "what is to be will be, and no cares of ours can arrest nor reverse the decree." It was perhaps one of the only subjects on which she and William Herndon agreed. His former law partner, he remembered, had long felt that "things were to be, and they came, irresistibly came, doomed to come; men were made as they are made by superior conditions over which they had no control; the fates settled things as by the doom of the powers, and laws, universal, absolute, and eternal, ruled the universe of matter and mind. . . . [Man] is simply a *simple tool*, a mere cog in the wheel, a part, a small part, of this vast iron machine, that strikes and cuts, grinds and mashes, all things, including man, that resist it."

In a letter to Eliza Gurney, a Quaker activist whom he came to know during the war, the president offered that the "purposes of the Almighty are perfect, and must prevail, though we erring mortals may fail to accurately perceive them in advance." Lincoln never shared the personal relationship with God in Christ that most of his coreligionists felt. His was a distant and unknowable God whose will was imperceptible to men and women. "We hoped for a happy termination of this terrible war long before this," he continued, "but God knows best, and has ruled otherwise. We shall yet acknowledge His wisdom and our own error therein. Meanwhile we must work earnestly in the best light He gives us, trusting that so working still conduces to the great ends He ordains. Surely He intends some great good to follow this mighty convulsion, which no mortal could make, and no mortal could stay."

It was one matter to believe in a divine plan, indiscernible to the men and women acting the script. But this did not strip people entirely of agency. Even as he remained uncertain how the war would end, or which side God favored, Lincoln grew sure, according to Gillespie, that God had chosen him for a specific purpose—"he came to believe himself an instrument foreordained" to save the Union and end slavery. Whether that cause was righteous was irrelevant. God chose people for all purposes, just and unjust, and Lincoln came to view himself as an agent of his will—"a mere instrument, an accidental instrument, perhaps I should say, of a great cause." "I claim not to have controlled events, but confess plainly that events have controlled me," he told a correspondent in 1864. "Now, at the end of three years struggle the nation's condition is not what either party, or any man devised, or expected. God alone can claim it. Whither it is tending seems plain. If God now wills the removal of a great wrong, and wills also that we of the North as well as you of the South, shall pay fairly for our complicity in that wrong, impartial history will find therein new cause to attest and revere the justice and goodness of God." Firm in his understanding of his role, believing slavery to be a sin but not at all certain that God willed it to be destroyed, he pressed forward with his purpose, seeing in his own actions a larger intent.

Lincoln's growing belief that he had been chosen to play a leading role in a history whose end was preordained may well have helped him weather the war's many reversals, defeats, and frustrations. John Hay, his trusted secretary, once described that "weary, introverted look" Lincoln often projected. "It is absurd to call him a modest man," Hay remarked. "No great man was ever modest." Lincoln's "intellectual arrogance and unconscious assumption of superiority" rankled many of his peers. As he vastly expanded the scope and authority of his office—raising great armies, sending young men into battle and assuming the responsibility for their deaths, expropriating the modern-day equivalent of a trillion dollars in slave "property"—Lincoln's quiet faith may have exerted a calming force in the darker days of the war, when other leading men wavered with each turn of fortune. "The Tycoon is in fine whack," Hay wrote his fellow secretary, John Nicolay. "I have rarely seen him more serene & busy. He is managing the war, the draft, foreign relations, and planning a reconstruction of the Union, all at once. I never knew with what tyrannous authority he rules the Cabinet, till now. The most important things he decides & there is no cavil. I am growing more and more firmly convinced that the good of our country absolutely demands that he should be kept where he is till this thing is over. There is no man in the country, so wise so gentle and so firm. I believe that God placed him where he is." In his belief that God *had* placed him where he was, Lincoln may have drawn the strength required to make dreadful decisions in the most impossible of circumstances.

In his arrogation of wartime powers, the president enjoyed the full-throated support of Northern clergymen. From jailing pro-secession editors and legislators and his crackdowns on the Copperhead press to the wartime draft—the first of its kind in United States history—Lincoln, by necessity, reinvented the presidency in ways that would have shocked earlier generations. Many clergymen welcomed it. J. M. Sturtevant, a Congregationalist minister and educator, believed that war would "furnish the very discipline we need," after decades of moral decay during which Americans had demonstrated "an ostentatious and costly self-indulgence; a lack of loyal admiration and reverence for a strong and energetic government; and a [tendency] to substitute the will of majorities, instead of justice, and the will of God." Henry Ward Beecher, well on his way to becoming the country's most prominent clergyman, went a step further, declaring a "divine right" of leaders in times of war. "Large portions of this country cannot be governed by anything but a monarchy now," he offered. "Whenever from any cause large portions of any community become barbarous, they necessitate monarchies, and the prevailing governments must either grow strong or fail entirely."

Alongside their growing acceptance of state authority, many Christians abandoned their prior faith in moral suasion and came to champion the coercion and violence necessary to fighting what they perceived as a holy war. As late as January 1861, Wendell Phillips continued to define "coercion" as a principally moral exercise—"Northern pulpits cannonading the Southern conscience, Northern competition emptying its pockets . . . civilization and Christianity beckoning the South into their sisterhood." But this view gave way to the realities of total war. In the same way that Black evangelical Christians like Frederick Douglass had long accepted violence as legitimate and necessary in the fight against slavery, white Protestants quickly came to view a militarized state as "the great common life of a nation, organized in laws, customs, institutions," in the words of Henry Bellows, a prominent Unitarian minister. Bellows was among those who decried "the kind of religion which will not defend the sacred interests of society, with all the power, physical and moral, which God and nature have supplied." Like a growing number of religious leaders, he lamented the "unhappy alienation of church and state" before the war and welcomed the advent of a centralized and battle-ready government.

If the Protestant establishment tended toward pacifism in the years prior to the war, it now swung wildly in the opposite direction. A popular syndicated column that first ran in the *Christian Herald and Presbyterian Recorder*, entitled Children's Corner, introduced Uncle Jesse, a fictional Union chaplain. Other religious publications soon picked up the series, effectively throwing their immense influence behind the effort to justify and even normalize battlefield violence. Uncle Jesse explained to young readers that the Union's cause was God's cause, and that with "Christ's sword" in hand, their fathers and older brothers were engaged in a righteous battle to redeem America. He described in vivid terms the "roar of cannon and the rattle of musketry" in battle— how some soldiers "had bullets through their limbs, some through their bodies, some through their faces. I saw men with their legs shot off. . . . In half an hour one-fifth of our soldiers were either killed or wounded." The American Tract Society, which before the war concerned itself with spreading the gospel to the unsaved, now published children's pamphlets like *Charlie the Drummer-Boy*, a story in verse about a brave Union drummer lad who loses his arm in battle:

It might have been worse too—the right arm instead.
I'm glad for my country I've suffered and fought;
I'll try to be brave now, and bear as I ought
This little misfortune that Providence sent
You will not mind, mother, if I am content.

Children's literature appearing in Christian publications taught boys that when it came their time to enter battle, they must not be "cowards," and girls that they must not "waste their bright glance and sunny smiles upon a boy who was a coward." Ultimately, "the more of a Christian a boy was, the better soldier he would prove."

Some clergymen acknowledged that they were counseling a jarring break with Christian pacifism. William L. Gaylord, a Congregationalist minister in New Hampshire, allowed that most recruits did not want to kill or be killed in battle, but doing so was a "stern and terrible necessity" in the service of a "just and holy cause." The Confederate cause, advanced by slaveholders who "bought and sold their fellow men as they would the dumb brute in the market" and who defamed "the holy name of Christianity," was "wholly antagonistic to the spirit of the Bible." Gaylord told Union volunteers that the "time to preach or pray to the South is ended. *Nay*—there is a gospel which we are bound to preach most faithfully to them. It is 'writ in rows of burnished steel.'" Speaking to a company of local volunteers on the eve of their departure, he deemed it their "sacred mission" to "strike down the arm of those bloody destroyers of order and peace, of law, justice, and humanity." He continued, "And I say the cause is a holy one. It is the cause of Christianity, and of God." By late 1862 the increasingly bellicose tone of organized Christianity in the United States was inescapable. Though each Union defeat invited its own litany of jeremiads, and each victory whipsawed clergy and laypeople to a state of euphoria, two themes remained constant: the Union's cause was God's cause, and God's cause required an Old Testament embrace of violence. When the New-York Conference of the Methodist Episcopal Church declared "no sacrifice too great, no time too long, to put down treason and traitors," it signaled a new acceptance of violence. The same was true when the Boston Methodist

Preachers' Meeting urged that "no terms should be made with traitors" and that the "leaders of this unprovoked and wicked rebellion" should suffer "the penalty of death." "We hold the National authority bound by the most solemn obligation to God and man to bring all the civil and military leaders of the rebellion to trial by due course of law, and when they are clearly convicted, to execute them."

Clergymen embraced armed struggle not just in word, but in deed. They became active military recruiters, as in the case of a pastor from Vermont who invoked the words of Joab—"be of good courage, and let us play the men for our people, and for the cities of our God"—in encouraging the young men in his congregation to enlist. Another minister told congregants, "Your country has called for your service and you are ready. . . . It is a holy and righteous cause in which you enlist . . . God is with us. . . . The Lord of hosts is on our side." A Methodist clergyman in Boston went even further: along with sixteen of his congregants, he enlisted in the Union army, as did a minister in Newton, who told churchgoers, "As a servant of my Divine Master, I do not call on you to go, but I say unto you, Come." It was a point of pride for the pastor of the First Methodist Church in New Haven that his congregation had sent more members into combat than any other church in the state. Methodist newspapers urged citizens to "plant largely," "raise all you can," and "save all you raise" to ensure the Union army would be properly fed and provisioned, and they called on all "able-bodied and patriotic young men everywhere, where circumstances will allow it, to enlist rapidly till half a million are thus enrolled." The editor of a religious journal offered that if he and his wife had "a son of sufficient age, [they] should not hesitate a moment to send him to the field of battle in such a cause . . . and should he fall in defending his country's flag, [they] should feel that he never would find a better time to die." It was not just that religious authorities sanctioned the war. They came increasingly to de-humanize the South, urging young men to become soldiers so that they might "tread treason and traitors under their feet as they would tread the life out of serpents and scorpions."

This new embrace of the Old Testament was not coincidental. A combination of technological advances in the instruments of warfare, and the necessity of either repelling an invading army or quelling an armed rebellion that many Southern civilians actively supported, quickly demanded a new way of thinking—about the craft of combat and battle, the morality of total war, and religion.

On the eve of the war, the regular army officer corps were a tightly knit group, many of whom had studied together at the United States Military Academy under Dennis Mahan, a professor of civil and mili-tary engineering, whose preferred method of war involved surgical strikes against enemy lines, but not all-encompassing campaigns against civil-ians, property, and infrastructure. This had been the army's winning formula in Mexico, where many Union and Confederate officers had first cut their teeth in battle. Leaders in both armies had known each other, and had grown up on the same code, for decades. To approach war in any other way than on shared terms of conduct was unthinkable.

The West Point code largely guided the Union's approach to warfare until mid-1862. Certainly, it was the governing philosophy of George McClellan, a devout Christian and resolute Democrat who served inter-mittently as commanding general of the army. McClellan was a superb organization man, unmatched in his ability to turn rough recruits into well-trained soldiers. He also bedeviled both Lincoln and Congress in his refusal to fight. Over a year and a half, he racked up a seemingly endless string of missed opportunities to pursue the enemy, defeat it in battle, and capture its capital city. Despite his considerable failures in battle, McClellan held his civilian superiors in utter contempt. Lincoln, his intellectual better, was an "idiot," "baboon," and "gorilla." The secretary of state, William H. Seward, was a "meddling, officious, incompetent little puppy," and the secretary of the navy, Gideon Welles, a "garrulous old woman." McClellan was a white supremacist and slavery apologist. His weak knees and arrogance notwithstanding, he was also genuine in the belief (and lectured the president to this effect) that war "should be conducted upon the highest principles known to Christian civilization. It should not be a war looking to the subjugation of the people of any State in any event. It should not be at all a war upon population, but against armed forces and political organization. Neither confiscation of property, political executions of persons, territorial organization of States, or forcible abolition of slavery should be contemplated for a moment. In prosecuting the war, all private property and unarmed persons should be strictly protected, subject only to the necessity of military operation." McClellan was clear: he forbade "all pillaging and stealing" and insisted upon the "highest Christian ground for the conduct of war."

McClellan's supercilious moralizing enraged the president's inner circle, as well as Republican members of Congress who expected their generals to fight. Even many Union soldiers who adored McClellan for turning them into a real army were eager to shed the kid gloves. One soldier noted that "the officers found it impractical, and next to impossible to observe . . . as our soldiers could not understand how that we were ever to whip the Rebels without hurting them." As the war dragged into its second year, and as Union forces met with stiff resistance—the swift, easy victory many people expected proving an illusion—both the West Point code and the "highest Christian ground" steadily lost influence. John Pope, one of several Union generals who briefly succeeded

McClellan, was one of the earliest proponents of total war. He issued an order allowing soldiers to live off the land and to destroy the homes of civilians who openly aided the Confederate army or government. Union soldiers broadly "rejoiced at the new orders," a private from Illinois wrote home. He and his comrades welcomed the freedom to "burn and destroy all rebel property and kill every [rebel] we meet till the rebellion is crushed." Other officers followed suit, including General Benjamin Butler, who oversaw a brutal occupation of New Orleans and declared enslaved people who fled behind Union lines to be "contraband"—rebel property that could be lawfully seized in the prosecution of the war.

Lincoln, who as a frontier boy could not stand to hunt, and who sincerely abhorred mob violence, was an early convert to Pope's way of thinking. By the summer of 1862 he approved a chain of military orders empowering Union forces to seize property, banish civilians behind enemy lines, and "subsist upon the country"—shorthand for taking produce, livestock, and other personal property to sustain the army's advance. Reflecting the evolution of Northern thoughts, in 1861 and 1862, respectively, Congress passed two Confiscation Acts, allowing for the seizure of rebel property, including both land and enslaved people. Finally, in January 1863 the president signed the Emancipation Proclamation, declaring all enslaved people in rebel states free, an act that changed the stakes overnight for Confederates, who now stood to lose their property and their way of life should they fail to win on the battlefield. Lincoln called his decree a "lever." The purpose of the war was still, officially, "restoring the union." But he could not achieve that end "without using the Emancipation lever" as he had done. These measures signaled a dramatic shift in the North's posture. In early 1861, its goal had been to corner (but not decimate) the Confederate army, and capture (not destroy) its capital and key cities. By late 1862, the objective was to bring the South to its knees, however much blood needed to be shed, or wealth destroyed.

All that was left was the matter of codifying the new approach. In December 1862, Lincoln established a commission charged with drafting rules to govern military conduct in battle. Francis Lieber, a German émigré and law professor at the law school at Columbia University (then called Columbia College), and the only civilian on the panel, drafted the order, which Lincoln issued in early 1863 as General Order No. 100, "Instructions for the Government of Armies of the United States in the Field." In his order, the president officially sanctioned practices that were, for all practical purposes, already prevalent and signaled a harsher fight not just against Southern armies, but against the South itself. Lieber's code held that "military necessity admits of all direct destruction of life or limb of *armed* armies, and of other persons whose destruction is incidentally *unavoidable* in the armed contests of war." Lieber maintained that "sharp wars are brief." So did Lincoln, who would soon elevate a new breed of generals—men like Ulysses S. Grant and William Tecumseh Sherman, who were sanguine about the cost in property and lives and people, including the lives of their own soldiers, needed to quash the rebellion. The year before, Frederick Douglass had scorned the army for fighting "the rebels with the Olive branch. The people must teach them to fight with the sword." Now, as *The New York World* observed in an editorial entitled "The End of Peaceable Warfare," the phase of combat when the Union battled "the rebels with both bullets and sugar-plums, is to cease." Secession was the work of Satan, "the great arch rebel himself," the editorial instructed readers, and "Divine *wrath* alone can deal with such crimes."

The adoption of Lieber's code signaled a sharp break with prevailing military norms and deeply offended many Southern leaders, who considered it both un-Christian and savage. They also understood that because the war would be fought primarily on Confederate ground, in practical terms, the new standard of war would disproportionately affect Southern civilians. In July 1863, Jefferson Davis took the unusual step of writing directly to Lincoln to "complain of the conduct of your officers and troops in many parts of the country, who violate all the rules of war by carrying on hostilities not only against armed foes but against non-combatants, aged men, women, and children." Union soldiers "not only seize such property as is required for the use of your forces, but destroy all private property within their reach, even agricultural implements." Such practices, he continued, clearly intended to "subdue the population of the districts where they are operating by the starvation that must result from the destruction of standing crops and agricultural tools." Davis was right, of course. The Union's new approach consigned the West Point code to obsolescence. In time, the North would lodge similar complaints against the Confederate army, whose violent war crimes against captured Black soldiers led Lincoln to suspend all prisoner exchanges.

Not everyone approved of Lincoln's pivot. Peace Democrats—Copperheads—venerated McClellan as the "Christian General" and managed to reconcile professions of Christian virtue with deep-seated antipathy toward African Americans. Though Lincoln continued to maintain that emancipation was a tactic to win the war, and not its principle aim, Copperheads seethed at the notion that Northern soldiers should sacrifice their lives, and be party to the South's destruction, in the service of freeing enslaved Black people. Samuel Cox, a Democratic congressman from Ohio, praised McClellan's "humane" approach to battle and regarded his removal from command as "a sacrifice to appease the Ebony Fetich." Even some Democratic generals quietly dissented. Winfield Scott Hancock, who earned distinction for his battlefield cool at Gettysburg, privately told his wife, "I have been approached again in connection with the command of the Army of the Potomac. . . . Under no conditions would I accept the command. I do not belong to that class of generals whom the Republicans care to bolster up."

It was a hard task to square the evolving reality of war with Christian love and pacifism. Doing so required new ways of thinking about what it even meant to be a good Christian. The Union's cause was righteous, but to uphold that cause, good Christians had to abandon their affinity for pacifism and accept violence as a necessity of the times. In their attempt to reconcile violence with Christianity, white evangelicals— some consciously, some unknowingly—followed in the footsteps of Black Protestants like Frederick Douglass. Religious scholars largely agree that by the eve of the Civil War, the New Testament, with its professions of Christian love and salvation, had replaced the Old Testament as the prevailing influence on white American churchgoers and Bible readers. Unlike Black Christians, who found wisdom and inspiration in the prophetic tradition—who understandably took a dimmer view of great civilizations in moral decline, and who drew inspiration from the story of the Exodus, and from heroes like David and Joshua—white evangelicals in the antebellum era felt more profoundly the narrative and moral tug of the gospels. That changed again after the first shot at Fort Sumter. "The Old Testament, in our current notions and sympathies, [had] been almost outlawed from human affairs," a white clergyman from Boston noted early in the war. "Now the days have come upon us, for which these strong-chorded elder Scriptures have been waiting. Their representations of God, as the Rewarder of the evil doer, the Avenger of the wrong . . . suit the day and the hour of the intense present."

In such a changed world, many religious Northerners naturally turned to the Hebrew Bible for justification and understanding. "In times of long-continued peace and public tranquility, the precepts of the New Testament seem more in accordance with true Christian feeling and experience," preached Levi Paine, a Congregationalist minister and abolitionist, when compared with the "fierce warfare waged by Joshua against the Canaanites, the warlike hymns of David, and the terrible denunciations of Isaiah and Ezekiel." This angry, more wrathful tradition exhibited "little of the spirit of true religion, and less the spirit of Christianity." But speaking in the direct aftermath of Shiloh, a horrific battle fought in 1862, and one of the bloodiest of the war, Paine felt that Christians might "begin to understand how the wars of Joshua and the imprecatory psalms of David can properly belong in the Bible now." "The stern necessities imposed upon our nation by a wicked and powerful rebellion, have done much to change the current of Christian devotion, and have shed a new light and interest on the dealings of God with his chosen people, Israel." The New Testament, he argued, was the "history of a *person* who was himself the model and example for all his followers, and whose precepts were intended for the guidance of Christians in their private and personal relations." The Old Testament, by contrast, was the "history of *a nation*, and its lessons are especially applicable to men in their civil and public relations." It now possessed "a new and peculiar interest."

In Charlestown, Massachusetts, Baptist minister George W. Gardner, also preaching in the aftermath of Shiloh, went even further. In a sermon entitled "Treason and the Fate of Traitors," he welcomed a return to the Old Testament's fire-and-brimstone justice, citing the prayers of Judah's King Hezekiah that God spare his people the wrath of a menacing Assyrian army. God sent an angel to earth, who killed 185,000 Assyrian soldiers. If God willed that the South be similarly destroyed, "Shall we not rejoice in it; shall we not give thanks to God for it?" "Look upon the drenched fields and deserted strongholds of nearly every rebel state," he demanded. "Think upon the terrible distress and ruin the rebellion has brought on its own head"—"pillage by devastating armies," horrors of "bloody fields," the "trenches of the rebel dead." Drawing on the Hebrew scriptures, Gardner bade his congregation to "not be shocked,—I shudder as much as you do at the heart-sickening details of a bloody victory," but "if the monster will not yield without his hecatomb of human sacrifices," then "let them fall from hands made nerveless by the missiles of death." "Treason is a sin against the nation," he instructed his congregation, and just as he sent the angel of death to do battle with Old Testament evildoers, God would surely "smite the presuming hand that is thus raised against the country, upon which he has so benignly smiled, and against himself."

THE OLD TESTAMENT HELPED CHRISTIANS JUSTIFY, OR MAKE SENSE OF, violence committed in their name, sometimes by their sons and brothers, often by their own hand. Many evangelical clergymen also embraced an expansive vision of state authority and state-sanctioned violence because the war enabled them to view the project of spreading a muscular form of Christian virtue as bound up tightly with the nation's survival. Before the war, most evangelicals held that the United States had a providential mission, but they tended to believe that churches and governments played different roles in the advancement of the millennial project. During the war, they ceased to make that distinction. When delegates from eleven Protestant denominations formed the National Reform Association in 1864 and proposed an amendment to the Constitution's preamble, they placed on full display an enhanced vision of the country's providential status. The amendment would have recognized "Almighty God as the source of all authority and power in civil government, the Lord Jesus Christ as the Ruler among nations, his revealed will as the supreme law of the land, in order to constitute a Christian government." Despite the official support of the Methodists, as well as two influential Presbyterian synods, Congress never considered and Lincoln politely filed away the proposed language.

Francis Wayland, a Baptist minister and former president of Brown University, spoke for many evangelicals when he identified the Union's cause as inseparable from God's. If democracy and civilization "cannot be maintained here, in the midst of a Protestant population, with a Bible in every house, and education as free as air and in the enjoyment of 'perfect liberty in religious concernments,'" he concluded, "then it may be reasonably believed that they can be sustained nowhere. Crushed and degraded humanity must sink down in despair, and centuries must elapse before this experiment can be made again under so favorable auspices." A. L. Stone, who held the pulpit at Boston's Park Street Church, placed the matter in sharp relief when he urged, "Strike for Law and Union, for Country and God's great ordinance of Government." Viewing their religious calling and patriotic duties as inseparable—believing that "firm and loyal adherence to our country in these times of trouble is obedience to God"—many Christians naturally came to accept state-sanctioned violence as a holy writ.

The relationship between the Northern evangelical churches and the federal government proved wholly symbiotic at times. As the war progressed and the Union army came to occupy larger portions of Confederate territory in the military departments of the Mississippi, the Tennessee, and the Gulf, the War Department seized Protestant churches—some of whose ministers, like their congregants, had fled with the arrival of Union troops—and placed them in the hands of Northern denominational authorities. By decree, all churches in occupied territory that had been affiliated with the Methodist Episcopal Church, South, were transferred to the authority of Bishops Edward Raymond Ames, Matthew Simpson, and O. C. Baker of the Methodist Episcopal Church. Southern Baptist churches "in which a loyal minister of said Church does not now officiate" fell under the auspices of the American Baptist Home Mission Society. The same was true of Presbyterian churches, whose governance and property the government transferred to the Board of Home Missions of the United Presbyterian Church. Northern denominational authorities responded by sending scores of ministers south, where many struggled to earn the confidence of congregants who understandably resented the imposition of Yankee preachers.

Years later, after the war, the experience still stung. Many Southerners resisted church reunification, citing, in one example, "the conduct of certain Northern Methodist bishops and preachers in taking advantage of the confusion incident to a state of war to intrude themselves into several of our houses of worship, and in continuing to hold these places against the wishes and protests of the congregations and rightful owners." Northern religious leaders remembered things differently. The "Church looked at the simple facts that many Southern pulpits were vacant and that others would become so," a Methodist official later argued, and as "the Government would not allow any but loyal men to fill their places . . . the Gospel, therefore, would not be preached at all to multitudes of people . . . unless the Government should open the way." In "asking the sanction of the Government," the Northern churches were doing what was only right. In receiving the government's endorsement, they entered into a wholly new relationship with the state.

At least for a time, evangelical leaders also believed—and some rejoiced—that the war had cemented the relationship between the government and the churches. Church leaders voiced profound pride that "the Christian sentiment of the country [had] grown to be the controlling element in the war" (the *Christian Herald and Presbyterian Reader*) and that the war itself had deepened the "religious spirit manifested by the people of this land. . . . Never before have there been such frequent, open, devout recognition of the authority of God as the ruler of nations, and of Jesus Christ, his son, as the Savior of the world by our public men" (Charles Hodge of the Princeton Seminary). Reverend C. B. Boynton, who served as chaplain of the House of Representatives, agreed that before the war, the country had "no definite religious character or purpose." As the war drew to a close, a new "religious sentiment," born out of "propagation and defense," had resulted in "an aggressive American Christianity."

Christianity, many evangelical leaders agreed, had been good for the war effort. And the war had been good for Christianity.

CHAPTER 9

SOLDIERS' WAR

S trange feelings come over one when he is in battle and bullets are whizzing around one," a Union soldier remarked during the war. "It is a wonderful place for one who is a Christian to test his faith." And test it they did. Of more than two million men who served in the Union army and navy during the Civil War, the vast number reflected the religious composition of the North itself: raised in communities that were rooted in evangelical Christian churches and institutions, they brought to the war the same spiritual heritage as the families they left behind, even as they experienced wartime religion through an altogether different lens. Not all soldiers and sailors were church members or believers, as was the case with the Northern population at large. An enlisted man confided to his wife that after he prayed audibly at a camp service, his fellow soldiers "called me the Saint and made fun of me. I let them ridicule me but I did not give up praying. I . . . am not ashamed to acknowledge my savior." If not all soldiers were believers, many who were did not identify as evangelicals. Catholics, Jews, and non-evangelical Christians fought and served in great numbers. But for those who came to military service already faithful, as well as for those who discovered faith on the battlefield, Christianity proved a powerful lens for understanding the drama most of them had volunteered to take part in, and for reconciling death—and their hand in inflicting it—on a scale no American had seen then or has seen since.

It is impossible to know how many soldiers were believers. From the start, many religious soldiers, as well as leaders of Christian lay and religious organizations, fretted that the "army is a fearful place for a young christian," as Henry Marsh of the Nineteenth Indiana wrote home. "I feel that to be in the army is as if in a bar room and a gambling salon." Another soldier agreed that the army was "no place for a decent man. Such oaths and swearing [he] never heard before, and such indecent language is enough to make one blush for his honor." A volunteer from Vermont lamented that "coarse jokes and vulgar obscenity" were ubiquitous among the men.

To be sure, camp life introduced hundreds of thousands of country boys to all manner of vice, from the mild (swearing, card playing, and gambling) and intermediate (drinking) to outright transgression (prostitution). In normal times, maintaining one's religious commitment required discipline. In war, the more so. Years later, John D. Billings of Massachusetts looked back on his experience as a soldier with an even-handed assessment. "That there were bad men in the army is too well known to be denied," he conceded, "but the morally bad soldiers were in the minority." Particularly in the first year of the war, before a combination of state-sponsored and private, philanthropic efforts to furnish soldiers with access to organized prayer and religious reading materials, the more pious among the troops bemoaned the low spiritual state of army life. "It is sad to contemplate the low ebb to which religion and morality have descended in the army," a private from Pennsylvania wrote with regret in a letter home. "And it may be easily accounted for. No one seems to take an interest in the spiritual well-being of the men."

There was a natural tension between training boys to be disciplined, hardened killers, and expecting them to remain pious and abstemious in the ways of men. John William De Forest, a Union officer, noted that while months of training and battle had rendered his troops better soldiers, "the men are not so *good* as they once were; they drink harder and swear more and gamble deeper." What was true of the enlisted troops was true of their superiors. "Officers who are members of the church, officers who once would not even play a game of cards, have learned to rip out oaths when the drill goes badly," De Forest continued. A soldier from Iowa observed much the same phenomenon when he remarked, "War is *hell* broke *loose* and benumbs all the tender feelings in men and makes them *brutes*." Some soldiers felt their sense of Christian propriety buckle under the strain of fear and temptation. "I feel for one I ought to live a far different life from what I do," a soldier from New Hampshire admitted mournfully. "I make resolutions that I will, but how frail I am, how soon do I forget them. It is hard to live a christian life when at home, under the influence of a christian wife and family, under the preached gospel, and surrounded by many christian friends, but oh how much harder in the army away from all these influences, but I pray God I may be kept from sin." Others, like Elisha Hunt Rhodes of the Second Rhode Island, found that their faith withstood the test. On his twentieth birthday, Rhodes took a moment to "thank God that he has kept me within his fold while so many others have gone astray, and trust that he will give me Grace to continue to serve Him and my country faithfully."

Army life was incompatible with Christian virtue in more tangible ways. Religious authorities complained bitterly that many officers insisted on drilling their men on Sundays, and in the case of the first battle of Bull Run, which fell on the Sabbath, some churchmen and pious officials in government believed that God had punished the Union for violating his day of rest and worship. "There is no Sunday in a time of war," a newspaper in Iowa remarked, and in large part, this observation held true. But army chaplains complained bitterly when officers made the "profane and deliberate choice" of working the troops on the Sabbath, so much so that in late 1861, George McClellan declared that his soldiers were fighting a "holy cause" and should "endeavor to deserve the benign favor of the Creator" by attending "divine service after the customary Sunday morning inspection." Not everyone jumped at the opportunity to pray. A sergeant from Michigan groused when he was assigned the task—to his mind, impossible—of corralling men for services. Some soldiers preferred rest and card playing to prayer. But by mid-1862, sufficient pressure grew that Lincoln felt compelled to codify McClellan's order. The president declared Sundays a day of rest "for man and beast" and decreed that "Sunday labor in the Army and Navy be reduced to the measure of strict necessity," in "deference to the best sentiment of a Christian people, and due regard for the Divine will." But with chaplains always in short supply, "no services today" became a common refrain in 1861 and 1862. "We have no religious services here," a soldier from Pennsylvania wrote home, "and everything is dead, dead, dead." But, he assured his parents, the "Lord is still with me."

AS THE WAR GROUND ON, THE GROWING PARTNERSHIP BETWEEN CHRIStian churches and the government resulted in a number of unprecedented public-private initiatives to ensure that Union troops enjoyed meaningful access to spiritual guidance and comfort. While the Confederacy lost access to Northern printing presses and tract societies, the American Bible Association furnished Union soldiers with over five million "pocket Bibles"—so many, in fact, that soldiers often found themselves carrying or discarding multiple copies of scripture. Towns like Ashby, Massachusetts, sent their volunteers off to war with revolvers, bowie knives, and copies of the New Testament. When in 1863 troops from the Nineteenth Iowa were aboard a steamboat headed south, a representative from a Christian organization met the men at a landing and passed out several crates of Bibles. Most of the soldiers ultimately threw the extra books overboard, as they were already awash in scripture.

Alongside its work with ecclesiastical organizations in claiming and staffing churches in occupied Southern territory, the government in Washington, DC, also forged official relationships with two Christian organizations that ministered to the spiritual and physical needs of soldiers and sailors.

The United States Christian Commission, founded in late 1861, drew all the major denominations together in an official effort to persuade soldiers "to become reconciled to God, through the blood of His Son, if they have not already done so, and if they have, then to be strong in the Lord, resolute for duty, earnest and constant in prayer, and fervent in spirit, serving the Lord." In cooperation with military and government officials, the Christian Commission sent five thousand agents into the field to distribute Bibles, tracts, hymnals, and other religious publications, and organize Christian meetings and services. The organization furnished soldiers with stamps and branded Christian Commission stationery—the envelopes read, "Soldier's Letter," to ensure care in delivery; the stationery header read, "This is a faithful saying and worthy of all acceptation, that Christ Jesus came into the world to save sinners, of whom I am chief"—and ministered to young men seeking spiritual comfort or guidance. The commission's leadership thought of itself as pragmatic. It enjoined delegates to go light on sermonizing. Their delivery should be "brief, kind . . . earnest . . . affectionate for the men, and fervent for Christ." Volunteers followed entire companies on foot, into battle, equipped with "a bucket to carry water or coffee in, and a cup to serve it out to the wounded." They ministered to dying men in field hospitals and helped surgeons and nurses remove the dead from battle-grounds to ensure that they received proper Christian burials—"in short, striving to do all that man can do to meet the wants of brethren far from home and kindred." In turn, soldiers left behind a trail of letters and diaries that suggest appreciation for the organization's work. The "Commission does not forsake us," one man wrote home. "It will follow us into the field." When a soldier from Pennsylvania lay grievously wounded in a hospital tent near Fredericksburg in the bitter winter cold in December 1862, a Christian Commission representative brought him a "tin bucket full of strong, hot coffee" and other "God-sent luxuries." It was the first the young man had ever learned of the commission, and he told his family of his profound gratefulness for the kindness. Another wounded soldier staggered in the midst of battle toward a row of tents on the periphery of the line before passing out. He woke to the sight of "some kind nurses bending over me, and all looking anxiously for my recovery." He later learned they were "the ladies of the Christian Commission, who had left home and all its luxuries to administer to the poor soldier in the field. God bless all those devoted women, and if they do not receive their reward on this earth may they receive it in heaven."

Alongside, and often in tense competition with, the Christian Commission, the United States Sanitary Commission also functioned as an arm of the government. Founded and funded by Christian activists, and headed by Henry Bellows, a Unitarian minister, the Sanitary Commission raised money from churchgoers to circulate food, medical supplies, clothing, and other essentials to soldiers in the field. Though similarly grounded in a spirit of Christian perfectionism, the Sanitary Commission's leaders ministered to the material needs of soldiers and eschewed the Christian Commission's efforts to proselytize and win souls. Both organizations enjoyed the official sanction of the civilian government and military brass, and in the thick of battle, they cooperated closely. But each commission eyed the other warily. Bellows viewed the Christian Commission as an amateurish outfit of do-gooders and fretted that "without accomplishing its own object, it will weaken and defeat ours." He privately dismissed George Stuart, the Christian Commission's president, as an "evangelical mountebank," reflecting in part the class and theological divisions between liberal Unitarians and the largely Methodist and Baptist leadership of the competitor organization. Other activists in the Sanitary Commission scoffed that their rivals diverted precious resources away from soldiers' real needs and instead spent recklessly on "tracts and broken down preachers." These differences notwithstanding, the official relationship between religious bodies and the government signaled a new chapter in American political history.

The civilian government in Washington, DC, as well as many religious members of the general officer corps, including George McClellan, earnestly believed that it was the responsibility of the army and navy to foster religion and spiritual well-being among soldiers and sailors—to minister to them in battle, as they lay wounded and perhaps dying, and during the many tedious months of camp life. The Christian Commission and Sanitary Commission filled gaps where the government had simply proven incapable of fulfilling this mission. Though in theory every regiment should have had a designated chaplain who served with an officer's rank, in practice, the War Department found that in June 1862, more than a year into the conflict, over 40 percent of regiments were without a chaplain, while another 6 percent had chaplains who were absent either on or without leave. This state of affairs belied Lincoln's issuance of General Orders Nos. 15 and 16, which required each unit to select a chaplain to support "the social happiness and moral improvement of the troops" and also provided for the employment of hospital chaplains, who worked alongside doctors and nurses. Simply put, it proved difficult to persuade Protestant ministers, Catholic priests, or Jewish rabbis to leave their pulpits for either a fixed or indeterminate period of service. They understandably worried about the spiritual needs of their congregations and parishes. Those regiments that had a chaplain in service often found the assigned clergymen sorely lacking in qualification or moral commitment. Edwin Bennett, an officer with the Fifth Massachusetts, conveyed widespread opinion among the men when he claimed that "at least seventy-five percent of the chaplains commissioned during the first year of the war were practically unfit for their work." This assessment was both uncharitable and an overstatement. Many clergymen of good standing served with distinction. But many soldiers echoed the sentiment of John McMahon of New York, who complained, "Our chaplains are a class of men that could not get employment at home and by underhanded work have got to be Chaplains."

Recognizing the problem, the government attempted to increase the supply of qualified chaplains after mid-1862. The effort met with mixed success, as many regiments had to rely on lay preachers or field agents from the Christian Commission to lead services and prayer meetings. Throughout the war, no more than six hundred chaplains were in service at one time, a number wholly inadequate to staff every regiment and field hospital. Nevertheless, almost two thousand four hundred clergymen—including seventeen Black ministers, one rabbi, and seventy Catholic priests—served as regimental or hospital chaplains, many of whom won high marks for their professionalism. Unsurprisingly, Methodists led the charge, furnishing 38 percent of Union chaplains, followed by Presbyterians (17 percent), Baptists (12 percent)—who preferred to offer their services through church organizations like the Home Mission Society—and Congregationalists (9 percent). "The men who offered themselves for this service differed greatly in age," recalled a chaplain years after the fact. "The life was rough. The older men found it too hard. The tangible results were slight." It often proved difficult to staff the right person for the job. "A regiment with three fourths Roman Catholics was not unlikely to have a Protestant chaplain. A Methodist or Baptist or Episcopalian would be in camp with men who were decidedly not of his way of thinking. . . . He might invite the men to a Sunday service," but given the vast differences in denominational background, "who cared to come?" Chaplains often felt obligated to "fall back on a common humanity broader than denomination," as it was their mandate to "be on terms of cordial sympathy with them all."

EVEN AS THEY ENCOUNTERED A COARSER LIFE—WHETHER THEY WERE as pious as Elisha Hunt Rhodes or as tempted as the young soldier from New Hampshire—and despite the shortage of qualified chaplains, soldiers turned in large numbers to Christian faith as a moral and spiritual lodestar. Union campgrounds were the collective scene of a massive, rolling wave of revivals that began in the winter of 1862–63 and continued well into the final days of the war. Historians estimated that between one hundred thousand and two hundred thousand Union troops were converted at these dramatic, often interdenominational demonstrations of faith, alongside hundreds of thousands more who reaffirmed their commitment to Christ. In reality, it is impossible to know, but by all accounts, "probably no army, in any age, has ever witnessed such outpourings of the Spirit of God as our own armies have experienced," in the words of a religious organizer. It was a "great national baptism," a clergyman proudly declared. "God will so pour out his spirit upon the army, the navy, and churches that millions of immortal beings will be converted, and the nation stand redeemed and sanctified."

Similar revivals, often larger, swept through Confederate army camps, so much so that a chaplain from Maine worried in the spring of 1863 that "God is reviving His work wonderfully at the South and in the army also." Some bursts of revivalism came in the wake of setbacks, like the Union's defeat at the first battle of Bull Run in 1861, McClellan's failed Peninsula campaign in the spring and summer of 1862, or the rout at Fredericksburg in December 1862. In the wake of these events, large religious meetings sprang up at army camps outside of Washington, DC, as well as in Chicago and St. Louis, where soldiers trained and expectantly prayed. Others followed great victories, such as the Union's dual triumph at Gettysburg and Vicksburg in July 1863, and Chattanooga in November 1863. Still others helped soldiers steel themselves for battle, as was the case in the spring of 1864, when Sherman's troops held a series of dramatic religious meetings as they prepared for their famous campaign in Georgia. Twice each day, at 1:00 p.m. and 7:00 p.m., "the church was crowded to overflowing," a bystander recalled, "not a foot of standing room unoccupied. The doors and windows were filled, and the crowds extended out into the street, straining their ears to catch the words of Jesus." One day, soldiers filed by the thousands to a nearby creek, "joining hands" and singing Christian hymns as their unbaptized brothers "went down into the water—some for immersion, some for sprinkling, and others for pouring, but all for baptism in the name of the Father, and of the Son, and of the Holy Ghost."

The revivals seemed to happen everywhere.

In Madison, Wisconsin, in 1863 a local unit had "some of the most interesting meetings . . . for the three weeks past, that I ever attended in my life," a soldier wrote home. "A great many have been brought from darkness into light, and have been . . . converted to Christ." In Louisiana at roughly the same time, a soldier from the Forty-Sixth Indiana noted that "quite a number in our Regt . . . have lately come out on the Lord's side." For some men, the revival meetings reinforced existing religious commitments that had buckled under the strain of war. Another soldier from Indiana who had been raised in an evangelical family admitted privately that he had surrendered to many of the temptations of army life—"the use of foolish and obscene language, the playing of foolish games, such as dominoes, checkers, chess and I regret to say sometimes handling vile cards." But hearing an old, familiar gospel hymn ringing out from a church tent, he realized, "By watching close and trusting in the Lord (not in myself), I can do better." Within days, he felt more his old self. "I think God is helping me."

Revivals often began as small, spontaneous displays of religious devotion before evolving naturally into movement events. In a diary entry dated September 1863, Elisha Hunt Rhodes noted, "Three of our men who are Christians attended a religious meeting at one of the camps in Gen. Wheaton's brigade. On the way home they kneeled down in the woods and prayed that God bless our Regiment. The next week six of them met for prayer, and last week about thirty were present. Tonight I was invited to join them. . . . About fifty men were present at first, but they soon began to come into the grove, and soon nearly every officer and man of our Regiment was listening to the service. I never saw such a prayer meeting before, and I know the Spirit of the Lord was with us." In the coming days, Rhodes and his fellow soldiers from the Second Rhode Island split logs in half to fashion rough seats in the clearing where the evening prayer meeting continued to build. So it went until the regiment packed up and moved on. Several months later, the men of the Seventy-Fifth and Eightieth Illinois, occupying parts of Louisiana, turned an abandoned sugar factory into a makeshift church where they staged "rousing religious meetings" each evening. Like Rhodes and his comrades, they soon found their provisional prayer space filled beyond capacity.

Soldiers from all parts of the country reported a "very excited meeting," the "best meeting I ever attended in the Army," "a very interesting meeting." Some, like Rhodes, were devout before the war and took heart that the "religious interest continues." Others, like LaForest Dunham of Illinois, found their faith in the army. "Ma I feal as iff God was on my side," he wrote. "I have resolved to be a christon the rest of my life." (By all accounts, Dunham was sincere. Writing home from a camp outside Atlanta in August, where he and the rest of Sherman's army was stuck in place, he reported home, "We have a prayer meeting every evening now while we ar in camp and it is doing a great deal of good.") At a service near Chattanooga, "between 50 and 60 men spoke of their religious experience and five or six men stood up and asked to be prayed for," a member of the Fifty-Ninth Illinois observed. A soldier from Iowa wrote of seeing twenty-seven soldiers converted at a single prayer meeting. Even amid heavy fighting, the revival meetings continued at the edge of battle, though "it seems strange to have the prayers punctuated by the vicious hiss or the dull thud of the Minnie ball flying overhead or striking some object," a soldier observed with detached irony.

For those soldiers who came new to Christian faith, or who renewed their commitment to Christ, these stirring and usually spontaneous meetings offered a measure of assurance and steadiness amid incomprehensively difficult circumstances. "I feel confident that I have found grace in the sight of god," wrote a soldier from Ohio in May 1864. "Why then should we be afraid to die." A nurse working at an army hospital in Baltimore wrote to the family of Austin Whipple and assured them that in the soldier's last minutes on earth, she had spoken to him about his salvation. Assuring her that he was right with God, he welcomed "whatever the Lord knew was best for him." As he slipped away, Whipple "looked as calm and peaceful as if in sleep. . . . It seemed to [her] that death for him had no terrors . . . he was willing to live or die as it seemed best to the Lord. The departed one has made a happy exchange and is safe with his savior, in whom he trusted."

Soldiers demonstrated a wide range of beliefs, but certain themes pervaded their letters and diaries. Where religious leaders on the Union home front devoted considerable focus to the righteousness of their cause, those who fought in the war were at least just as, if not more, focused on acceptance. They ruminated on whether the Union was on God's side (it was), and God on the Union's side (God was), but the immediate reality that they might die in battle trained their thoughts on a more immediate question: Did God have a plan for them? One officer told his wife, "I am getting to be a believer in pre-destination. It is the most comfortable belief a soldier can have." He likely did not mean "predestination" in its original, Calvinist connotation but instead gave voice to a fatalism that many of his comrades shared in the lead-up to battle. For one man who sustained wounds in battle but survived the fight, it was clear that "Nothing but the kind Providence of God would have led [him] safely through such a fire." A volunteer from Michigan similarly reported home that God had led him to improbable survival during an exchange of fire outside Atlanta. It was a common refrain: "Providence . . . protected me in my rough pathway"; "A merciful Providence has again taken me through the ordeal of battle unscathed"; "My escape was providential & I have reason to return thanks to Him who rules the destinies of battle." Just as soldiers felt sure that their survival was God's will, they took comfort in knowing that if they fell in combat, that, too, was part of God's plan. "I sometimes think that I can plainly see a Providential hand connected with our co. so far," a soldier from Ohio wrote. His company had suffered few casualties, but it might not always be so. "I do not put my arm trust in any arm of flesh nor in heavy battalions of men," he continued, "but in Him who rules the armies & holds the destiny of the nation in His hands." More like Lincoln, and less like those on the home front, who often felt *sure*, many soldiers came to view God's plans as a mystery. "We must trust to providence," Henry Kauffman of Ohio told his wife, just as an officer from the Eleventh Illinois assured his wife, Ann, that whether he lived or died, he would serve his country "with a firm reliance of God's all wise providence that it will result in good, in carrying out His Sovereign Will."

Understandably, many men turned to their Bibles before charging into battle, and while in the thick of combat, they would "load, fire, and pray," in the words of a volunteer from West Virginia, hoping that God would see them through the other side. Another soldier accepted Christ in the lead-up to battle and told a Methodist chaplain, "If I fall in battle, let my mother know of this transaction. It will afford her great joy." Like those they left behind on the home front, soldiers took comfort in the belief that "this world is but a short period of our existence." "These are trying times," Samuel Piper of the 158th Pennsylvania wrote to his wife, "and we should all humble ourselves and try to live as we should and as we will wish we should have done when we come to die. We should live always with God before our eyes and endeavor to serve him continually. At best our days are few and evil, and we should live agreeable together in this world so that we may be better prepared to enjoy our heavenly home above; a few days, weeks, months or years at farthest we will be called upon to leave our earthly home and if we live right the days allotted to us here below the change will be a good one. If not it will certainly be a very bad one."

ALONGSIDE THE SURGE IN RELIGIOUS ACTIVITY IN UNION ARMY CAMPS, soldiers came to embrace the churches' increasing advocacy of abolition, in many cases well in advance of the broader civilian population. At the start of hostilities, soldiers and sailors generally represented the full range of views on display in their communities. Some enlisted to strike a blow against slavery. Most joined the fight to preserve the sanctity of the Union. Others, including many border state soldiers, agreed with a young recruit from Tennessee who wrote, "I can hate [Abraham Lincoln] and still love the Union . . . no state has a right to secede." Many men also voiced deeply racist sentiment, like a battle-hardened volunteer who resented fighting for "a detestable Black man." But as the conflict raged on, soldiers found that "the rebellion is abolitionizing the whole army," as a member of the Third Wisconsin told a local newspaper. For most men, the realities of war—and the need to strike a direct blow against the institution that was responsible for it—resulted in this new and hardened view. "Men of all parties seem unanimous in the belief that to permanently establish the Union, is to first wipe [out] the institution of slavery." A private from Missouri elaborated that because "it was slavery that caused the war," peace could not come until "the eternal overthrow of slavery" gave way to a more perfect Union. Much as Lincoln and Congress came to believe that slavery both caused the war and posed a strategic manpower advantage to the South—and therefore needed to be eliminated—soldiers in the field came to recognize the same urgency behind abolition. A young man from Illinois gave voice to this sentiment when he observed that he and many of his comrades "like the Negro no better now than we did then but we hate his master worse and I tell you when Old Abe carries out his Proclamation he kills this Rebellion and not before. I am henceforth an *Abolitionist* and I intend to practice what I preach."

A combination of factors drove the radicalization of Union soldiers, and much of it was not religious in nature. Many came into direct contact with enslaved people and slavery for the first time in their lives. They witnessed firsthand the institution's cruelty—the way it tore families apart, its repudiation of Christian morality, its violence (including sexual violence) against enslaved people. Even soldiers who remained hardened racists found that they could "have a good deal of sympathy for the *slave*, but . . . like the *Negro* the farther off the better." Soldiers also grew deeply resentful of Copperhead politicians who, in their opinion, undermined the war effort by agitating against conscription and enlistment and fueling the South's belief that a protracted conflict would ultimately result in a peace settlement, with slavery intact. The more that Peace Democrats appealed to popular racism, commonly employing crude racial epithets, the more many soldiers denounced such "a specimen of Trash the damned Copperheads have been sending" in the field. No Copperhead was more reviled than Congressman Clement Vallandigham, a slavery apologist and outspoken war critic who was convicted by an army court of inciting opposition to the war effort and banished behind Confederate lines. When he learned that Vallandigham had been released from custody and intended to run for governor of Ohio, Chauncey Welton, a soldier and self-identified Democrat, fumed with disgust. The "news fell like a thunderbolt upon this regiment," he told his father, who still supported the Democratic ticket. Chauncey implored his parents to recognize that "any man who upholds Vallandigham at all never can be called anything but my enimy. . . . There is no one on the face of this earth that is despised and hated by every soldier as mutch as the copperhead is."

Many soldiers also encountered Black Christian worship for the first time—among local Black populations in occupied Southern territory, and Black soldiers, the majority of whom were Southern freedmen. "Their meetings are very interesting," a white soldier from Pennsylvania observed. The fervor and "singing and manner of Worship" fascinated white soldiers who were born a generation removed from Cane Ridge or the charismatic Methodist revivals of the early nineteenth century. For young men raised on a more staid form of worship, the emotive style of Black services seemed either exotic, amusing, or praiseworthy. A skeptical chaplain from Massachusetts begrudgingly acknowledged that Black worshippers were "honest and in earnest in their devotions," while another white soldier reported home that he had attended "an able sermon by a negro, which although in crude language was deeply felt by all." He wrote, "I firmly believe he was more sincere in his preaching than our Chaplain often is, for his words seemed to go right to the heart." In 1863, John Hay, the president's secretary, was granted a military rank and traveled to South Carolina to confer with army officials in the field. Like other soldiers, he was profoundly moved—if also confused—by the fusion of worship styles imported decades or centuries earlier from Africa and a distinctly prophetic, Old Testament brand of Christianity that was also increasingly in evidence in white churches.

"Song by a Florida slavegirl," Hay recorded in his diary. "We will fight for liberty. The children join. Sergeant Proctor delighted. 'Roll Jording Roll.'"

"Went to the colored Schools," he noted. "Miss Harris and Miss Smith"—white abolitionists from Massachusetts and New Hampshire, respectively—"in charge of the Abcdarians . . . Light mulatto girls and white children. All singing together."

> Say my brother aint you ready
> Get ready to go home
> For I hear de word of promise
> At de breaking of the day
> Ill take de wings of de morning
> & fly away to Jesus
> Ill take de wing of de morning
> & Sound de Jubilee.

On Paris Island, Hay and his party "went to the Plantation house," where formerly enslaved people "sang some strange & wild songs."

Like hundreds of thousands of Union soldiers, he was captivated by this first exposure to the sounds and cadences of black Christian worship. "They swayed to & fro as they sang with great feeling," he observed. "An old woman who came over fr. Africa. Says she was grown when she came."

> Genl. Hunter sitting on the tree of life
> To hear the wind of the Jordan roll

Roll J.R.R. J. Roll
(Ch.)
March de Angel March
March de Angel March
My soul is rising heavenward
To hear the wind of the Jording roll.
I ax old Saton why follow me so?
Satan aint got nothing to do with me.
Hold yr. light (Bis) on Canaan's shore.
Oh Sister Ketchum dont you want to get religion
Down in the lonesome valley, (my lord).
And meet my Jesus there—

In their interactions with freedmen, white soldiers came to recognize Black people as Christians, even if their form and style of worship was different. The sense of religious kinship deepened their commitment to abolishing an institution most came to view as both undemocratic and in conflict with Christian teachings.

We have some idea of how pervasive soldiers' support for abolition grew as the war progressed. In 1862 most states had not yet adopted provisions for absentee balloting, so very few enlisted men and officers had the opportunity to cast votes in the off-year election. That fall, the Republican Party suffered heavy losses. In 1863 states like Ohio, where Vallandigham stood as the Democratic nominee for governor, introduced absentee ballots for soldiers, whose votes helped Republicans recover their losses in key bellwether regions of the country. The following year, soldiers broke disproportionately for the Republican Party, delivering as much as 78 percent of their votes to Abraham Lincoln, who ran on a platform in support of a constitutional amendment to abolish slavery.

Though soldiers' embrace of abolition flowed from different sources, many of them fundamentally pragmatic and secular, the concurrent growth of abolitionist and religious fervor in Union army camps was more than coincidental. Soldiers like Elisha Hunt Rhodes did not distinguish between their Christian faith and the twin causes for which they fought—the Union and abolition. "I trust I entered the Army with pure motives and from love of country," Rhodes reflected in the final days of service. "I have tried to keep myself from evil ways and believe I have never forgotten that I am a Christian. . . . I feel that I can go home to my family as pure as when I left them as a boy of 19 years. I have been successful in my Army life simply because I have always been ready and willing to do my duty. I thank God that I have had an opportunity of serving my country freeing the slaves and restoring the Union."

CHAPTER 10

NATIONAL REGENERATION

Early in his presidency, Thomas Jefferson declined a request by a group of Baptists in Connecticut to declare a national fast day, observing that the Constitution had erected "a wall of separation between Church and State." The Civil War had blown that wall away. It was only natural that churches should support their government in its time of need, and that government would lean on the churches for material and moral support. Less clear was whether religious leaders and institutions should meddle in politics—the partisan competition between Democrats and Republicans. Before the war, few Christians would have advocated for the encroachment of religion into politics. By the 1860s, that resistance crumbled as evangelicals lent their voices and votes to the Republican cause. This did not occur in a vacuum. It built over time. Evangelical Christianity and American popular democracy grew up contemporaneously and bore more than a superficial resemblance to each other. John Helm, who knew the Lincoln family in Kentucky, noted the similarities between Methodist camp meetings and the "log cabin and hard cider" campaign of 1840, when the Whig Party "took to beat the democrats and sung them," patterning dramatic political rallies after the popular style of Protestant revivals. That both revivals and political rallies might seem like interchangeable forms of public entertainment did not sit well with all churchmen, including a Methodist minister from Ohio who found that the log cabin campaign had "so engrossed the minds . . . even of the members of the Church" that it sapped their enthusiasm for building and extending the Christian fellowship. But even in the days before slavery consumed politics and rent the major churches in two, most religious leaders and laypeople accepted a soft convergence of religion and politics. They agreed that Christians should vote in accordance with their spiritual commitments. "Go . . . before you vote to your closet," implored one minister, "and ask God to give you light and direction." Churches in the antebellum period frequently hosted prayer meetings on the eve of state and federal elections, and evangelicals generally agreed with Horace Bushnell that it was their special obligation to exclude from public office those candidates "stained with *drunkenness, Sabbath-breaking, profaneness, gambling, or murder.*"

There was a difference, however, between welcoming a Christian presence in politics and choosing sides. "How will the Presbyterians, or Baptists, or Protestant Episcopalians, or Methodists vote?" a political editor posed to his readers. "They are known to be divided on every leading question of policy, and to vote without reference to any religious creed or dogma." Two things were true: Notwithstanding very specific state and regional dynamics where certain denominations tended to support one party over the other, nationally, evangelicals were just as divided between Whigs and Democrats as were non-evangelicals. Yet at the same time, Whig leaders, who fashioned themselves as the Christian party, tended to wear religion on their sleeves, while Democrats were usually more circumspect in joining their spiritual and political commitments. In part, this grew out of the Democratic Party's increased reliance on German and Irish Catholic immigrants, who resented Protestant moralizing, and Protestant nativism, which experienced a sharp uptick after the 1830s. It also reflected the Whigs' commitment to social uplift and reform causes—education, Sabbath observance, temperance—which dovetailed with projects near and dear to the evangelical united front. Democrats were churchgoers, too, but many Whigs cast them as infidels, enemies of "Marriage, Morality and Social Order" on a mission to "OVERTHROW THE CHURCH." Whiggery was a minority political alignment for most of its short existence, but where its fires burned strongest, party leaders often held rallies inside Protestant churches. In 1840 prominent ministers including Lyman Beecher (Congregationalist/Presbyterian) and Arthur Elliot (Methodist) even spoke at Whig rallies, beseeching the crowds to defeat Democrats "in the name of the Great Jehovah."

The steady creep of politics into the churches intensified in the 1850s, as the sectional debate snapped the major denominations in two and as the parties realigned around the slavery question, with Democrats generally supporting or at least tolerating its extension into the territories, and the new Republican Party opposing it. In 1856, Democrats in Pennsylvania complained of "fanatical Baptist and Methodist preachers . . . hurling their anathemas at us from their pulpits on Sundays and from the stump on week days." They had a point. Evangelical clergymen were aligned as never before in opposition to the Kansas-Nebraska Act, and some—notably, Henry Ward Beecher, who took a temporary leave of absence from his pulpit at Brooklyn's Plymouth Church to serve as an official Republican Party stump speaker—entirely blurred the line between their clerical and political commitments. Churches throughout the North hosted rallies for the Republican presidential nominee, John C. Frémont. Ministers offered benedictions at party meetings. Others infused their sermons with strong antislavery messages, which, if not avowedly partisan, surely intended to stoke support for the new party. National papers took notice when the candidate and his wife attended services on the eve of the election at Beecher's church.

This same fervor carried into the 1860 election, which saw not only many evangelical clergymen dabble in Republican politics, but also the party's ranks dominated by committed Protestant lay figures. Gilbert Haven, the Methodist minister and abolitionist, rejoiced that Lincoln's election would "assur[e] the speedy abolition of slavery." John Andrew of Massachusetts and Austin Blair of Michigan, devout and active lay members in the Unitarian church, marshaled religious support in their successful campaigns for governor. John Wentworth, the mayor of Chicago and a once-and-future congressman, preached that Abraham Lincoln would "break every yoke and let the oppressed go free." Joshua Giddings, no longer in Congress but active on the stump, told audiences that the election concerned no less than the "advancement of Christian civilization." While on the hustings, it was not uncommon for Republican candidates to cast the electoral contest as fraught with religious import. George Julian, a radical antislavery congressman from Indiana, and Giddings's son-in-law, called it "a fight . . . between God and the Devil—between heaven and hell!" While addressing New York City's Wide-Awakes—young men who donned oilcloth capes and staged dramatic, torchlight parades in support of the Republican cause—another party spokesman affirmed that the coming election would pit "Christ's doctrine of righteousness" against unalloyed "evil." After the election, leading church organizations passed resolutions urging that no further compromises be made with seceding states. In many ways, the Republican

Party had become the new Christian party, both in how it styled itself and in how many people—including many Democrats—perceived it.

And yet even as late as 1860, evangelicals in the North likely divided their votes between the parties—if not evenly, then in sufficient numbers to make it unclear that one or the other enjoyed the full-throated support of Northern Protestants. Even in Springfield, his hometown, only three of the city's clergymen voted for Lincoln, in part reflecting the city's Democratic bent (Lincoln swept the farm areas outside Springfield), but also a likely knock-on effect from his local reputation as a heretic and nonbeliever. Nationally, many of the most vocal leaders of the main denominations supported the Republican ticket, but they were ahead of the laity in fusing their religious and political identities.

The gap between clergy and laypeople closed quickly. The war's evolution from a struggle to maintain the Union to a battle for the liberation of four million enslaved human beings ultimately brought the Protestant churches and their members into close alignment with the Republican Party in a way that influenced not just the next several decades of American politics, but the coming era of American Protestantism. At the heart of this transformation was the churches' strong embrace of emancipation as a war aim and outcome.

MOST EVANGELICAL LEADERS AND INSTITUTIONS IN THE NORTH FOL-lowed a steady course from nominal opposition to slavery in the first decades of the century, to full-throated opposition to its extension (but lukewarm support, if any, for its abolition) in the 1850s, to outspoken backing for abolition during the Civil War. Before the war, many preachers—even those who opposed slavery—held back from publicly embracing abolition for fear of promoting dissension within their churches or disunion between the states. As late as September 1861, a Connecticut minister, Ichabod Simmons, affirmed, "The war is not being conducted for the purpose of liberating the Southern slaves; it is the government saving itself." But for most Christian leaders who once viewed abolition as a hot-button issue that would only divide Americans against each other, the Secession Crisis of 1860–61 flipped the equation. Now, according to Gilbert Haven, the "shock of arms united them. The one saw that Union now meant universal liberty. The other that abolitionism meant Union, and only under its banner could the nation be preserved. Equal rights were seen to mean every man's rights." That the proponents of slavery had foisted disunion on the country, and the opponents of slavery sought to defend it, rendered abolition not just respectable, but a religious imperative.

Lincoln's announcement in September 1862 that he intended to emancipate Southern enslaved people, and his final proclamation, issued on January 1, 1863, met with widespread approval among most evangelical church leaders. They took it as proof that "God is working out in his own providential way a solution of the mighty problem, and our part is to stand still and see the salvation of God," as a Presbyterian minister in New Jersey explained to his congregation. Even Old School Presbyterians, not known for their antislavery ardor, came to believe they were living in historic times—historic in the biblical sense of the word— and that it was God's "will that every vestige of human slavery . . . should be effaced, and that every Christian man should address himself with industry and earnestness to his appropriate part in the performance of this great duty." Reflecting the increasingly martial spirit of evangelical Christianity, the General Assembly rejoiced that the president had responded to "powerful and wicked treason" by decreeing slavery's "extinction by military force." Moral suasion was no longer the method by which Christians would extinguish wickedness.

If during the first year of the war evangelicals had despaired that Lincoln was too lenient—too sluggish in his embrace of emancipation as a war measure and objective—by the time of his proclamation, they increasingly echoed his language, much as he adopted theirs. "The character of the war will be changed," Lincoln told a government official not long after he issued his order. The war for union would now become a war "of subjugation," and the old South would "be destroyed and replaced by new propositions and ideas." A Congregationalist minister from Salem, Massachusetts, made essentially the same argument when he noted, "The cause of the war is clearly slavery; and we tried for a long time . . . to fight the war, and save the sin; and God would not suffer it. . . . The Proclamation of the President puts us right. Now we are openly and directly on the side of God; and now we may hope to have his favor." Of course, where Lincoln remained unconvinced that God was on his or the Union's side, the clergyman stood firm in his belief that the country had chosen correctly in the struggle between "Light and Darkness, Christianity and Barbarism," and that God would "enable us to crush . . . once and for all" slaveholders and their government. For many devout evangelicals, emancipation was a sign of "the approaching Providence"—the "National Regeneration"—a measure of perfection that prepared the world for the coming millennium. God would now "fight for the nation as He has not yet fought for it," the *Pittsburgh Christian Advocate* believed. Its issuance was a "turning point of the war," the *Christian Times and Illinois Baptist* affirmed. Edmund Fairchild, a Free Will Baptist who served as president of a small religious college in Michigan, believed that "the day of our redemption draweth nigh . . . Justice . . . and Right and Heaven are with us!" Not only did the proclamation herald a new chapter in America's millennial project, it generated a new imperative to bring the fight to the South. Now that "human freedom" had emerged as "the issue in the conflict," the Wisconsin Methodist Conference "deemed it alike the duty of the citizen and the Christian to prosecute the war."

Speaking at an AME church just three days before Lincoln issued his final proclamation, Frederick Douglass declared it a "sacred Sunday" and time for "poetry and song." In acknowledgment of the document's provision for the raising and arming of Black soldiers, in the coming weeks he summoned biblical language in calling on African Americans to "sound once more the trumpet of war" and invoked the memory of Denmark Vesey, Nat Turner, and John Brown—three martyrs who died for their incitement of rebellions by enslaved people—to declare a "contest with oppression" in which "the Almighty has no attribute which can take sides with oppressors."

By early 1864, Douglass, whose voice had been one of the earliest to advocate an abolition war, believed that what had begun as a battle devoid of great meaning had evolved into a project of "National regeneration," a term rife with religious import. He claimed to be "neither appalled nor disappointed" that the war had slogged on so long or cost as many lives as it did. "The longer the better if it must be so—in order to put an end to the hell black cause out of which the Rebellion has risen." Regeneration, after all, often required suffering and penance. It was a theme he had sounded many times before. But Douglass also signaled grudging admiration for the political and military leaders who led that regenerative effort. "President Lincoln introduced his administration to the country as one which would faithfully catch, hold, and return runaway slaves," he preached. Now, the administration was committed to passing the Thirteenth Amendment, codifying the legal death of slavery. "Our Generals, at the beginning of the war, were horribly Pro-Slavery. They took to slave-catching and slave-killing like ducks to water. They are now very generally and very earnestly in favor of putting an end to Slavery."

Support for emancipation proved an easy bridge to political engagement. Even as early as 1862, when in his annual message to Congress Lincoln called for a program of voluntary, compensated emancipation, church leaders exhibited a noticeable surge of activity that straddled the line between advocating for emancipation and openly supporting the Republican Party. Religious outlets including the *Congregational Journal*, *Zion's Herald and Wesleyan Journal*, *The Presbyterial Quarterly Review*, and the *Christian Advocate and Journal* lent full-throated support for the president's proposal. Though some clergymen found the concept of gradual emancipation a half measure, or even a moral affront, Methodist Episcopal conferences in New York, New England, and northern Indiana, as well as the General Synod of the Evangelical Lutheran Church, endorsed the president's plan. When, later that year, Congress passed and Lincoln signed a manumission scheme for the District of Columbia, compelling slaveholders to emancipate their enslaved people, but providing compensation of up to $300 per enslaved person to offset their financial losses, most religious authorities "hailed with joy" (the New England Methodist Episcopalian Church). "Thank God this reproach is wiped out," cheered the *Western Christian Advocate*.

Even more than in prior cycles, churchmen leaned into the 1862 off-year election campaign. The Methodist Episcopal Conference of Wisconsin instructed coreligionists that it was their duty to elect men of high moral caliber—men who supported emancipation in both the border states and the South. In Lincoln's home state, the Illinois Annual

Conference of the Methodist Episcopal Church expressed "the deepest abhorrence [for] any public servant who by his votes or speeches, or influences, has endeavored to embarrass the Government in crushing the rebellion at any cost"—a statement aimed squarely at Copperhead Democrats, but also some War Democrats who opposed Lincoln's war policies and emancipation measures. So it went throughout the North. In Dodge, Wisconsin, the Baptist association, representing a denomination in which authority was traditionally dispersed, told voters, "To save the Union is a noble work; but the salvation and enthronement of a great moral principle which is really more warred against than is the Union, seems to us the paramount duty of the hour." In Massachusetts, a prominent Baptist minister went a step further, telling the state Republican convention, "God gives us certain means, let us use them." When Democrats and conservative Republicans joined forces in Massachusetts in an effort to deny Charles Sumner, an outspoken radical, reelection to the US Senate, a wide coalition of clergymen, Sunday school teachers, and religious newspapers spanning leading Protestant denominations joined forces to stump on his behalf. Sumner was reelected.

Clergy and lay leaders generally lent full support to Republican candidates at the state and federal levels in 1862, but enough Protestant voters broke ranks to deliver a decisive victory to the Democratic Party that fall. A Methodist minister in Indiana privately mused that many evangelical voters switched party allegiances as a "first reaction" to the Emancipation Proclamation. Another Methodist minister recorded in his diary that some of his trustees had blocked essential repairs to the church in opposition to his outspoken support of the president and the preliminary Emancipation Proclamation. "The country," one of his trustees complained, was on the cusp of being "ruined by abolition preachers."

Given the swing of the political pendulum, many evangelical voters clearly *had* rejected the Republican Party, even as lay and religious leaders grew more avowed in their commitment to abolition and embrace of partisan politics. It would remain to be seen whether the pattern would hold in 1864.

⚜

LINCOLN MAY NOT HAVE BEEN A NATURAL-BORN POLITICIAN. HE STUMbled plenty in his early tenure as a state legislator, and his single term in Congress was anything but successful. But over the years he developed a shrewd ability to perceive which way the political winds blew. Notwithstanding the likelihood that he developed a genuine sense of spirituality during the war, he also appreciated the growing importance of the churches in motivating the Northern public and the outsize role that evangelical voters might play in the 1864 presidential election, should they vote as a bloc. Governing in an era long before the development of public polling, the president could count only on anecdotal evidence and personal instinct. Both led him to believe that evangelicals would, for the first time, be a largely united and powerful political force. Though Lincoln kept an open-door policy that maddened his staff and cabinet members, meeting all manner of visitors each week, with seemingly little concern for his schedule and focus, he went out of his way to receive influential lay and clerical leaders, as well as representatives from the principal religious service organizations. Theodore Tilton, a Christian layman and fervent abolitionist; Henry Ward Beecher; and Matthew Simpson all enjoyed ready access to the Executive Mansion. The president met frequently with delegations from the Presbyterian, Baptist, Methodist, and Quaker churches and societies, and from the US Sanitary

Commission. When the American Baptist Home Mission Society presented the administration with resolutions of backing and encouragement, Lincoln responded by thanking them for the almost "unanamous" support which the Christian communities are so zealously giving to the country, and to liberty." He was flattering his audience while recognizing their importance to the Union war effort. He also yoked their support to the cause of emancipation, which by 1864 had become a cornerstone of his reelection platform. "When, a year or two ago, those professedly holy men of the South, met in the semblance of prayer and devotion," he continued, "and, in the name of Him who said 'As ye would all men should do unto you, do ye even so unto them' appealed to the christian world to aid them in doing to a whole race of men, as they would have no man do unto themselves, to my thinking, they contemned and insulted God and His church, far more than did Satan when he tempted the Saviour with the Kingdoms of the earth. The devils attempt was no more false, and far less hypocritical. But let me forbear, remembering it is also written 'Judge not, lest ye be judged.'" Given how controversial emancipation remained among the broader electorate, Lincoln took a considerable risk in signaling to religious leaders that the war *was* very much about slavery, and that rebellion in the name of slaveholding was sinful.

Not everyone appreciated the president's solicitousness toward evangelical supporters. Earlier in the war, William Tecumseh Sherman, famously a curmudgeon, groused, "I wish that [General Henry] Halleck would put a Guard over the White House to keep out the Committees of preachers, Grannies and Dutchmen that absorb Lincoln's time and thought." Some non-evangelicals voiced their resentment of the president's open embrace of religious reformers and political priests. Lincoln "seems to imagine that he is a sort of half way clergyman," a strict Illinois Calvinist complained, "and even our people & soldiers have the same confused and paralyzing ideas."

As Peace Democrats became more outspoken in their opposition to the war, church leaders grew more strident in aligning themselves with the Republican Party. In Ohio, they uniformly opposed the gubernatorial aspirations of former congressman Clement Vallandigham. Running his campaign in absentia from Canada, Vallandigham continued to advocate restoration of "the Union as it was and . . . the Constitution as it is." Churches in Ohio lined up against Vallandigham, whom even many wobbly Republicans and War Democrats regarded as a traitor to his country. The Western Reserve Convention of the United Brethren declared that it would be "incompatible with the principles and spirit" of the church to vote for the notorious Copperhead. The state's Congregational conference affirmed the "righteousness of the war" and denounced the "fractious spirit of Democrats." Methodist outlets openly endorsed Vallandigham's principal opponent, the War Democrat John Brough, who ran on a fusion ticket with the Republicans. "Lord God Almighty bless John Brough, the candidate . . . who is called upon to bear the ark of our cause," a prominent Methodist minister prayed. "Give him favor among this people, that he may have a most unequal majority . . . and God have mercy on poor Vallandigham. . . . Lord pardon [his] sins." Vallandigham lost the election in a rout.

Lincoln's active engagement of religious leaders ultimately paid handsome dividends in the bitterly fought election of 1864. In his bid to become the first two-term president since Andrew Jackson, Lincoln faced off against George McClellan, the former general and commander of the Union army. Exceeding even their high level of involvement in previous election cycles, prominent evangelicals campaigned enthusiastically for Lincoln, whom many considered—as did Schuyler Colfax, the

Speaker of the US House of Representatives and an active member in his local Reformed church—"the instrument with which our God intends to destroy slavery." The chairman of the American Baptist Home Mission Society urged a national convention of Baptists to rally behind the president and his party, holding that he "believed fully that God has raised up His Excellency for such a time as this." This notion—that Lincoln was in some fashion God's agent on earth—became an increasingly common means by which clergymen and Christian activists justified both their engagement in partisan politics and their tendency to frame support for the Republican cause as a moral and religious imperative.

It was not simply that some or even most church leaders evinced support for the Republican party. For the first time, leading evangelical denominations formally endorsed a partisan ticket. Regional Methodist conferences and Baptist associations explicitly asked members to vote Republican in the fall elections. So did Congregationalist organizations, several Presbyterian synods, and individual churches. Religious bodies often took care to wrap their political endorsements in patriotic cloth. The election was not so much a contest between Democrats and Republicans as it was, in the words of the Methodist *Repository*, a matter of showing "true and honest loyalty to our government." The *American Presbyterian*, affiliated with the New School, did not need to use the word "Democrat" when it scorned those who would "embarrass and seek to overthrow the Government in the very crisis of the awful struggle . . . to seek to baffle and confound it by sowing discord, discontent and despondency among the people. . . . What is this but *Disloyalty!*" Even Old School Presbyterians locked arms with their more evangelical brethren. The *Presbyter*, a Cincinnati-based church organ, endorsed a resolution that "any person teaching and maintaining that American slavery is not a sin, and is justified by the word of God, is justly liable to censure." It then offered an unequivocal endorsement of the Republican ticket.

It made matters easier that the Democratic National Convention, meeting in Chicago in late August, hung an albatross around McClellan's neck by adopting a peace platform and calling for a negotiated settlement that would allow the South to reunite with slavery still intact. Many Northern voters dubbed this a "surrender platform" and viewed it as near treasonous. For Christians, it provided additional rationale for bringing religion into politics. "Peace through Victory," a Congregationalist minister from New York intoned, in a sharp rebuke to Peace Democrats who would abandon Black people's lives in the pursuit of reunion. When the Union scored a series of critical victories weeks before voting began, a professor at the Union Theological Seminary wrote, "The hand of God is to me so conspicuous in this struggle, that I should almost as soon expect the Almighty to turn slaveholder, as to see this war end without the extinction of its guilty cause." If George McClellan as president would bargain away the hard-won military advances that Northerners had achieved on the battlefield, or reverse course on abolition, it was the duty of all Christians to vote Republican. The alignment of church, state, and party was complete.

Religious activists treated the fall campaign as a holy mission. Theodore Tilton took to the hustings throughout the Northeast, rallying religious voters to the Republican cause. Henry C. Wright, a clergyman and missionary, stumped for Lincoln in Illinois and Michigan. Marius Robinson, Theodore Weld, and Ichabod Codding—theologians who cut their teeth as "Lane Rebels" in the 1840s—also campaigned far and wide. A leading religious newspaper implored clergymen to instruct their congregants each Sunday on the importance of defeating the Democrats and their treacherous peace platform. And if "pew-holders refrained from attending church," the editors continued, "the pastor should immediately visit them at home, in their stores or work-places." They need not have worried. Prominent clerics like Henry Ward Beecher, Granville Moody of Ohio, and Robert Breckinridge of Kentucky—and hundreds of political clergymen, particularly in the battleground states of the Midwest—stumped for the party with impunity. They signaled little concern for those of their coreligionists made uncomfortable by the casual comingling of the spiritual and secular. On the eve of the election, Matthew Simpson rallied the faithful at New York City's Academy of Music. In a special election version of his famous "war speech"—part sermon, part patriotic exhortation—the bishop waved a bloody battle flag belonging to New York's Fifty-Fifth Infantry Regiment and declared that though the "blood of our brave boys is upon it" and the "bullets of rebels have gone through and through it . . . there is nothing on earth like that old flag for beauty, lone may those stars shine." Those assembled took to their feet and let out wild cries and cheers as Simpson called on all Christians to vote for "the railsplitter . . . President" in the upcoming canvass.

Democrats, who for three years nursed growing frustration with political preachers, loudly complained that the Protestant churches and their leaders, lay and clerical alike, had thrown in wholesale with the Republican cause in a manner that broke faith with the separation of church and state. William D. Potts, a clergyman from Newark, New Jersey, so strongly disapproved of this trend that he published a 127-page treatise denouncing both Lincoln and the Republican Party, and Protestant preachers who had turned their pulpits into political stages. Conceding that he was well in the minority, Potts lamented that Americans "have been taught to respect the Clergy and credit their preaching. But we are compelled to fear that Satan has assumed the ministerial office, and occupies, unmolested, a large proportion of the pulpits, spreading enmity and destruction all around!" Such dirges only confirmed that at every level, from local churches and their members—from regional synods and conferences to the highest levels of denominational leadership—evangelical Christians were marrying their religious and political faith like never before.

When a clergyman wrote to the president, assuring him that the nation's Christian establishment was "doing whatever we can for you and the country," he hardly exaggerated. Lincoln, after all, had been chosen in the nation's most critical moment "by the Providence of God," and it was the duty of Christians to see that he remained in the Executive Mansion. So pervasive was the evangelical influence in the fall campaign that one secular newspaper casually observed, "If McClellan is elected he must breast and overcome almost the entire ecclesiastical and ministerial force of the land. . . . These are the men, together with those who are found in the house of God on the Sabbath and who countenance the spiritual gathering of the week time." Count Adam Gurowski, a Polish émigré whose diaries offer keen insight into Washington, DC, during the war, privately concurred, noting that religious newspapers "at times appreciate the events and men from a standpoint by far higher and clearer than that of the common press . . . these preaching and writing divines . . . are the genuine apostles of the spirit of our age."

The president needed all the help he could muster. Lincoln's new general-in-chief, Ulysses S. Grant, had initiated a mammoth, coordinated offensive against the Confederacy but suffered a series of costly setbacks that spring and summer. In Georgia, General William Tecumseh Sherman was stuck outside Atlanta. Even on the outskirts of Washington, DC, Confederate Jubal Early and his men threatened the very safety of the Union's capital city. Many Republican leaders urged Lincoln to withdraw from the race, lest the military quagmire, soon entering its fourth year, result in an electoral rout up and down the ballot. Even the president acknowledged that "unless some great change takes place" on the battlefield, he would be *"badly beaten"* in the November election. In late August, Lincoln drafted a private memorandum in which he recorded for history that it seemed "exceedingly probable that this Administration will not be re-elected. Then it will be my duty to so co-operate with the President elect, as to save the Union between the election and the inauguration; as he will have secured his election on such ground that he can not possibly save it afterwards."

The autumn campaign was arguably the most vicious and racially charged in American history, then or since. At Lincoln's urging, the Republican Party—rebranded temporarily as a fusion National Union Party, with some War Democrats joining in a momentary coalition— had adopted a convention plank advocating a constitutional amend-ment banning slavery. Democratic newspaper editors coined a new term, "miscegenation," and accused the president of fighting a war to impose race amalgamation on the country. They claimed that Lincoln was in fact "the outcrop of a remote African in his ancestry."

Reflecting Democrats' disgust with the seeming bond between the leading evangelical churches and the Republican Party, the president's political enemies issued a stinging satire, *The Lincoln Catechism*, which dubbed the president "Abraham Africanus the First" and included a mock rewrite of the Ten Commandments:

> Thou shalt have no other God but the negro.
> Thou shalt make an image of a negro, and place it on the Capitol
>   as the type of the new American man.

Thou shalt swear that the negro shall be the equal of the white
man. . . .

Thou shalt commit murder—of slaveholders.

Thou mayest commit adultery—with the [escaped enslaved people].

Thou shalt steal—everything that belongeth to a slaveholder. . . .

Thou shalt covet the slave-holders man-servant and his maid-
servant.

The tract also reimagined the Sermon on the Mount to reinforce the
party's appeal to white racism ("Give to a negro that asketh not, but
from the poor white man turn thou away") and took a gratuitous aim at
leading civic and religious lights of the Republican Party ("When though
prayest, go to the Academy of Music, or to Cooper's Institute, that thou
mayest be seen of men, after the manner of Cora Hatch and Henry
Ward Beecher"). (Hatch was a well-known spiritualist, and therefore an
easy target for Democrats who despised "ultraisms.") For good measure,
the booklet's cover included a cartoon of Lincoln, rendering him as a
Black man.

However dim his prospects seemed in late summer, military developments soon changed the political tide. On September 1, Atlanta surrendered to William Tecumseh Sherman, delivering a massive blow to the
Confederacy and a critical military and political win for the president.
Days later, Ulysses S. Grant essentially propped up the Republican cause
by issuing a public letter that promised (in the words of John Nicolay,
the president's private secretary) "an encouraging view of the military
situation, and tells the country the true road to peace is through hard
fighting till the rebellion is put down." In October, Union forces under
Philip Sheridan's command encircled and defeated Jubal Early. The war,

it seemed, had taken a dramatic turn, and with it, so did Lincoln's political fortune.

In the end, the election proved a rout for the Democratic Party. Lincoln carried every state except New Jersey and Missouri, winning the popular vote by a margin of 55 percent to 45 percent, and the electoral college by a lopsided 212 votes to 21. His party also swept congressional and state elections. It seemed, as John Hay, the president's other secretary, observed earlier in the war, that if many of the professional politicians did not regard Lincoln as "their 'kind of cat,'" still, "the people want him. . . . There is no mistaking that fact." Notwithstanding his overwhelming victory, Lincoln was stung by the acid tone of the campaign. "It is a little singular," he told Hay, "that I who am not a vindictive man should have always been before the people for election in canvasses marked for their bitterness; always but once: When I came to Congress it was a quiet time. But always besides that the contests in which I have been prominent have been marked with great rancor."

On Election Day, a great majority of evangelical voters appear to have heeded the instruction of their leaders to "march as churches in our processions, as churches to the polls" (the *New York Independent*) or, as Gilbert Haven urged, march "to the ballot-box, an army of Christ, with the banner of the cross." Lincoln and his party carried the election largely on the strength of their lopsided support among native-born Protestants, particularly those in rural areas, in a time when most Americans still worked and resided on farms. Assessing the president's decisive victory, the editor of a Methodist newspaper observed that there "probably never was an election in all history into which the religious elements entered so largely, and so nearly all on one side." Nationally, voters from several non-evangelical denominations, including mainline Episcopalians and Old School Presbyterians, likely broke in McClellan's favor, as did Baptists in the lower Midwest states. McClellan also carried the Catholic vote. But Lincoln was the overwhelming favorite among Baptists nationally, as well as New School Presbyterians, Methodists, Congregationalists, Quakers, Unitarians, and several smaller Protestant denominations. It was the first time that evangelicals voted as a bloc, representing both the emergence of a new religious influence in politics and the full politicization of evangelical religion. Years later, the devout Congregationalist Henry Wilson, a senator from Massachusetts who served as vice president under Ulysses S. Grant, claimed that the Republican Party "contained more . . . moral worth than was ever embodied in any political organization in any land . . . created by no man . . . brought into being by Almighty God himself." If his assessment was audacious, it was also widely shared in a particular moment when evangelical Christians felt themselves living in historic times and understood their obligations to extend from the battlefield of war to the battlefield of partisan politics.

CHAPTER 11

NO SORROW LIKE OUR SORROW

The four months between Lincoln's reelection and second inaugural were momentous for the president, and for the nation he led. The string of Union victories that helped turn the electoral tide in the Republican Party's favor continued unabated. In December, William Tecumseh Sherman's army, having cut a swath through Georgia, plundering everything in sight on its "march to the sea," captured Savannah. Union forces also defeated the Confederates near Nashville that month, essentially destroying the Army of Tennessee.

In January, the president threw the full weight of his office behind an effort to secure approval in the House of Representatives of a constitutional amendment abolishing slavery. The war was nearing its end. Lincoln had grounded the Emancipation Proclamation in his wartime powers as commander in chief. A cessation of hostilities would undermine the legal basis of that order, and it was not inconceivable that the courts might order the re-enslavement of millions of African Americans, including many who fought in the Union army. The new Congress, which was scheduled to convene in December 1865, was sure to pass the measure, as Republicans had routed their opponents in the recent election. Lincoln even had the option of calling the new Congress into session early. But he was under intense pressure to negotiate peace with the Confederacy, and he needed the amendment to make abolition a sine qua non. Only when they realized that slavery could not be saved would the rebels lay down their arms.

In pursuit of his goal, Lincoln likely sanctioned and in some cases directly negotiated the brazen use of patronage appointments to buy off a requisite number of lame-duck Democratic congressmen who had lost their seats in the fall election. He personally whipped hard for the amendment, visiting a Democratic congressman whose brother had fallen in battle, to tell him that his kin "died to save the Republic from death by the slaveholders' rebellion."

"I wish you could see it to be your duty to vote for the Constitutional amendment ending slavery," he told the legislator. He also ordered Congressman James Alley, one of the amendment's supporters: "I am the President of the United States, clothed with immense power, and I expect you to procure those votes." Or at least that was how Alley remembered the conversation almost a quarter century after the fact. In the end, the House passed the Thirteenth Amendment, which the president, in an unusual and constitutionally unnecessary step, personally signed on February 1. The churches naturally cheered passage of the amendment, hailing, in the words of Congregationalist minister George Tuthill, the day that "Slavery . . . shall exist no more." Across the North, clergy and church conferences lent vociferous support for ratification at the state level. When the New Jersey legislature first voted down ratification, the state's Methodist Episcopal conference and Baptist convention issued stinging rebukes. The Baptist *Christian Watchman* reflected the views of many evangelical Christians when it noted with warm approval that if the country was born on July 4, 1776, it was "born again" on January 31, 1864. The amendment embodied the great national regeneration for which religious men and women had waited expectantly for years.

On March 4, with the war's close well on the horizon, Lincoln delivered his second inaugural address before a large crowd, forty thousand strong, on the east portico of the Capitol Building, whose dome—under construction through the first years of the war—was now complete. An hour before he was scheduled to take the oath of office, a heavy rain fell, leaving the streets mud covered and nearly impassable, and the onlookers "bedraggled and drenched," "streaked with mud from end to end," as newspaperman Noah Brooks observed. As Lincoln stepped up to the lectern, the sun broke through the clouds.

The president's remarks were brief: just 701 words, lasting perhaps 5 minutes—the shortest inaugural address since George Washington's second term in office, and shorter than every presidential inauguration speech since, excepting Franklin D. Roosevelt's fourth and final address in 1945. It was also a wholly different style of address from anything that preceded or followed it—deeply spiritual, borrowing heavily from the style of the King James Bible, reflective of Lincoln's personal spiritual journey and crafted to lend religious meaning to a war that would soon draw to a close, but whose aftershocks Americans would continue to feel for decades to come.

"On the occasion corresponding to this four years ago, all thoughts were anxiously directed to an impending civil-war," he told the nation. "All dreaded it—all sought to avert it. . . . Both parties deprecated war; but one of them would *make* war rather than let the nation survive; and the other would *accept* war rather than let it perish. And the war came."

Like many of his countrymen, Lincoln understood the conflict in providential terms. It was willed by God—an inevitability that simply "came," despite the wishes of people of good faith, on both sides, who lacked agency in the grander scheme of a divine plan.

At the time of disunion, he continued, "one eighth of the whole population were colored slaves, not distributed generally over the Union, but localized in the Southern part of it. These slaves constituted a peculiar and powerful interest. All knew that this interest was, somehow, the cause of the war. To strengthen, perpetuate, and extend this interest was the object for which the insurgents would rend the Union, even by war; while the government claimed no right to do more than to restrict the territorial enlargement of it. Neither party expected for the war, the magnitude, or the duration, which it has already attained." God's purposes, as always, were mysterious.

By 1865, many of Lincoln's countrymen, particularly those who shared in the millennial faith of the evangelical churches, had grown secure in the conviction that God was on their side, and that they were on God's. Lincoln remained as irresolute as ever. In reflecting on the bloody conflict between North and South, he observed, "Both read the same Bible, and pray to the same God; and each invokes His aid against the other. It may seem strange that any men should dare to ask a just God's assistance in wringing their bread from the sweat of other men's faces; but let us judge not that we be not judged. The prayers of both could not be answered; that of neither has been answered fully. The Almighty has His own purposes. 'Woe unto the world because of offences! for it must needs be that offences come; but woe to that man by whom the offence cometh!'" Invoking a lexicon that was deeply resonant with American Protestants, he cut to the heart of the matter:

If we shall suppose that American Slavery is one of those offences which, in the providence of God, must needs come, but which, having continued through His appointed time, He now wills to remove, and that He gives to both North and South, this terrible war, as the woe due to those by whom the offence came, shall we discern therein any departure from those divine attributes which the believers in a Living God always ascribe to Him? Fondly do we hope—fervently do we pray—that this mighty scourge of war may speedily pass away. Yet, if God wills that it continue, until all the wealth piled by the bond-man's two hundred and fifty years of unrequited toil shall be sunk, and until every drop of blood drawn with the lash, shall be paid by another drawn with the sword, as was said three thousand years ago, so still it must be said "the judgments of the Lord, are true and righteous altogether."

Lincoln's message was unmistakable: Slavery was an offense against God. Both sides, North and South, had brought "this terrible war" upon themselves by sustaining its cruelty and injustice over so many generations. Death, destruction, and bereavement, felt on such an unprecedented scale, were God's way of punishing a degenerate nation. They were also a form of justice for every Black American kept in chains, sold away from his or her family, whipped and beaten and murdered.

For millions of Bible-reading Americans, the president's invocation of scripture was immediately evident.

"Woe unto the world because of offences! for it must needs be that offences come; but woe to that man by whom the offence cometh!" (Matthew 18:7)—a passage in which Jesus instructs his disciples that if their feet led them to sin, they must cut off their feet—if their eye led them to sin, they must remove the offending eye, for they should prefer "to enter into life with one eye, rather than having two eyes to be cast into hell fire." Americans had sinned, and God demanded awful sacrifices for their regeneration.

"If God wills that it continue, until all the wealth piled by the bondman's two hundred and fifty years of unrequited toil shall be sunk, and until every drop of blood drawn with the lash, shall be paid by another drawn with the sword, as was said three thousand years ago, so still it must be said 'the judgments of the Lord, are true and righteous altogether'"—a paraphrase of Psalm 19:9, which warns that "the fear of the Lord *is* clean, enduring for ever: the judgments of the Lord *are* true *and* righteous altogether." Lincoln's use of the term "bondman," rather than "bondsman," was also a knowing appropriation of the King James Bible's way of describing Hebrew enslaved people.

In his closing lines, Lincoln lifted inspiration from James 1:27 ("Pure religion and undefiled before God and the Father is this, To visit the fatherless and widows in their affliction, *and* to keep himself unspotted from the world"). "With malice toward none; with charity for all; with firmness in the right, as God gives us to see the right, let us strive on to finish the work we are in; to bind up the nation's wounds; to care for him who shall have borne the battle, and for his widow, and his orphan—to do all which may achieve and cherish a just, and a lasting peace, among ourselves, and with all nations."

Neither before nor since has a United States president so openly infused a public speech with religious sentiment and phrasing. Frederick Douglass, present in the audience, considered it "more like a sermon than a state paper." The address directly mentioned God fourteen times, referenced prayer three times, and quoted or paraphrased the Bible four times. Resonant with evangelicals in its promise of national regeneration, it also reflected the deeply seated fatalism of a president who remained drawn to his parents' faith, with its denial of human agency and belief in a distant and impersonal God whose will was inscrutable to human beings. The war came. Slavery was *somehow* its cause. "Neither party expected for the war, the magnitude, or the duration. . . . Neither anticipated that the *cause* of the conflict might cease with, or even before, the conflict itself should cease. Each looked for an easier triumph, and a result less fundamental and astounding." God would hold Americans accountable for their sins. In holding them accountable, he alone would dictate the price of grace. However far a road Lincoln had traveled, his God more closely resembled Tom Lincoln's than Henry Ward Beecher's.

Lincoln had been measuring and rehearsing these themes for some time. In his letter to Eliza Gurney several months earlier, he declared the will of the Almighty mysterious and unknowable and allowed that it might be his intent to punish the North and the South equally for the sin of slavery. A few months earlier, in a letter to leaders of the American Baptist Home Mission Society, the president denounced those who "contemned and insulted God and His church" by citing the Bible as moral justification for slavery. "The devil's attempt" to corrupt Jesus Christ was "no more false," he wrote. "But let me forebear, remembering it is also written, 'Judge not, lest ye be judged.'" In a nation of devout Christians certain they were right with God, and secure in their personal relationship with Christ, Lincoln remained an iconoclast.

Hours after he delivered his address, Lincoln told Thurlow Weed, the newspaper editor and Republican political boss from New York, "I expect [it] to wear as well as—perhaps better than—any thing I have produced; but I believe it is not immediately popular. Men are not flattered by being shown that there has been a difference of purpose between the Almighty and them. To deny it, however, in this case, is to deny that there is a God governing the world. It is a truth which I thought needed to be told; and as whatever of humiliation there is in it, falls most directly on myself, I thought others might afford for me to tell it." Only recently, the president had affirmed that "the religion that sets men to rebel and fight against their government" in the defense of slavery "is not the sort of religion upon which people can get to heaven." Unlike so many religious Northerners, Lincoln was none too certain that he or his countrymen had earned the right to grace either.

ABOUT A MONTH AFTER LINCOLN DELIVERED HIS SECOND INAUGURAL address, and just days after Robert E. Lee surrendered his army at Appomattox Court House, John Wilkes Booth shot and mortally wounded the president as he and Mary attended a play, *Our American Cousin*, at Ford's Theatre in Washington, DC. It was Good Friday, a day saturated with meaning for Christians.

In the moments following the attempt on his life, the president was moved across the street to a private residence, where, stretched out on a bed too small to accommodate his lanky frame, he "breathed with slow and regular respiration throughout the night," as John Hay, who had rushed to his side, later recalled. A miscellany of friends, family, government officials filed in and out of the bedroom: Robert Todd Lincoln; Gideon Welles; Elizabeth Dixon, the wife of Connecticut senator James Dixon, and a close friend of the First Lady; Secretary of War Edwin Stanton; Generals Henry Halleck and Montgomery Meigs; and Vice President Johnson, who briefly paid his respects. Robert broke down in tears several times and leaned on Charles Sumner for support. "As the dawn came and the lamplight grew pale," Hay remembered, the president's "pulse began to fail; but his face, even then, was scarcely more haggard than those of the sorrowing men around him. His automatic moaning ceased, a look of unspeakable peace came upon his worn features, and at twenty-two minutes after seven he died. Stanton broke the silence by saying: Now he belongs to the ages."

As word quickly spread of the president's assassination, people across the nation joined together in a collective expression of almost inconsolable grief. To many Americans, the fact that the president was martyred on Good Friday lent the event a terrible religious import, as though Lincoln, like Christ before him, had been sacrificed for the atonement of a sinful nation. Churches that would have been crowded that weekend with holiday worshippers now teemed with mourners who sought meaning and solace that "Black Sunday." When Maxwell Gaddis, a Methodist minister, arrived on Saturday evening at his church in Cincinnati, he found it jammed to capacity, with thousands more people lined up outside. He moved his nighttime service to nearby Pike's Opera House, where over four thousand citizens heard him preach. He still needed to turn away several hundred more. So it went across the North, where Christians did not merely turn to their clergymen to make sense of the national tragedy. They all but demanded it. When a replacement minister in Medway, Massachusetts, preached the Sunday morning service but made no mention of the assassination, members of the Baptist congregation passed a resolution scoring him for his insensitivity and demanding that he leave town within fifteen minutes. A week after the assassination, the minister at Trinity Episcopal Church in Washington, DC, faced an "intensely crowded audience tumultuous with excitement, and under circumstances connected with [his] parochial position and southern birth, that called for all the prudence and preparation possible."

The intensity of public mourning was without parallel in American history. Northerners treated Lincoln's funeral, coming as it did in the final days of the war, as a collective expression of grief for all that they had lost—not only a president, but sons, brothers, and husbands who had fallen in service to their country. On Tuesday, April 18, thousands of mourners filed quietly through the East Room of the Executive Mansion to pay their respects to the late president, whose body lay upon a raised catafalque. The next day, he was transported by a military procession to the US Capitol, where he served his single term in Congress almost two decades earlier, and would now lie in state. Hundreds of Black mourners lined the streets in front of the White House to pay their respects. "The sight was novel," a reporter for the *Chicago Tribune* remarked. "Four years since a procession of this description could no more have passed unmolested through the streets of the National Capital than it could have passed over Long Bridge from Virginia into the District of Columbia without passes from their slave driving masters." By accident rather than design, the US Colored Troops Twenty-Second led the sequence to the Capitol.

On Friday, April 21, a week after the assassination, a train carrying the bodies of Abraham Lincoln and his beloved son Willie, who was to be reinterred alongside him, left Washington, DC, for Springfield, repeating for the most part the tour of Northern cities that the late president had visited four years earlier as he traveled to the capital to assume his duties. The train made stops in Baltimore, Harrisburg, Philadelphia, New York, Albany, Buffalo, Cleveland, Columbus, Indianapolis, and Chicago, where millions of people attended public viewings and participated in prayer and funeral services. Traveling at a speed of no more than twenty miles per hour, but often as slowly as five, the funeral train afforded millions more the opportunity to pay their respects. In every small town and city along the way, mourners lined the tracks and crowded the train depots. As the train passed through Lancaster, Pennsylvania, two of the town's most prominent citizens, Thaddeus Stevens and James Buchanan, longtime political and personal foes, lifted their hats in somber respect. In New York City, young Theodore Roosevelt viewed the procession from the second floor of his parents' town house near Gramercy Park, as two hundred African American soldiers joined the official procession. Ultimately, some five million Americans paid their respects, either at public viewings of the president's casket or in funeral processions along packed city streets.

At the family's request, Matthew Simpson, the fighting war bishop with whom Lincoln had come to enjoy a close relationship, delivered the funeral sermon in Springfield, after which the president and Willie were laid to rest at Oak Ridge Cemetery on May 4. It was early spring, and the graveyard was blooming with lilacs, an image that Walt Whitman captured in his elegy, "When Lilacs Last in the Dooryard Bloom'd."

LIKE THEIR CONGREGANTS, CLERGYMEN REACTED WITH HEARTACHE AT the loss of a much-beloved leader. "Words express nothing," Edwin Webb of the Shawmut Congregational Church in Boston observed. "The sun is less bright than before, and the very atmosphere seems to hold in it for the tearful eye a strange ethereal element of gloom. . . . It is manly to weep to-day." Ministers struggled to find their words, admitting to their flocks that they felt an "indescribable stupefaction." "There has been, on this side of the world, no sorrow like our sorrow, so far as we can read back the history of the men who have dwelt here," the rector of

St. Paul's Chapel in New York mourned. "Regarded in its cause and in its manner of manifestation, it stands beyond comparison in its awful grandeur." In East Saginaw, Michigan, the pastor of the First Baptist Church summed up the nation's sense of loss simply: "America mourns as she never mourned before." A Union soldier from Vermont voiced the confusion and test of faith that many Christians felt at first news of the president's death. "Why did a just and merciful God permit this thing to happen?" he asked painfully. *The Ladies' Repository*, a Methodist publication, agreed that the assassination was "one of the inexplicable mysteries of Providence."

For African Americans, the president's death delivered an especially terrible blow. Lincoln's decision to turn the war for the Union into a holy war against slavery, and his unwavering commitment to enshrining universal freedom in the Constitution, made him a resonant figure for Black Christians—those born free and those born into bondage. "We, as a people, feel more than all others that we are bereaved," said the spiritual leader of the African Methodist Episcopal Zion Church in Troy, New York. "We had learned to love Mr. Lincoln as we have never loved man before. . . . We looked up to him as our saviour, our deliverer. His name was familiar with our children, and our prayers ascended to God in his behalf. [Had he] passed away according to the natural course of nature, we could have consoled ourselves with the thought that it was God's will it should be so. But falling as he did by the hand of the wicked, we derive our consolation only from the assurance that by his upright-ness, his honesty and his principles of Christianity, he is now enjoying that rest that remains for the just." A Black preacher at Cincinnati's Zion Baptist Church went even further. Had Lincoln's assassin given them "the choice to deliver him or ourselves to death, we would have said, take me; take father or mother, sister, brother; but do not take the life of the father of this people."

Though few of them had ever met Lincoln, many Christians who felt a personal relationship with Jesus Christ, who also died on Good Friday, similarly felt "profound personal grief" at the loss of their president. Living in the end days of a war that had cost the North so dearly in life and treasure, it was "as when a dear old father, a beloved mother, or a brother is torn relentlessly from our breast." A Methodist minister in Buffalo observed, "Unconsciously to ourselves, we felt a deep personal interest in him, an affection for him." Speaking of the late president almost as he might have spoken of Christ, Gilbert Haven, the Methodist minister and veteran abolitionist, offered that "never did a ruler so love his people. . . . He held every one in his heart of hearts; he felt a deep and individual regard for each and all; he wept over the nation's dead boys at Gettysburg as heartily as over his own dead boy in Washington." Haven likely erred in supposing that "their death, more than his own child's, was the means of bringing him into experimental acquaintance with Christ." For Lincoln, Willie's death was a spiritual turning point. But Haven was surely right in offering that the president's grief over the Union dead inspired in Lincoln a "godly sorrow."

Northern churchgoers united in their sense of bereavement in the days following Lincoln's death. They also expressed almost uncontrollable rage. Channeling and sharing in their congregants' fury, many ministers determined that the New Testament, while normally of greater relevance on Easter Sunday, was inadequate to the work of reconciling with the decapitation of the elected government. "In such a juncture our Government needed an infusion of the Old Testament severity rather than the New Testament tenderness," a Presbyterian minister from New

York reflected just a few days later. A country that had learned to lend spiritual license to the violent and coercive measures necessary to quash a rebellion and win a war now turned its anger on not just the assassins, but the South itself, which many Christians had become familiar with castigating as an ungodly region of unregenerate sinners. Henry Morehouse, a clergyman from Michigan, promised that the "taint of this assassination" would forever "cleave to the people of the South wherever they go. . . . Southern 'chivalry' has earned for itself the title of barbarism; Southern civilization . . . has shown itself to be a whited sepulcher full of corruption within."

Alonzo Quint, a Congregationalist minister who had served for a time as chaplain to the Second Massachusetts, delivered a typically fiery broadside in which he derided the archetypal "Southern Gentleman"—the "patriarchal protector" of lore, known for his "boundless hospitality and grace"—as a fraud. The war had exposed Southerners en masse as "revengeful, treacherous, murderous." The Southern gentleman "was a liar and a cheat. . . . His lordly mansion was, nine times in ten, unfit for a sty of northern pigs." Having ministered to his unit on the battlefield, Quint came to know the South. Speaking from the pulpit, he disparaged it as a land of "barbarians." He deplored "Southern Chivalry" as nothing more than "to assassinate an unarmed man." Such cutting and sweeping denunciations of Southern culture and character were common from Northern pulpits on Black Sunday and the days immediately following. Mostly forgoing expressions of Christian forgiveness and charity, clergymen reinforced the anger of churchgoers, assuring them that the assassination of Abraham Lincoln revealed Southerners as (in the words of a Presbyterian minister from upstate New York) unrepentant sinners "representing treason, disloyalty. Impatience of control, passion, disregard of the principle of majority rule, oppression of the weak, deeper degradation of the degraded," their leaders nothing more than "factious demagogues who would rather 'rule in hell than serve in Heaven.'"

In the days and weeks following Lincoln's assassination, the threads of religious transformation wound themselves together in a tight and sturdy knot. Faith in the retributive wisdom of the Old Testament—conviction that God's will and state authority were equally, and divinely, inviolate—a new comfort with violence and coercion in the enforcement of religious and civic order. This Christian culture would have been un-recognizable to the pre-war generation. "We have lost all sentiment of clemency," a minister in New York observed. A Presbyterian clergyman from Illinois noted that in the closing days of the war, some Northerners developed a natural sympathy for the vanquished Confederates. "Since they had not succeeded in destroying the government, we were falling into the absurdity of pitying their want of success and their misfortune. This murder, perpetrated in their behalf, and by their inspiration, has violently checked that tide." In his funeral sermon, Matthew Simpson called for every Southern officeholder and for "every officer educated at the public expense . . . who turned his sword against the vitals of the country [to] be doomed to a traitor's death."

In subsequent months and years, tempers would quell, and churches would gravitate back to a message of Christian love and mercy. But some of the tendencies on display in April 1865 would inform a more muscular and politically engaged variant of Protestantism in the years following the Civil War.

Sorrow and anger haunted church services in the weeks after Lincoln's death. So did a search for meaning. However appalled they were by Booth's murderous act, and even as they laid the blame for Lincoln's assassination squarely at the feet of Southern traitors, many Christians saw in the president's death the hand of providence. "Events are God's teachers," a New York pastor told his congregants. "Shall we say, that the hand of the assassin, which struck at so noble a life, did it for any fault of his? Or shall we say, that God permitted for a greater good to us, to our country, to our posterity," that Lincoln die for the nation's sins? Reflecting the careful balancing act that evangelicals performed in weighing the scope of human agency against God's will and design, ministers insisted that "the Lord . . . permitted this shocking deed" but "has not caused it. He is the cause of no evil whatsoever. . . . All evil has its origin in man himself, and is occasioned by the abuse or perversion of his divinely given freedom." Others believed that, like Christ, Lincoln had fulfilled the mission for which God had chosen him and would now be called home to an eternal resting place. Abraham Lincoln "died because his work was done," a Baptist preacher confidently asserted. "The purpose which God had to accomplish through his instrumentality had been fulfilled."

Some religious people even believed that Lincoln might have been too decent and forgiving a man to meet the "stern duties of the coming time," when a victorious North would render justice upon the defeated South. "Let us look for the good hand of our God in this calamitous visitation." James Garfield, a war veteran then serving in Congress, and known as "the praying Colonel" for the intensity of his religious conviction, maintained that God had permitted Lincoln's assassination because the president had been "the kindest, gentlest, tenderest friend" the South could hope to reckon with in the aftermath of the war. "It would really seem . . . that this tragedy almost parallels that of the Son of God, who died saying, 'Father, forgive them: they know not what they do.' So here the rebellion has removed the barrier between themselves and justice . . . and he, dying with words of tenderness and magnanimity upon his lips, forgave them all they had done. In taking away this life, the rebels have left the iron hand of the people to fall upon them."

Above all, church leaders believed, as the Presbyterian minister Charles Robinson of Brooklyn proclaimed, that a "martyr's blow has sealed the covenant we are making with posterity." Reflecting popular faith in America's providential mission to speed the coming of the millennium, Robinson reminded his faithful that the North "has stood for the rights of men, the truth of the Gospel, the principles of humanity, the integrity of the Union, the power of Christian people to govern themselves, the indefeasible equality of all the creatures of God in natural conditions of existence, no matter what be the color of their skin." Lincoln's death was a tragic sacrifice but also a stepping stone on the march toward one thousand years of peace. Robinson was of course wrong. Violent resistance to Reconstruction, Northern fatigue and capitulation, and a century of Jim Crow would prove his faith to be at least somewhat misplaced. But in the wake of Lincoln's death—the first time an American president had ever fallen by an assassin's bullet—the government survived, the war was won, and, according to Henry Ward Beecher, "Republican institutions have been vindicated in this experience as they never were before. . . . God, I think, has said by the voice of this event, to all the nations of the earth, 'Republican liberty, based upon true Christianity, is firm as the foundation of the globe.'" William Dean Howells, the young novelist who had penned Lincoln's official campaign biography in 1860, agreed. He shared the belief that Lincoln's death hung "upon every American like a personal calamity," but "thank God they cannot assassinate a whole Republic; the People is immortal."

AS THEY SOUGHT TO MAKE SENSE OF THE WAR AND OF LINCOLN'S DEATH, most evangelical Christians appear to have agreed with the late president that slavery was "somehow, the cause of the war." In the same way that Lincoln may have viewed Willie's death as the personal loss he must bear in a war that would cleanse the nation of its worst sin, Christians took comfort in knowing that the president sacrificed his own life to absolve the country of its crimes. Some remained angry, like Phillips Brooks. "I charge this murder where it belongs, on Slavery," he intoned from the pulpit. Slavery had robbed the country of "the gentlest, kindest, most indulgent man that ever ruled a State!" But to others, like E. S. Atwood of Salem, Massachusetts, Lincoln would only grow greater in death for the deeds he committed in life. "Let Abraham Lincoln be known to posterity by no other name than that of the Great Emancipator," he urged, "and his fame is secure. No other man ever dared so much in such a cause."

CHAPTER 12

THE UNRAVELING

Evangelical Christianity was a central, organizing influence as millions of Northerners—civilian and military, Black and white, men and women, lay and clergy—experienced and came to terms with the Civil War. The war changed religion itself, especially the culture of evangelical Protestantism, as much as it changed believers. It was not the first time that religion helped ordinary people make sense of mass mobilization and unspeakable carnage. But it was America's first experience with *total* war. It was also America's first modern armed conflict, with sophisticated weapons and technology that made the conflict both bloodier and more immediate. What began as a skirmish around states' rights and the inviolability of the Union developed into a freedom struggle of historic proportions. Against this backdrop, religion helped soldiers steel themselves for battle, reconciled their families to the inevitable loss of loved ones on the battlefield, and prepared a sinful nation to envision a different future—one in which slavery, America's original sin, would be forever expurgated. For evangelicals, the war altered, at least on a temporary basis, the relationship between religion and state. A spiritual movement rooted in pacifism and moral suasion came to embrace state coercion and violence in the furtherance of God's providential vision for the United States. Clergymen learned to view politics as the natural extension of their Christian ministry. The Old Testament bridged the divide between white and Black worshippers, uniting them in a prophetic tradition that seemed uniquely suited to the times.

It was different in the South, where even before the war, Christians tended to forswear the reforming spirit of the evangelical united front—the isms. God had not favored their cause. The Bible offered a measure of consolation, but the experience of defeat reinforced the sectional divide between Christians. In the South, Protestantism retreated ever inward, focusing on the business of saving souls, one by one, keeping itself aloof from the business of government and politics.

For the victorious North, the war left a lasting imprint, blurring the line between the secular and spiritual worlds. Generations of American presidents—from James Garfield, a Republican, to Woodrow Wilson, a Southern-born Democrat—grew more comfortable in weaving religious themes and appeals into their official addresses. Mainline churches continued to see a role for religion in public life and aggressively engaged in all manner of causes. Whereas in the antebellum era, Protestant reformers focused on saving souls and influencing individual behavior through moral suasion, now they actively embraced politics, working to win not just souls, but votes, for causes ranging from labor reform and good municipal government to anti-liquor and vice laws.

In the late nineteenth century, liberal Christians involved themselves with gusto in the Social Gospel, a new movement that fused the reform instinct of the antebellum evangelical united front with the political spirit of wartime Protestantism. "You become a Christian by choosing the Christian life and beginning immediately to do the duties which belong to it," wrote Washington Gladden, a Congregationalist minister who hailed from New York's burned-over district and became the movement's leading light. Social Gospelites rolled up their sleeves and campaigned for candidates and causes in the North's growing urban centers. Safer and cleaner housing. Public infrastructure. The right of workers to organize and strike. Honest government, clean of corruption and graft. To those who argued that religion had no place in dictating the affairs of politics, business, or labor, Gladden replied, "We must make men believe that Christianity has a right to rule this kingdom of industry, as well as all the other kingdoms of the world." Such thinking might have seemed heterodox in 1850, but the war made many Christians comfortable with the confluence of sacred belief and secular power.

The Social Gospel represented one, but not the only, outgrowth of the muscular brand of Protestantism that emerged from the 1860s. More socially conservative Christians threw themselves into a broad array of coercive social reform campaigns. Anthony Comstock, founder of the New York Society for the Suppression of Vice—an offshoot of the Young Men's Christian Association—built a powerful coalition that worked toward criminalizing contraceptive devices, abortion, prostitution, and pornography. Frances Willard, a devout Methodist, led the Women's Christian Temperance Union, an organization devoted to the legal prohibition of the manufacture or sale of alcohol. The WCTU also concerned itself with a broader array of social reforms, including age of consent laws to protect young women from exploitation, and statutes to encourage Sabbath observance. Unlike the evangelical reform movements of the mid-nineteenth century, the brand of reform championed by religious leaders like Comstock and Willard focused on state intervention—and state power—rather than moral suasion at the individual level. Like their liberal counterparts in the Social Gospel movement, evangelicals concerned with vice and morality had learned during the Civil War to see a natural confluence between church and state.

Despite this continuity, the unity that Northern evangelicals forged in the cauldron of war began to crack in the last decades of the nineteenth century. For one, even with the reunification of the North and the South, the mainline churches remained divided along regional lines: to this day Southern Baptists retain their own organization, while the Methodist Church did not reunite until 1939. Mass immigration, which delivered millions of immigrants—twenty million, approximately, between 1880 and 1920, many of them Catholic and Jewish—also undermined the nation's fragile religious consensus. Many people feared that America was fast on its way to becoming a polyglot nation in which Protestants would be just one group among many, vying for cultural and political influence.

The ground shifted in science and education as well. Public school students of the Civil War generation had been raised on textbooks like McGuffey's Eclectic Readers, which drove home the interconnected virtues of Sabbath observance, frugality, hard work, and Bible reading. At Northern colleges, most of which claimed church affiliation in the nineteenth century, students still read classic works like Bishop Joseph Butler's *Analogy of Religion, Natural and Revealed, to the Constitution and Course of Nature* (1736) and William Paley's *Natural Theology* (1802), which held that the Bible formed the basis of all science and that its tenets were so fundamentally true and verifiable that any ordinary person could, by virtue of his innate common sense, realize God's truth.

The evangelical consensus also faced another threat in modern science's challenge to the once-unshakable belief that the Bible was inerrant, and that all people were equally equipped to recognize its truth. Perhaps no volume did more to undermine evangelical faith in biblical literalism than Charles Darwin's *On the Origin of Species* (1859), which held that humans had evolved organically. Concurrent developments in biology, physics, chemistry, and astronomy led some theologians, including—and notably—Henry Ward Beecher, to make gestures toward reconciling science and religion. Scholars were simply discovering too much about matter, energy, and the cosmos to sanction literal readings of scripture. Beecher audaciously proposed that God was an "engineer and architect and . . . master builder" who devised some form of material creation—perhaps evolution and natural selection, perhaps other, still-undiscovered processes—in order to invent and perfect humans. Christians should not fear scientific discoveries like Darwin's, Beecher argued. Instead, they should realize that God "is at work in natural laws." That modern men and women were finally coming to understand science was merely proof that "He is shining in great disclosures [and] teaching the human consciousness all around." Lyman Abbott, another outspoken modernist, even went so far as to argue that "whether God made the animal man by a mechanical process in an hour or by a process of growth continuing through the centuries is quite immaterial to one who believes that into man God breathes a divine life."

Theologians like Beecher and Abbott were raising the stakes high. If the Old Testament story of creation—of Adam and Eve and the Garden of Eden—was more allegory than straight history, then the entire Bible might very well be open to interpretation. This is precisely what Charles A. Briggs, a professor of biblical theology at Union Theological Seminary in Manhattan, argued in 1893. That year, the Presbytery of New York placed Briggs on trial for "teaching that errors may have existed in the original text of the Holy Scripture." In his own defense, the noted Presbyterian scholar held that "the only errors [he] found or ever recognized in Holy Scripture have been beyond the range of faith and practice, and therefore they do not impair the infallibility of Holy Scripture as a rule of faith and practice." In other words, the Bible's importance lay in its *ideas and meaning*, which were incontestable, and not in its literal recording of history, which modern scholarship proved fallible. But who would divine biblical meaning? The Presbytery of New York worried about exactly this question when it booted Briggs out of the ministry.

In writing about the early twentieth-century struggle over religion and science, historians generally designate the contending parties as "fundamentalists" and "modernists," or "fundamentalists" and "liberals." These terms are accurate to a point. Many conservative Christians *did* fear the encroachment of scientific theory on religion and looked askance at the reforming and political spirit of the Social Gospel movement. In 1910 members of the Presbyterian General Assembly identified five theological "fundamentals" that scientists and religious modernists could not challenge: scriptural inerrancy, the virgin birth of Christ, personal salvation in Christ, Christ's resurrection, and the authenticity of Christ's earthly miracles. Defenders of tradition turned to the same language when they published *The Fundamentals*, a series of twelve paperback volumes that answered the Christian modernists and liberals with a ringing defense of biblical literalism. In 1919 some of the more conservative members of the traditional camp formed the World Christian Fundamentals Association, and in 1920 journalists began lumping most conservative Christians together as "fundamentalists."

But in the early twentieth century, and throughout the better part of the 1920s, "fundamentalism" was not as well-defined a religious movement as it is today. It was really a loose coalition of Protestant theologians and worshippers who opposed key strains of modernism—particularly to the emergent tendency within the leading Protestant denominations to bring the Bible into concert with science. The movement was cross-sectional, with important pockets in the North, but it was strongest in the South. Fundamentalists generally championed biblical inerrancy, or a literal reading of scripture. Some, but not all, also believed in *dispensational* premillennialism—a doctrine that prophesied Christ's imminent return to earth, *followed* by a thousand-year reign of peace. They took the book of Revelation in full earnest—especially its coded forecast of the great social upheaval and moral degradations that would precede Christ's return to earth. Humankind's recent descent into baseless slaughter during World War I, loosened sexual and gender mores, wanton materialism and avarice—all seemed to point to an imminent reckoning with the creator.

The conflict between fundamentalists and modernists grew ever more intense in the early twentieth century. By the 1920s it threatened to rend several of the largest Protestant denominations in two. To millions of ordinary Americans, it mattered a great deal whether or not the Bible's account of the genesis was historically verifiable. People who were uneasy about the unraveling of Victorian culture—those who rejected urban America, with its heightened ethnic, racial, and religious pluralism, its celebration of consumption and personal satisfaction, its abandonment of old sexual norms and gender codes—tended to embrace fundamentalism as a bulwark against further social change. In the South, which remained predominantly rural, fundamentalism proved wildly popular. But fundamentalism was not just the preserve of rural Southerners. Just as the conflict over slavery rent the nation's major denominations along sectional lines in the 1840s, the new debate over religion and modernity threatened to split the *northern* Baptist, Methodist, and Presbyterian churches—and not just along urban and rural lines. The conservative evangelical torrent that swept through America between the 1890s and the 1920s was every bit as much an urban as it was a rural phenomenon.

Alongside the rise of fundamentalism, new interdenominational movements emerged to challenge the old evangelical consensus. The Holiness movement, originally a movement *within* the Methodist Church, soon attracted people from outside the Wesleyan ranks who were drawn to the promise of second blessing and to a less formal, more charismatic form of worship. Many middle-class Methodists, who celebrated their denomination's wartime journey from revivalist roots to domesticated, patriotic respectability, were uncomfortable with the Holiness movement and were happy to see its adherents depart their ranks and go their own way. Alongside the emergence of independent organizations like the Pilgrim Holiness Church and the Church of the Nazarene, a new Pentecostal movement took hold both in the South and the West, drawing an unusual combination of Black and white congregants in cities like Los Angeles to a form of worship that included healing and speaking in tongues.

Not all breakaway congregations broke so sharply with the old evangelical consensus. But some of the most popular revivals of the late nineteenth century operated outside the walls of the mainline denominations. In the late 1870s the conservative evangelist Dwight Moody took this Protestant crusade to America's teeming industrial cities, most of them in the Northeast and Midwest, and on the West Coast, warning tens of thousands of new urbanites of Jesus Christ's imminent return to earth, and of the urgency behind their conversion and embrace of the gospel. Moody was typical of the modern generation of revivalists: unschooled in the finer points of theology, lacking any real investment in denominational distinctions, and thoroughly literal in his reading of scripture, he viewed religion as a personal matter and preached the necessity of individual salvation. City folks formed a virtual throng to hear God's impassioned troubadour. He offered them hope, order, and community in a world that seemed ever more chaotic, impersonal, and dissolute.

IF THE CIVIL WAR FORMED THE HIGH-WATER MARK OF EVANGELICAL unity and power, it nevertheless established precedents that took hold in future decades. It paved the way for a muscular brand of Christianity to assert itself in the nation's political life. It fashioned an alternative to moral suasion and pacifism in the furtherance of God's providential mission. It also presaged the power that evangelicals would later wield, as well as the risks they would incur, by blurring the line between church and state. In the 1970s, after withdrawing from public life in the 1920s, a broad coalition of conservative evangelical Christians reengaged in politics, asserting themselves in debates over same-sex relationships, reproductive rights, contraception, school prayer, and women's rights. As a united front, they emerged more powerful than in any moment since the Civil War. Southern Baptists were an anchor of this new coalition, as were megachurches and evangelical organizations outside the mainline denominations. (Mainline churches, in turn, shrunk in size, relative to their influence in the nineteenth century, and drifted leftward in politics.) As was the case during the Civil War, flexing political muscle in the secular arena came at a cost: it required evangelical activists to refashion what it meant to be a good Christian. In the 1860s, that meant an embrace of force and coercion in the service of preserving the Union and destroying slavery. In the 2020s, it means forging common ground with revanchist politicians and media personalities whose belief system runs far afield from Christian notions of benevolence, grace, and piety.

Abraham Lincoln, who was both a lifetime iconoclast *and* an uncanny student of public opinion, was the first president to channel the spiritual currents of his electorate into a powerful political movement. Though he was never a conventional believer, his spiritual evolution was sincere, and it prepared him to work within the evangelical united front to help Americans understand the historic times in which they lived, and their role in that story. The strength he derived from his faith in divine intention, despite his uncertainty, to the very end, that God willed that the Union win the Civil War, enabled him to hold the Union together through violence and to initiate the death of slavery, making him in many ways a latter-day answer to the Hebrew prophets whose stories he had absorbed as a young boy, lying on his back in Tom Lincoln's log cabin in Indiana—a skeptical, but always assiduous, student of the Bible, firm in the "natural idea that he was going to be something." Though his brand of Christian faith was not evangelical by common definition, in his appeal to the prevailing religious sensibility of the country—in his deft mobilization of Protestant churches, and in his knowing invocation of religious language and themes to help Americans understand the times in which they lived—Lincoln was, arguably, the nation's first evangelical president.

ACKNOWLEDGMENTS

Historians rely on a network of academic and public scholars to help them sharpen and refine their ideas. When I left higher education fifteen years ago, I knew that I would continue to write and publish, but I worried I would do so without the benefit of that critical exchange.

I was fortunate to join the ranks of contributing writers at *Politico*, where, over the years, I've had the opportunity to pressure test early versions of my work, or ideas that later evolved into book-length projects. Writing for the magazine, which places a premium on engaging, longform storytelling, has also made me a better writer. The team at *Politico*, including Elizabeth Ralph, Dylon Jones, Margy Slattery (now at *The Atlantic*), and the late Blake Hounshell have been a steady source of feedback, encouragement, and support. I'm grateful they keep me around!

For all its problems, social media has afforded scholars working across diverse fields an opportunity to share their work more broadly with the public. It's also helped connect academics and writers who might otherwise not have known one another personally. It's been a great pleasure getting to know the "Twitterstorians" — hundreds of professional scholars who are active across Twitter and other social media channels. Through this informal network, I've had the chance to keep abreast of scholarly trends and meet a range of writers whose own work, even when not directly related to this book, inform my own work. My special thanks to Kevin M. Kruse and Julian Zelizer of Princeton University, who have invited me back into the academic fold to participate in conferences and edited volumes, and who serve in many respects as the unofficial mayors of this merry band of historians.

The team at Viking Press has been a marvel to work with. My longtime editor, Wendy Wolf, has been a constant source of good counsel and reinforcement. Her eye for telling an important story in a compelling and interesting way is, to my mind, unrivaled, and I hope that her influence shines through in this volume. I'm deeply grateful to Wendy and her editorial assistant, Paloma Ruiz, for all they've done to bring this book from rough concept to reality. My deep thanks as well to the broader Viking team: Nicole Celli, Angelina Krahn, Daniel Lagin, Johnathan Lay, Gabriel Levinson, David Litman, Andrea Monagle, and Ben Petrone. It takes a village to publish a book, and this is a pretty great village to live in.

I wrote my first book with Viking a decade ago. When it was published, my daughters were toddlers. They vaguely understood why I disappeared for hours at a time on weekends to tap away at my keyboard. Today, Lillian (12) and Naomi (9) take an active interest in history and politics. Their intellectual curiosity and love of learning provide a well of inspiration, as does the delight they bring to learning. Lillian also brought her artistic talent to bear in taking the photo for this book jacket. I couldn't be prouder of them, or more grateful for their love.

ACKNOWLEDGMENTS

My wife, Angela, is a steady source of support and encouragement. More important by far, she is my companion and coconspirator in everything—the only person who gets the inside joke and shares in the ups and downs, the wonder of raising our daughters, and the joy in building a life together. I'm so grateful for her love and partnership.

This book is dedicated to the memory of my mother, Elaine Zeitz, and my aunt, Deede Snowhite; and to my father, Carl Zeitz, and my uncle, Larry Snowhite. They inspired a lifelong love of learning and curiosity about the world that keeps me writing all these years later.

NOTES

PREFACE

ix **"eminently Christian president":** J. G. Holland, *Holland's Life of Abraham Lincoln* (Lincoln: University of Nebraska Press, 1998), 542.

ix **"Christ teaches it":** Holland, *Holland's Life of Abraham Lincoln*, 237.

ix **an overnight bestseller:** Joshua Zeitz, *Lincoln's Boys: John Hay, John Nicolay, and the War for Lincoln's Image* (New York: Viking, 2014), 234.

ix **Successive generations of amateur:** Mark A. Noll, "Lincoln's God," *Journal of Presbyterian History* 82, no. 2 (Summer 2004): 82–83.

x **"made it impossible":** Richard J. Carwardine, "'Simply a Theist': Herndon on Lincoln's," *Journal of the Abraham Lincoln Association* 35, no. 2 (Summer 2014): 19.

x **But was Abraham Lincoln:** For an early scholarly consideration, see Richard N. Current, *The Lincoln Nobody Knows* (New York: Hill and Wang, 1958), chap. 3.

x **"an un-believer in Christianity":** Carwardine, "'Simply a Theist,'" 20.

xiv **By numbers alone, organized:** Mark A. Noll, *The Civil War as a Theological Crisis* (Chapel Hill: University of North Carolina Press, 2006), 12–13.

PART I

CHAPTER 1: UNDISTINGUISHED FAMILIES

3 **"it is a great piece":** John L. Scripps to William Herndon, June 24, 1865, *HI*.

---

3 **Other politicians might:** John M. Hay and John G. Nicolay, *Abraham Lincoln: A History* (New York: Century, 1890), 2:266.

4 **"is not much of it":** Abraham Lincoln to Jesse Fell, December 20, 1859, *CW* 3:511.

4 **"My parents were both":** Lincoln to Fell, December 20, 1859, *CW* 3:511.

4 **"a wandering laboring boy":** Autobiography Written for John L. Scripps, ca. June 1860, *CW* 4:61.

4 **"had run off":** David Herbert Donald, *Lincoln* (New York: Simon & Schuster, 1996), 21.

4 **"the illegitimate daughter":** Donald, *Lincoln*, 19–23.

6 **"very careless about":** Augustus Chapman to William Herndon, before September 8, 1865, *HI*.

6 **"When first my father":** "The Bear Hunt," ca. 1846, *CW* 1:386.

6 **Abe had an ax:** Autobiography Written for John L. Scripps, *CW* 4:61–62.

7 **"she knew she was":** Dennis F. Hanks to William Herndon, June 13, 1865, *HI*.

7 **"ragged & dirty":** Hanks to Herndon, June 13, 1865, *HI*.

7 **"Soaped—rubbed and washed":** Hanks to Herndon, June 13, 1865, *HI*.

8 **In an era when many:** Kenneth J. Winkle, *The Young Eagle: The Rise of Abraham Lincoln* (Dallas: Taylor Trade Publishing, 2001), 14.

8 **But Abe and Sarah Johnston:** Sarah Bush Lincoln interview, September 8, 1865, *HI*.

8 **"was like the other people":** Michael Burlingame, *Abraham Lincoln: A Life* (Baltimore: Johns Hopkins University Press, 2008) 1:9.

9 **Survival demanded a collective outlook:** Winkle, *The Young Eagle*, 12–13; and William Lee Miller, *Lincoln's Virtues: An Ethical Biography* (New York: Alfred A. Knopf, 2002), 28–29. On the rhythms of the protomarket economy, see Charles Sellers, *The Market Revolution: Jacksonian America, 1815–1846* (New York: Oxford University Press, 1991), 3–33.

9 **In Kentucky they:** Allen C. Guelzo, "Abraham Lincoln and the Doctrine of Necessity," *Journal of the Abraham Lincoln Association* 18, no. 1 (Winter 1997): 66–67.

9 **Thomas ultimately helped:** John F. Cady, "The Religious Environment of Lincoln's Youth," *Indiana Magazine of History* 37, no. 1 (March 1941): 17, 19–20.

9 **"criterions by which":** Bertram Wyatt-Brown, "The Antimission Movement in the Jacksonian South: A Study in Regional Folk Culture," *Journal of Southern History* 35, no. 4 (November 1970): 512.

10 **"exclusively the work":** Wyatt-Brown, "The Antimission Movement," 512.

10 **"in Election by grace":** Guelzo, "Abraham Lincoln and the Doctrine of Necessity," 67.

10 **In Maryland, antimissionists:** Wyatt-Brown, "The Antimission Movement," 512.

10 **"new men and new measures":** Wyatt-Brown, 511.

11 **Certainly he would have:** Mark A. Noll, "Lincoln's God," *Journal of Presbyterian History* 82, no. 2 (Summer 2004): 86.

12 "a wild region": Lincoln to Fell, CW 3:511.
12 "My childhood-home": "My Childhood-Home I See Again," February 25, 1846, CW 1:367–68.
13 "was not Energetic": Matilda Johnston Moore interview, September 8, 1865, HI.
13 "to the house from work": John Hanks interview, 1865–66, HI.
13 "read a little": Sarah Bush Lincoln interview, HI.
13 "being a day laborer": John B. Helm to William Herndon, June 20, 1865, HI.
14 "didn't like physical": Sarah Bush Lincoln interview, HI.
14 "constant and I may": Dennis F. Hanks to William Herndon, June 13, 1865, HI.
14 Cousin Sophie Hanks reported: Michael Burlingame, The Inner World of Abraham Lincoln (Urbana: University of Illinois Press, 1994), 38.
14 "never bawled but dropt": Dennis F. Hanks to Herndon, June 13, 1865, HI.
14 Even on the morning: Burlingame, The Inner World of Abraham Lincoln, 39.
15 Cousins and neighbors: Nathaniel Grigsby, Silas Richardson, Nancy Richardson, and John Romine interview, September 14, 1865, HI.
15 "farming, grubbing, hoeing": John Hanks to William Herndon, June 13, 1865, HI.
15 "father taught him to work": Grigsby et al. interview, HI.
15 When a neighbor: Burlingame, The Inner World of Abraham Lincoln, 37–38.
15 Years later, as his deep: Abraham Lincoln to Eliza Browning, April 1, 1838, CW 1:118.
16 "read the Bible some": Sarah Bush Lincoln interview, HI.
16 "make him quit": Matilda Johnston Moore interview, September 8, 1865, HI; Dennis Hanks interview, September 8, 1865, HI.
16 "Abe always had": Burlingame, The Inner World of Abraham Lincoln, 237.
17 Families in this period: Joyce Appleby, "New Cultural Heroes in the Early National Period," in The Culture of the Market: Historical Essays, ed. Thomas L. Haskell and Richard F. Teichgraeber III (New York: Cambridge University Press, 1996), 174, 178.
17 "a good quiet citizen": John Hanks interview, May 25, 1865, HI.
17 He was, by the estimation: Nathaniel Grigsby to William Herndon, September 4, 1865, HI.
18 "Card for his Relations": Dennis F. Hanks to William Herndon, January 26, 1866, HI.
18 "singular that you": Abraham Lincoln to Thomas Lincoln, December 24, 1848, CW 2:15.
18 "You are not lazy": Abraham Lincoln to Thomas Lincoln and John D. Johnston, December 24, 1848, CW 2:16–17.
19 "thought that Abe did": Dennis F. Hanks to William Herndon, January 26, 1866, HI.
19 Whatever the case, Lincoln: Leonard Swett to William Herndon, January 15, 1866, HI.
19 Their differences notwithstanding: John D. Johnston to Abraham Lincoln, May 25, 1849, Abraham Lincoln Papers, Library of Congress.

19 **"all we can to render your stay agreeable"**: Augustus H. Chapman to Abraham Lincoln, May 24, 1849, Abraham Lincoln Papers, Library of Congress.

20 **"nothing which could do any good"**: Abraham Lincoln to John D. Johnston, January 12, 1851, CW 2:96–97.

21 **His convictions lay**: Abraham Lincoln, "The Perpetuation of Our Political Institutions," address before the Young Men's Lyceum, Springfield, Illinois, January 27, 1838, CW 1:115.

CHAPTER 2: EVERY SOUL IS FREE

23 **"the very season and age"**: Nathan O. Hatch and Mark A. Noll, eds., *The Bible in America: Essays in Cultural History* (New York: Oxford University Press, 1982), 3.

24 **"the Lord's day is profaned"**: Jon Butler, Grant Wacker, and Randall Balmer, *Religion in American Life: A Short History* (New York: Oxford University Press, 2000), 71–72.

24 **90 percent of all congregations**: Jon Butler, *Becoming America: The Revolution Before 1776* (Cambridge, MA: Harvard University Press, 2001), chaps. 1, 5.

25 **George Whitefield, an Anglican**: Butler, Wacker, and Balmer, *Religion in American Life*, 128–29.

25 **"Your wickedness makes"**: Jonathan Edwards, *The Works of Jonathan Edwards, A.M.*, ed. Edward Hickman (London: John Childs & Son, 1839), 2:9.

26 **Second Great Awakening**: Nathan O. Hatch, *The Democratization of American Christianity* (New Haven, CT: Yale University Press, 1989), 3–4.

26 **Peter Cartwright, a Methodist**: Peter Cartwright, *Magazine of the Wesleyan Methodist Church*, vol. 26 (1803), 84.

27 **A minority influence**: Richard J. Carwardine, *Evangelicals and Politics in Antebellum America* (New Haven, CT: Yale University Press, 1993), 5.

27 **"the battle ax"**: Hatch, *The Democratization of American Christianity*, 49.

27 **"fainting, shouting, yelling"**: Hatch, 52.

28 **All told, by 1855**: Carwardine, *Evangelicals and Politics*, 6, 43.

29 **"Christianity pervades the United States"**: James Dixon, *Personal Narrative: A Tour through a Part of the United States and Canada* (New York: Lane and Scott, 1849), 176.

29 **"ought to be viewed"**: Robert Baird, *Religion in the United States of America* (Glasgow: Blackie and Son, 1844), 415.

30 **"We believe in the absolute"**: Linda Jeanne Evans, "Abolitionism in the Illinois Churches, 1830–1865" (PhD diss., Northwestern University, Evanston, IL, 1981), 190.

30 **"I am often slothful"**: Butler, Wacker, and Balmer, *Religion in American Life*, 55. See also Edmund S. Morgan, *The Puritan Dilemma: The Story of John Winthrop* (New York: Little, Brown, 1958), 134–55.

31 **Caleb Rich, an early founder:** Hatch, *The Democratization of American Christianity*, 172.

31 **"Why, then, I can":** Hatch, 172.

32 **The doggerel was probably:** Charles Grandison Finney, *Sermons on Various Subjects* (New York: S. W. Benedict, 1835), 71.

32 **"God has made":** Paul E. Johnson, *A Shopkeeper's Millennium: Society and Revivals in Rochester, New York, 1815–1837* (New York: Hill and Wang, 1978), 3.

32 **"It should in all cases":** Johnson, *A Shopkeeper's Millennium*, 96.

32 **"men are free agents":** Lyman Beecher, *Autobiography, Correspondence, Etc. of Lyman Beecher*, ed. Charles Beecher (New York, 1865), 1:554.

32 **"You lie! You can repent":** William G. McLoughlin Jr., *Modern Revivalism: Charles Grandison Finney to Billy Graham* (New York: Ronald Press, 1959), 28–29.

33 **In his famous:** Charles Grandison Finney, *Sermons on Various Subjects* (New York: S. W. Benedict, 1835), 22, 38.

33 **"absolutely ashamed of it":** McLoughlin, *Modern Revivalism*, 23–25.

33 **Barton Stone, a Presbyterian:** Hatch, *The Democratization of American Christianity*, 172–73.

34 **"are no sects":** Mark A. Noll, introduction to *God and Mammon: Protestants, Money, and the Market, 1790–1860*, ed. Mark A. Noll (New York: Oxford University Press, 2002), 4.

35 **"We are not personally acquainted":** Hatch, *The Democratization of American Christianity*, 173–74.

35 **"Let us be republicans":** Nathan O. Hatch, "Sola Scriptura and Novus Ordo Seclorum," in *The Bible in America: Essays in Cultural History*, 66.

38 **"The direct action of great minds":** Theron Metcalf, *An Address to the Phi Beta Kappa Society of Brown University* (Boston: Lily, Wait, Colman, and Holden, 1833), 4.

38 *Every Man his own Lawyer:* Gordon S. Wood, *The Radicalism of the American Revolution* (New York: A. A. Knopf, 1992), 361.

38 **"the unalienable right of private judgment":** Wood, *The Radicalism of the American Revolution*, 362.

38 **Tocqueville, whose travel chronicles:** Alexis de Tocqueville, *Democracy in America* (New York: Knopf Doubleday, 1990), 1:43

39 **"knowledge has induced":** David Daggett, *An oration, pronounced in the brick meeting-house, in the city of New-Haven, on the Fourth of July, A.D. 1787* (New Haven, CT: T. and S. Green, 1787).

39 **"Ten thousand Reformers":** Hatch, *The Democratization of American Christianity*, 81.

39 **"in a direct way":** Hatch, "Sola Scriptura and Novus Ordo Seclorum," 60.

40 **"I said in my heart":** Hatch, 69.

40 **"Every member shall":** Hatch, 72.

40 "Bible was the only Confession": Hatch, 72.

40 "utterly unable to accept": Hatch, 75.

41 "Know then that every": Hatch, 68.

41 "By 1850, women": A. Gregory Schneider, *The Way of the Cross Leads Home: The Domestication of American Methodism* (Bloomington: Indiana University Press, 1993), 169.

42 "tastes, habits, and character": Colleen McDannell, *The Christian Home in Victorian America, 1840–1900* (Bloomington: Indiana University Press, 1986), 128–32.

42 The relationship between evangelical: Albert J. Raboteau, *Canaan Land: A Religious History of African Americans* (New York: Oxford University Press, 1999), 3–20.

43 In 1794 Black Methodists: See Richard S. Newman, *Freedom's Prophet: Bishop Richard Allen, the AME Church, and the Black Founding Fathers* (New York: New York University Press, 2004); and James T. Campbell, *Songs of Zion: The African Methodist Episcopal Church in the United States and South Africa* (Chapel Hill: University of North Carolina Press, 1998).

44 "You slaves will": Albert J. Raboteau, *Slave Religion: The "Invisible Institution" in the Antebellum South* (New York: Oxford University Press, 1978), 213.

44 "Church was what": Raboteau, *Slave Religion*, 213.

45 "One morning I was walking down": Raboteau, 259.

45 Most white evangelicals believed: Nicholas Guyatt, *Providence and the Invention of the United States, 1607–1876* (New York: Cambridge University Press, 2004), 1–8.

46 For Black evangelicals, Christianity: On the lasting importance of the prophetic tradition among Black religious and lay leaders, see David L. Chappell, *A Stone of Hope: Prophetic Religion and the Death of Jim Crow* (Chapel Hill: University of North Carolina Press, 2004).

46 "God rules in the armies": David Walker, *Appeal to the Coloured Citizens of the World* (Boston: published by the author, 1830).

47 "we were surprised": Noll, introduction to *God and Mammon*, 4–5.

47 For Francis Grund: Noll, 5.

47 Finney's famous revivals: John Corrigan, *Business of the Heart: Religion and Emotion in the Nineteenth Century* (Berkeley: University of California Press, 2002), 26–27.

48 the same way that capitalism: Robin Klay and John Lunn, "Protestants and the American Economy in the Postcolonial Period: An Overview," in *God and Mammon*, 39–40.

49 Finney, who championed: Hatch, *The Democratization of American Christianity*, 198–99.

49 "The Carnal Mind is Enmity": Whitney R. Cross, *The Burned-Over District: The Social and Intellectual History of Enthusiastic Religion in Western New York, 1800–1850* (Ithaca, NY: Cornell University Press, 1982), 174.

49 **"in three months"**: Johnson, *A Shopkeeper's Millennium*, 109.

49 **"the anxious may come"**: McLoughlin, *Modern Revivalism*, 95.

50 **the most renowned**: Scott Gac, *Singing for Freedom: The Hutchinson Family Singers and the Nineteenth-Century Culture of Reform* (New Haven, CT: Yale University Press, 2007), 1–18.

CHAPTER 3: FLOATING PIECE OF DRIFTWOOD

53 **Settling in Illinois**: Paul M. Angle, *"Here I Have Lived": A History of Lincoln's Springfield*, rev. ed. (New Brunswick, NJ: Rutgers University Press, 1935), 33–34.

53 **But in the following days**: John G. Nicolay and John M. Hay, *Abraham Lincoln: A History* (New York: Century, 1890), 1:47–49.

54 **"Boots off, hat"**: Charles E. Hovey and Elijah P. Lovejoy, "Two Old Letters: One from Elijah P. Lovejoy, 1837; the Other from Gen. Charles E. Hovey, 1858." *Journal of the Illinois State Historical Society* 2, no. 4 (January 1910): 44–48.

54 **Lincoln was later fond**: William H. Herndon and Jesse W. Weik, *Herndon's Lincoln: The True Story of a Great Life* (North Scituate, MA: Digital Scanning, 1999), 79.

54 **cut "entirely adrift"**: Charles H. Coleman, *Abraham Lincoln and Coles County, Illinois* (New Brunswick, NJ: Scarecrow Press, 1955), 41.

55 **"friendless, uneducated, penniless"**: Abraham Lincoln to Martin Morris, March 26, 1843, CW 1:320.

55 **One admiring historian**: William E. Barton, D. H. Rutledge, A. Lincoln Free, and George M. Marsh, "Abraham Lincoln and New Salem," *Journal of the Illinois State Historical Society* 19, no. 3/4 (October 1926–January 1927): 81.

55 **Lincoln would devote roughly**: Kenneth J. Winkle, *The Young Eagle: The Rise of Abraham Lincoln* (Dallas: Taylor Trade Publishing, 2001), 57.

55 **"our farmers, our mechanics"**: Benjamin P. Thomas, *Lincoln's New Salem* (Carbondale: Southern Illinois University Press, 1954), 17.

55 **"log houses and cabins"**: Thomas, *Lincoln's New Salem*, 25.

57 **"used to sit up"**: N. W. Branson to William Herndon, August 3, 1865, *HI*.

57 **William Greene, who clerked**: William G. Greene to William Herndon, May 30, 1865, *HI*.

57 **"New Salem he devoted"**: William Mentor Graham to William Herndon, July 15, 1865, *HI*.

57 **Lincoln also absorbed newspapers**: Branson to Herndon, August 3, 1865, *HI*.

57 **"Salem in those days"**: Abner Y. Ellis, Statement for William Herndon, January 23, 1866, *HI*.

58 **His friendship with Jack Armstrong**: Douglas L. Wilson, *Honor's Voice: The Transformation of Abraham Lincoln* (New York: Vintage Books, 1999), chap. 1.

58 **"gave him so much satisfaction"**: Autobiography Written for John L. Scripps, ca. June 1860, CW 4:64.

59 **likely fell in love with**: Wilson, *Honor's Voice*, chap. 4.

59 **Each year, his neighbors:** Thomas, *Lincoln's New Salem*, 51–52.

60 **"sea of sectarian":** *Julian M. Sturtevant: An Autobiography*, ed. Julian M. Sturtevant Jr. (New York: F. H. Revell, 1896), 160–61.

60 **"way to heaven":** Thomas, *Lincoln's New Salem*, 54.

60 **both movements bitterly:** *The Autobiography of Peter Cartwright: The Backwoods Preacher*, ed. W. P. Strickland (New York: Carlton & Porter, 1857), 46.

61 **"the fatal misfortune":** Mark A. Noll, "Lincoln's God," *Journal of Presbyterian History* 82, no. 2 (Summer 2004): 79.

61 **"belonged to no religious sect":** James Gourley (WHH Interview), 1865–1866, *HI*.

61 **"was the language of respect":** James H. Matheny to William Herndon, November 1866, *HI*.

61 **"pick up the Bible":** James H. Matheny (WHH Interview), 1865–1866, *HI*.

61 **"especially when young":** John T. Stuart (WHH Interview), December 2, 1866, *HI*.

61 **"further against Christian beliefs":** John T. Stuart (WHH Interview), March 2, 1870, *HI*.

62 **"At that time I had":** George Spears to William Herndon, November 3, 1866, *HI*.

62 **As early as 1837:** "Second Reply to James Adams," October 18, 1837, CW 1:106.

62 **Six years later:** Abraham Lincoln to Martin Morris, March 26, 1843, CW 1:320. See also William Lee Miller, *Lincoln's Virtues: An Ethical Biography* (New York: Alfred A. Knopf, 2002), 155.

62 **The two men likely:** Conversation with Hon. Wm. Butler, Springfield, June 13, 1875, in *An Oral History of Abraham Lincoln: John G. Nicolay's Interviews and Essays*, ed. Michael Burlingame (Carbondale: Southern Illinois University Press, 1996), 18–21.

63 **In 1834, Cartwright:** Douglas L. Wilson, *Lincoln before Washington: New Perspectives on the Illinois Years* (Urbana: University of Illinois Press, 1997), chap. 4.

64 **He had grown notably:** Jean H. Baker, *Mary Todd Lincoln: A Biography*, rev. ed. (New York: W. W. Norton, 2008), 127–28.

64 **At the heart of his:** John B. Weber to William Herndon, November 1, 1866, *HI*.

64 **"Lincoln wrote a work":** Hardin Bale to William Herndon, May 29, 1865, *HI*.

64 **"one of the circumstances":** John Hill to William Herndon, June 27, 1865, *HI*.

65 **"Handbill Replying to Charges of Infidelity":** "Handbill Replying to Charges of Infidelity," July 31, 1846, CW 1:382.

65 **"I was inclined to believe":** "Handbill," July 31, 1846, CW 1:382.

66 **"alleviated Calvinism":** William G. McLoughlin, *The Meaning of Henry Ward Beecher: An Essay on the Shifting Values of Mid-Victorian America, 1840–1870* (New York: Alfred A. Knopf, 1970), 12.

66 **"the innate depravity of Man":** Jesse W. Fell to Ward Hill Lamon, September 22, 1870, *HI*.

67 **Herndon, who became:** David Herbert Donald, *Lincoln* (New York: Simon & Schuster, 1996), 15.

67 **"absurd and impious":** Thomas Paine, "Predestination," https://thomaspaine
.org/works/essays/religion/predestination.html.

67 **"We see our own earth":** Thomas Paine, *The Age of Reason: Part I*, https://
thomaspaine.org/works/major-works/the-age-of-reason-part-1.html.

68 **James Keyes, a resident:** James W. Keyes, Statement for William Herndon,
1865–1866, *HI*.

68 **Another associate concurred:** Fell to Lamon, September 22, 1870, *HI*.

68 **Joseph Gillespie, a friend:** Joseph Gillespie to William Herndon, January 1,
1866, *HI*.

68 **Jesse Fell, who had known:** Fell to Lamon, September 22, 1870, *HI*.

69 **"Passion has helped us":** Lincoln, "The Perpetuation of Our Political Institutions," January 27, 1838, *CW* 1:108–15.

71 **He hoped, in the words:** Elizabeth Abell to William Herndon, February 15,
1867, *HI*.

CHAPTER 4: THE EVANGELICAL UNITED FRONT

73 **"a sentiment as much":** Auguste Levasseur, *Lafayette in America in 1824 and
1825; or, Journal of Travels, in the United States* (New York: White, Gallagher
& White, 1829), 1:260.

73 **"characteristic of this country":** George Wilson Pierson, *Tocqueville and Beaumont in America* (New York: Oxford University Press, 1938), 181.

74 **"a Union of purpose":** *Niles' National Register*, July 1, 1843.

74 **Several years later, the editors:** Timothy L. Smith, *Revivalism & Social Reform:
American Protestantism on the Eve of the Civil War*, rev. ed (Baltimore: Johns
Hopkins University Press, 1980), 226.

74 **If Christians did:** Smith, *Revivalism & Social Reform*, 227.

75 **The American Bible Society, founded:** Paul Boyer, *Urban Masses and Moral
Order in America, 1820–1920* (Cambridge, MA: Harvard University Press,
1978), 22–24.

75 **"come in from the country":** Boyer, *Urban Masses*, 37.

76 **For its sheer prodigiousness:** Ronald G. Walters, *American Reformers, 1815–
1816* (New York: Hill and Wang, 1978), 31.

76 **"No class has such opportunities":** *Atlantic Monthly* 1, no. 7 (May 1858):
862–63.

77 **"politico-religious age":** Smith, *Revivalism & Social Reform*, 15.

77 **Arthur and Lewis Tappan surely:** Bertram Wyatt-Brown, *Lewis Tappan and the
Evangelical War against Slavery* (Cleveland: Press of Case Western Reserve
University, 1969), 34–35.

77 **"gradually and almost imperceptibly":** Wyatt-Brown, *Lewis Tappan*, 60–61.

79 **"St. Arthur de Fanaticus":** Wyatt-Brown, 67.

79 **Unsurprisingly, abolitionism thrived:** Walters, *American Reformers*, 80–81.

80 **Most were committed:** Walters, 161.

81 slaveholding as sinful: James Brewer Stewart, *Holy Warriors: The Abolitionists and American Slavery*, rev. ed. (New York: Hill and Wang, 1996), 45.

81 "not only *overshadows*": Stewart, *Holy Warriors*, 45.

82 "We did not anticipate": Stewart, 73.

82 Joshua Giddings, who for eleven: James Brewer Stewart, *Joshua Giddings and the Tactics of Radical Politics* (Cleveland: Press of Case Western Reserve University, 1970), 24–31.

83 "No real distinction": Daniel Walker Howe, *The Political Culture of the American Whigs* (Chicago: University of Chicago Press, 1979), 178.

84 "possessed by the desire": Frederick J. Blue, *Salmon P. Chase: A Life in Politics* (Kent, OH: Kent State University Press, 1987), x.

84 He described the struggle: Blue, *Salmon P. Chase*, 44.

85 "I am deeply and sorrowfully": John R. McKivigan, *The War against Proslavery Religion: Abolitionism and the Northern Churches, 1830–1865* (Ithaca, NY: Cornell University Press, 1984), 67.

85 Religious abolitionists who experienced: Charles K. Whipple, "Relations of Anti-Slavery to Religion," No. 19, *Anti-Slavery Tracts* (New York: American Anti-Slavery Society, 1855–1856).

86 In short, religious abolitionists: McKivigan, *The War against Proslavery Religion*, 21.

86 "slavery is a sin": Linda Jeanne Evans, "Abolitionism in the Illinois Churches, 1830–1865" (PhD diss., Northwestern University, Evanston, IL, 1981), 83–84.

87 On paper, most: "The Methodist General Conference," *New York Times*, May 5, 1860.

87 "the voluntary enslaving": *General Assembly of the Presbyterian Church in the United States, 1789–1820* (Philadelphia: Presbyterian Board of Publication, 1820), 692.

87 Thus in 1836 the Presbyterian: Harriet Beecher Stowe, *A Key to Uncle Tom's Cabin* (Boston: Jewett, 1854), 414.

88 "We thought and felt": George M. Frederickson, "The Coming of the Lord: The Northern Protestant Clergy and the Civil War Crisis," in *Religion and the American Civil War*, ed. Randall M. Miller, Harry S. Stout, and Charles Reagan Wilson (New York: Oxford University Press, 1998), 115–16.

89 "every man who holds Slaves": George Bourne, *Picture of Slavery in the United States of America* (Middletown, CT: Edwin Hunt, 1834), 11.

90 "it is not 'God's method'": Evans, "Abolitionism in the Illinois Churches," 12–13.

90 "speak to them as friends": McKivigan, *The War against Proslavery Religion*, 34.

91 "the complete divorce": Evans, "Abolitionism in the Illinois Churches," 79.

91 Reflecting this spirit: McKivigan, *The War against Proslavery Religion*, 68–69.

92 Congregationalists generally refused: Evans, "Abolitionism in the Illinois Churches," 193.

93 "The Anti-Slavery Society is avowedly": McKivigan, *The War against Proslavery Religion*, 60.

93 Some radical abolitionists: Stewart, *Holy Warriors*, 114–15.

93 Despite the activists' frustration: Stewart, 50.

94 "The whole system of slavery": Stewart, 50.

95 Like other Black evangelicals: David W. Blight, *Frederick Douglass: Prophet of Freedom* (New York: Simon & Schuster, 2018), 157–58, 228.

96 "The church and the slave": Blight, *Frederick Douglass*, 114–15.

96 "Some things are settled": Frederick Douglass, "The Kansas Nebraska Act," Speech at Chicago, October 30, 1854, in *Frederick Douglass: Selected Speeches and Writings*, ed. Philip S. Foner, rev. ed. (Chicago: Lawrence Hill Books, 1999), 301.

96 "Supreme Court . . . not the only power in the world": Blight, *Frederick Douglass*, 279.

97 "two or three dead slaveholders": Blight, 242–43.

97 "For a *white* man": Frederick Douglass, "Is It Right and Wise to Kill a Kidnapper?," June 2, 1854, in Foner, *Frederick Douglass*, 277–80.

97 By the mid-1850s, Douglass: Frederick Douglass, "Peaceful Annihilation of Slavery Is Hopeless," in Foner, *Frederick Douglass*, 344.

98 Far from proscribing violence: Stewart, *Holy Warriors*, 157.

98 "these violent massacres": Richard J. Carwardine, *Evangelicals and Politics in Antebellum America* (New Haven, CT: Yale University Press, 1993), 283–84.

99 "to incite slave rebellion": Eden Burroughs Foster, *Four Pastorates: Glimpses of the Life and Thoughts of Eden B. Foster* (Lowell, MA: George M. Elliott, 1883), 73.

100 "I can scarcely believe": C. C. Goen, *Broken Churches, Broken Nation: Denominational Schisms and the Coming of the Civil War* (Macon, GA: Mercer University Press, 1985), 69.

100 Another delegate observed: Goen, *Broken Churches*, 69.

100 "question is not between": Goen, 71.

101 "I knew, if the Southern": *The Autobiography of Peter Cartwright*, ed. W. P. Strickland (New York: Carlton & Porter, 1857), 423–24.

101 Meeting in New York: Reprinted in *Proceedings of the General Antislavery Convention Called by the British and Foreign Antislavery Society* (London, 1841), 284.

102 "The division of the Methodist": Goen, *Broken Churches*, 85.

103 "ignorance of the Bible": Goen, 128.

103 "APOSTACY FROM THE GOOD": Goen, 128.

103 "If Slavery indeed be": Goen, 75.

104 Religious newspapers, which: Whitney R. Cross, *The Burned-Over District: The Social and Intellectual History of Enthusiastic Religion in Western New York, 1800–1850* (Ithaca, NY: Cornell University Press, 1982), 104.

NOTES

104 **"We heard a shout":** Allan Nevins, *Ordeal of the Union,* vol. 1, *Fruits of Manifest Destiny: A House Dividing, 1852–1857* (New York: Charles Scribner's Sons, 1947), 388.

104 **Abel Stevens, editor:** Ralph A. Keller, "Methodist Newspapers and the Fugitive Slave Law: A New Perspective for the Slavery Crisis in the North," *Church History* 43, no. 3 (September 1974), 324.

104 **Matthew Simpson struck:** Keller, "Methodist Newspapers," 330–31.

105 **The special committee appointed:** Keller, 328.

106 **"In Christ, not in":** Gilbert Haven, *Sermons, Speeches, and Letters on Slavery and Its War [. . .]* (Boston: Lee and Shepard, 1869), 29.

106 **"The march of events":** Smith, *Revivalism & Social Reform,* 220–21.

CHAPTER 5: VOTE AS YOU PRAY

107 **"From 1849 to 1854":** Abraham Lincoln to Jesse Fell, December 20, 1859, CW 3:512.

110 **"about the only public question":** Joseph Gillespie to WHH, January 31, 1866, HI.

111 **"whole life was a calculation":** Leonard Swett to WHH, January 17, 1866, HI.

111 **"You know I dislike slavery":** Abraham Lincoln to Joshua Speed, August 24, 1855, CW 2:320–23.

112 **It was a remarkably intemperate:** Richard N. Current, *The Lincoln Nobody Knows* (New York: Hill and Wang, 1958), 6, 12–13.

113 **But he implored voters:** William Lee Miller, *Lincoln's Virtues: An Ethical Biography* (New York: Alfred A. Knopf, 2002), 261–62.

114 **"My faith in the proposition":** Miller, *Lincoln's Virtues,* 263.

114 **"We implore Christians":** Miller, 294.

115 **"raise a hell":** David M. Potter, *The Impending Crisis: America before the Civil War, 1848–1861* (New York, Harper & Row, 1976), 160.

115 **"a great political sectional":** *Congressional Globe,* vol. 28, part 1, 621.

115 **But he did not overstate:** Richard J. Carwardine, *Evangelicals and Politics in Antebellum America* (New Haven, CT: Yale University Press, 1993), 236–38.

116 **By 1857 the tide:** James Brewer Stewart, *Holy Warriors: The Abolitionists and American Slavery,* rev. ed. (New York: Hill and Wang, 1996), 169.

117 **"Those who admit":** John R. McKivigan, *The War against Proslavery Religion: Abolitionism and the Northern Churches, 1830–1865* (Ithaca, NY: Cornell University Press, 1984), 147.

117 **"exhausted soil, old":** Eric Foner, *Free Soil, Free Labor, Free Men: The Ideology of the Republican Party before the Civil War* (New York: Oxford University Press, 1970), 41.

118 **Joshua Giddings, whose antislavery:** James Brewer Stewart, *Joshua Giddings*

276

and the Tactics of Radical Politics (Cleveland: Press of Case Western Reserve University, 1970), 40.

118 **They were long committed:** McKivigan, *The War against Proslavery Religion*, 146.

118 **Regarding slavery as:** *The Thirteenth Annual Report of the American and Foreign Anti-slavery Society, with the Addresses and Resolutions* (New York: American and Foreign Anti-Slavery Society, 1853), 16.

118 **"the high distinction":** Lincoln, debate at Quincy, October 13, 1858, CW 3:256.

119 *in the right to eat the bread*: Lincoln, debate at Ottawa, August 21, 1858, CW 3:249.

119 **"spreading civilization and Christianity":** Douglas, debate at Ottawa, August 21, 1858, CW 3:12.

119 **Douglas repeatedly attempted:** Douglas, debate at Quincy, October 13, 1858, CW 3:275.

119 **"The Savior, I suppose":** Lincoln, speech at Chicago, July 10, 1858, CW 2:501.

120 **"Does it not enter":** Lincoln, debate at Alton, October 15, 1858, CW 3:310.

121 **Christopher Brown, a young:** Christopher C. Brown (WHH Interview), 1865–66, *HI*.

121 **"placed himself and family":** David S. Reynolds, *Abe: Abraham Lincoln in His Times* (New York: Penguin Press, 2020), 333–34; and James Smith to WHH, January 24, 1867, *HI*.

121 **Lincoln's oldest son:** Robert Todd Lincoln to WHH, December 24, 1866, *HI*; and John T. Stuart to WHH, March 2, 1870, *HI*.

122 **"The good old maxims":** Lincoln, speech at Cincinnati, September 17, 1858, CW 3:462.

122 **"LET US HAVE FAITH":** Lincoln, address at Cooper Institute, New York City, February 27, 1860, CW 3:550. See also David Herbert Donald, *Lincoln* (New York: Simon & Schuster, 1996), 237–38; and Harold Holzer, *Lincoln at Cooper Union: The Speech That Made Abraham Lincoln President* (New York: Simon & Schuster, 2004).

123 **In Lincoln's home state, Methodist:** See Linda Jeanne Evans, "Abolitionism in the Illinois Churches, 1830–1865" (PhD diss., Northwestern University, Evanston, IL, 1981).

123 **Little wonder that the Republican:** Richard J. Carwardine, *Lincoln: A Life of Purpose and Power* (New York: Vintage Books, 2006), 123, 127–128.

124 **Official biographies took:** Richard J. Carwardine, "Lincoln, Evangelical Religion, and American Political Culture in the Era of the Civil War," *Journal of the Abraham Lincoln Association* 18, no. 1 (Winter 1997): 27–57.

124 **"Black republicanism has":** Carwardine, *Lincoln*, 128.

124 **It rankled Democrats:** Carwardine, 128.

125 **"Without the assistance of that":** Lincoln, farewell address at Springfield, Illinois, February 11, 1861, CW 4:190.

126 **"most happy indeed"**: Lincoln, address to the New Jersey Senate at Trenton, February 21, 1861, CW 4:236.

PART II

CHAPTER 6: AND THE WAR CAME

129 **"The people are impatient"**: David Herbert Donald, *Lincoln* (New York: Simon & Schuster, 1996), 30.

130 **The western campaign:** James M. McPherson, *Battle Cry of Freedom: The Civil War Era* (New York: Oxford University Press, 1988), 392–427; and Allen G. Guelzo, *Fateful Lightning: A New History of the Civil War & Reconstruction* (New York: Oxford University Press, 2012), 200–13.

131 **"What will the country say?":** Michael Burlingame, *Abraham Lincoln: A Life* (Baltimore: Johns Hopkins University Press, 2008), 2:498.

131 **"The judgements of God":** George C. Rable, *God's Almost Chosen Peoples: A Religious History of the American Civil War* (Chapel Hill: University of North Carolina Press, 2010), 77.

133 **"This melancholy history":** John Cotton Smith, *Two Discourses on the State of the Country* (New York: John A. Gray, 1861), 4.

133 **"For the continuance":** James H. Moorhead, *American Apocalypse: Yankee Protestants and the Civil War, 1860–1869* (New Haven, CT: Yale University Press, 1978), 27.

134 **Drawing on John the Apostle's:** Frederick Douglass, "The Decision of the Hour," June 16, 1861, in *Frederick Douglass: Selected Speeches and Writings*, ed. Philip S. Foner, rev. ed. (Chicago: Lawrence Hill Books, 1999), 463.

134 **"I think to lose Kentucky":** Eric Foner, *The Fiery Trial: Abraham Lincoln and American Slavery* (New York: W. W. Norton, 2010), 176–79; and Allan Nevins, *The Ordeal of the Union*, vol. 5, *The Improvised War* (New York: Charles Scribner's Sons, 1959), 331–33.

134 **unanimously passed a resolution:** Sean A. Scott, *A Visitation of God: Northern Civilians Interpret the Civil War* (New York: Oxford University Press, 2011), 39.

134 **From Kalamazoo, Michigan:** Victor B. Howard, *Religion and the Radical Republican Movement, 1860–1870* (Lexington: University Press of Kentucky, 1990), 13.

135 **From southern Illinois:** Howard, *Religion and the Radical Republican Movement*, 14–15.

137 **Sermons that cast the war:** Rable, *God's Almost Chosen Peoples*, 85.

137 **Henry McNeal Turner, a bishop:** Henry McNeal Turner, "The Plagues of This Country," *Christian Recorder*, July 12, 1862, in *Freedom's Witness: The Civil War Correspondence of Henry McNeal Turner*, ed. Jean Lee Cole (Morgantown: West Virginia University Press, 2013), 44–48.

138 **"The whole affair":** Henry McNeal Turner, untitled, *Christian Recorder*, September 13, 1862, in Cole, *Freedom's Witness*, 63.

138 **Days before Lincoln signaled:** W. W. Patton, "A Paper Read Before the Maryland Historical Society, Baltimore," December 12, 1887 (Baltimore: Peabody Publication Fund, 1888), 12–13.

139 **A Methodist minister spoke generally:** Rable, *God's Almost Chosen Peoples*, 35.

139 **The war shattered:** Rable, 35.

140 **For every cautious:** Rable, 65.

140 **"imprecations of David":** George Warren Gardner, *Treason and the Fate of Traitors: A Sermon Preached in the First Baptist Church [. . .]* (Boston: Davis and Farmer, Printers, 1862), 10.

140 **"the blockade, the manufacture of arms":** Gardner, *Treason and the Fate of Traitors*, 8.

CHAPTER 7: LOSING WILLIE

143 **"'Well, Nicolay,' said he":** John G. Nicolay, journal entry, February 20, 1862, JGN-LC.

143 **In the months that followed:** Jean H. Baker, *Mary Todd Lincoln: A Biography*, rev. ed. (New York: W. W. Norton, 2008), 208–17; and David Herbert Donald, *Lincoln* (New York: Simon & Schuster, 1996), 336.

144 **A passing acquaintance:** LeGrand B. Cannon to WHH, October 7, 1889, *HI*.

144 **Spiritualism was neither:** David S. Reynolds, *Abe: Abraham Lincoln in His Times* (New York: Penguin Press, 2020), 630–31.

145 **"He comes to me":** Donald, *Lincoln*, 427.

146 **Colburn would later claim:** Nettie Colburn Maynard, *Was Abraham Lincoln a Spiritualist?* (Philadelphia: Rufus C. Hartranft, 1891), 74–75.

146 **It was the first modern:** Drew Gilpin Faust, *This Republic of Suffering: Death and the American Civil War* (New York: Vintage Books, 2008), 39–41, 55–56; and Gary Laderman, *The Sacred Remains: American Attitudes toward Death, 1799–1883* (New Haven, CT: Yale University Press, 1996), 97.

147 **It was a lonely death:** Faust, *This Republic of Suffering*, 9, 11.

147 **"Death is so common":** Elisha Hunt Rhodes, *All for the Union: The Civil War Diary and Letters of Elisha Hunt Rhodes*, ed. Robert Hunt Rhodes (New York: Crown, 1991), 76.

148 **"appeared willing to do":** Sean A. Scott, *A Visitation of God: Northern Civilians Interpret the Civil War* (New York: Oxford University Press, 2011), 201–2.

148 **"Because thine heart was tender":** Scott, *A Visitation of God*, 202.

148 **"I have always believed him":** Scott, 203.

148 **spiritual condition of soldiers:** Scott, 201–3.

148 **"cowardly giving way to fear":** Faust, *This Republic of Suffering*, 24.

148 **"Nobody was in sight":** Rebecca Harding Davis, *Bits of Gossip* (Boston: Houghton Mifflin, 1905), 120.

149 **In the decades just prior:** Scott, *A Visitation of God*, 206–7.

151 **"Up to the Hills":** Faust, *This Republic of Suffering*, 179.

151 **A popular song verse:** Faust, 177.

151 **One of the most widely:** Elizabeth Stuart Phelps, *The Gates Ajar* (Boston: Fields, Osgood, 1868).

151 **John Sweet, a Baptist:** Faust, *This Republic of Suffering*, 185.

152 **Weeks after Lincoln's assassination:** John G. Nicolay to WHH, May 27, 1865, *HI*.

152 **"Mr. Lincoln loved Nicolay":** Richard J. Carwardine, "'Simply a Theist': Herndon on Lincoln's Religion," *Journal of the Abraham Lincoln Association* 35, no. 2 (Summer 2014): 27.

152 **His call for:** Lincoln, "Proclamation Appointing a National Fast Day," March 30, 1863, *CW* 6:155–56.

153 **"these victories have":** Lincoln, "Proclamation of Thanksgiving," July 15, 1863, *CW* 6:332.

154 **Charles McIlvaine an evangelical:** Scott, *A Visitation of God*, 136.

154 **Elizabeth Duncan was:** Scott, 81, 136.

154 **His rhetorical pivot:** Lincoln, "Remarks to Baltimore Presbyterian Synod," October 24, 1863, *CW* 6:535–36.

155 **When a crowd serenaded:** Lincoln, "Response to a Serenade," July 7, 1863, *CW* 6:319–20.

155 **Just prior to the Union's:** William E. Gienapp and Erica Gienapp, eds., *The Civil War Diary of Gideon Welles, Lincoln's Secretary of the Navy: The Original Manuscript Edition* (Urbana: University of Illinois Press, 2014), 54.

155 **Still, at the urging:** Lincoln, Emancipation Proclamation, January 1, 1863, *CW* 6:30.

156 **Orville Browning, a Republican:** Michael Burlingame, ed., *An Oral History of Abraham Lincoln: John G. Nicolay's Interviews and Essays* (Carbondale: Southern Illinois University Press, 1996), 4–5.

156 **Mary, who was in:** Mary Todd Lincoln (WHH notes on interview), September 1866, *HI*.

157 **His close friend:** Joshua F. Speed to WHH, January 12, 1866, *HI*.

157 **"was reading the bible":** Burlingame, *An Oral History of Abraham Lincoln*, 5.

157 **he confessed to a delegation:** Richard J. Carwardine, *Lincoln: A Life of Purpose and Power* (New York: Vintage Books, 2006), 224.

157 **An artist who lived:** Francis B. Carpenter to WHH, December 24, 1866, *HI*.

158 **When Noyes Miner:** Carwardine, *Lincoln*, 227.

159 **to a nation of devout Christians:** For a superb close reading of the biblical tonality of the Gettysburg Address, see James P. Byrd, *A Holy Baptism of Fire & Blood: The Bible & the American Civil War* (New York: Oxford University Press, 2021), 217–21.

159 **"We all have faith":** Laderman, *The Sacred Remains*, 127–30.

160 **His message, if subtle:** Joshua M. Zeitz, "Remembering the Gettysburg Address," *New York Times*, November 21, 2013.

CHAPTER 8: THE WILL OF GOD PREVAILS

162 "The will of God prevails": Meditation on the Divine Will, September 2, 1862, CW 5:403–4.

162 Such thinking became increasingly: David S. Reynolds, *Abe: Abraham Lincoln in His Times* (New York: Penguin Press, 2020), 721–22.

163 "just rebuke from God": Richard J. Carwardine, *Lincoln: A Life of Purpose and Power* (New York: Vintage Books, 2006), 225.

163 "It is your high mission": Carwardine, *Lincoln*, 225.

164 "I hope it will not be irreverent": Abraham Lincoln, "Reply to Emancipation Memorial Presented by Chicago Christians of All Denominations," September 13, 1862, CW 5:420.

164 "in its profoundest": *Chicago Tribune*, August 4, 1864.

164 Studies of wartime Cincinnati: George D. Harmon, "The Pennsylvania Clergy and the Civil War," *Pennsylvania History* 6, no. 2 (April 1939), 101.

164 Individual denominations often blurred: George M. Frederickson, "The Coming of the Lord: The Northern Protestant Clergy and the Civil War Crisis," in *Religion and the American Civil War*, ed. Randall M. Miller, Harry S. Stout, and Charles Reagan Wilson (New York: Oxford University Press, 1998), 118–20.

165 "official organ of the Methodist": Sean A. Scott, *A Visitation of God: Northern Civilians Interpret the Civil War* (New York: Oxford University Press, 2011), 229–30.

165 Henry Clay Fish, a prominent: Henry Clay Fish, *The Valley of Achor a Door of Hope; or The Grand Issues of the War* (New York: Sheldon, 1863), 22.

166 That formulation often blurred: Scott, *A Visitation of God*, 24.

166 "Methodism is loyalty": Phillip Shaw Paludan, *A People's Contest: The Union & Civil War, 1861–1865* (Lawrence: University Press of Kansas, 1988), 347–48.

166 Methodist leaders encouraged: William Warren Sweet, *The Methodist Episcopal Church and the Civil War* (Cincinnati: Methodist Book Concern Press, 1912), 83.

167 Speaking the familiar language: Lincoln, Proclamation of a Special Fast Day, August 16, 1861, CW 4:482.

167 In another prayer day proclamation: Lincoln, Proclamation Appointing a Special Fast Day, March 30, 1863, CW 6:156.

167 By contrast, Jefferson Davis: Reynolds, *Abe*, 724.

167 Lincoln parted ways: Carwardine, *Lincoln*, 225.

167 Edwin Stanton, who served: John Hay and John G. Nicolay, *Abraham Lincoln: A History* (New York: Century, 1890), 5:138.

168 "Christians must carry": Scott, *A Visitation of God*, 4.

168 Antislavery ministers like: Scott, 20.

168 John Reynolds, a Democrat: *Illinois State Register*, January 12, 1863.

168 In the days just after: Scott, *A Visitation of God*, 166.

168 Opponents of "political preaching": Scott, 221–24.

169 early in the war, a pastor: Paludan, *A People's Contest*, 345.

169 John C. Gregg, a Methodist: James P. Byrd, *A Holy Baptism of Fire & Blood: The Bible & the American Civil War* (New York: Oxford University Press, 2021), 208.

170 The Boston Methodist Preachers': Sweet, *The Methodist Episcopal Church*, 67.

170 In Newark, New Jersey: Sweet, 73–74.

170 How could one reach: Byrd, *A Holy Baptism of Fire & Blood*, 245.

170 But American evangelicals: James H. Moorhead, *American Apocalypse: Yankee Protestants and the Civil War, 1860–1869* (New Haven, CT: Yale University Press, 1978), 5.

170 "extending civilization, republicanism": Moorhead, *American Apocalypse*, 6.

171 When, during a Christian religious: Scott, *A Visitation of God*, 227.

172 Lincoln was "a fatalist": Henry Clay Whitney, *Life on the Circuit with Lincoln* (Boston: Estes and Lauriat, 1892), 267.

172 "what is to be": Allen C. Guelzo, "Abraham Lincoln and the Doctrine of Necessity," *Journal of the Abraham Lincoln Association* 18, no. 1 (Winter 1997): 57.

172 "things were to be": Guelzo, "Abraham Lincoln and the Doctrine of Necessity," 57.

172 In a letter to Eliza Gurney: Lincoln to Eliza P. Gurney, September 4, 1864, *CW* 7:535.

173 Even as he remained uncertain: Joseph Gillespie to WHH, December 8, 1866, *HI*, 505.

173 "a mere instrument": Lincoln, reply to Oliver P. Morton at Indianapolis, February 11, 1861, *CW* 4:193.

173 "I claim not to have": Lincoln to Albert G. Hodges, April 4, 1864, *CW* 7:282.

174 John Hay, his trusted: John Hay, "The Heroic Age in Washington," unpublished manuscript, JH-BU.

174 "The Tycoon is": John Hay to John G. Nicolay, August 7, 1863, reel 5, frames 1434–37, JH-BU.

175 Henry Ward Beecher, well: Henry Ward Beecher, *Patriotic Addresses: In America and England, from 1850 to 1855, on Slavery, the Civil War, and the Development of Civil Liberty in the United States* (New York: Fords, Howard & Hulbert, 1891), 387.

175 As late as January 1861: Wendell Phillips, "The Unholy Alliance," *New York Times*, January 22, 1861.

175 "the great common life": George M. Frederickson, *The Inner Civil War: Northern Intellectuals and the Crisis of the Union*, rev. ed. (Urbana: University of Illinois Press, 1993), 70.

176 A popular syndicated column: Harry S. Stout, *Upon the Altar of the Nation: A Moral History of the Civil War* (New York: Penguin Books, 2006), 100–3.

177 William L. Gaylord, a Congregationalist: William Luther Gaylord, *The Soldier God's Minister: A Discourse Delivered in the Congregational Church,*

Fitzwilliam, N.H. [. . .] (Fitchburg, MA: Rollstone Job Printing Office, 1862), 7, 17–18.

177 **By late 1862 the increasingly:** Sweet, *The Methodist Episcopal Church,* 68, 72.

178 **They became active military:** Byrd, *A Holy Baptism of Fire & Blood,* 63.

178 **Another minister told congregants:** Paludan, *A People's Contest,* 348.

178 **A Methodist clergyman in Boston:** Sweet, *The Methodist Episcopal Church,* 69.

178 **Methodist newspapers urged:** Sweet, 117–18.

179 **They came increasingly to dehumanize:** Sweet, 121.

180 **Lincoln, his intellectual better:** James M. McPherson, *Battle Cry of Freedom: The Civil War Era* (New York: Oxford University Press, 1988), 359; and David Herbert Donald, *Lincoln (*New York: Simon & Schuster, 1996), 319.

180 **"should be conducted upon":** George B. McClellan, *Letter of the Secretary of War, Transmitting Report on the Organization of the Army of the Potomac* (Washington, DC: Constitutional Union Office, 1864), 105.

180 **"the officers found it impractical":** Stout, *Upon the Altar of the Nation,* 121.

181 **Union soldiers broadly:** Stout, 141.

181 **"without using the Emancipation lever":** Interview with Alexander W. Randall and Joseph T. Mills, *CW* 7:507.

182 **Francis Lieber, a German émigré:** *Instructions for the Government of Armies of the United States in the Field,* prepared by Francis Lieber, LL.D., Originally Issued as General Orders No. 100, Adjutant General's Office, 1863 (Washington, DC: Government Printing Office, 1898), article 15.

182 **The year before, Frederick Douglass:** Frederick Douglass, "The Slaveholders' Rebellion," July 4, 1862, in *Frederick Douglass: Selected Speeches and Writings,* ed. Philip S. Foner, rev. ed. (Chicago: Lawrence Hill Books, 1999), 503.

182 **"the rebels with both bullets":** "The End of Peaceable Warfare," *New York World,* quoted in Byrd, *A Holy Baptism of Fire & Blood,* 131.

183 **Samuel Cox, a Democratic congressman:** Stout, *Upon the Altar of the Nation,* 281.

184 **Winfield Scott Hancock, who:** Stout, 281.

184 **"The Old Testament, in our":** Andrew Leete Stone, *Emancipation: A Discourse Delivered in Park Street Church, on Fast Day Morning, April 3, 1862* (Boston: Henry Hoyt, 1862), 4, https://www.loc.gov/item/92838832.

185 **"In times of long-continued peace":** Levi L. Paine, *Political Lessons of the Rebellion: A Sermon Delivered at Farmington, Connecticut, on Fast Day, April 18, 1862* (Farmington, CT: Samuel S. Cowles, 1862), 1, 6.

186 **"Shall we not rejoice":** George W. Gardner, *Treason and the Fate of Traitors: A Sermon Preached in the First Baptist Church [. . .]* (Boston: Davis and Farmer, 1862), 5–17.

187 **When delegates from eleven:** Frederickson, "The Coming of the Lord," 123.

187 **Francis Wayland, a Baptist minister:** Paludan, *A People's Contest,* 346.

187 **Viewing their religious calling:** Sweet, *The Methodist Episcopal Church,* 51.

188 **By decree, all churches:** Sweet, 98–109.

189 **the war had cemented:** Frederickson, "The Coming of the Lord," 123.

CHAPTER 9: SOLDIERS' WAR

191 **"Strange feelings come":** Bell Irvin Wiley, *The Life of Billy Yank: The Common Soldier of the Union* (Baton Rouge: Louisiana State University Press, 1952), 73.

191 **An enlisted man confided:** Sean A. Scott, *A Visitation of God: Northern Civilians Interpret the Civil War* (New York: Oxford University Press, 2011), 89.

192 **From the start, many religious:** Steven E. Woodworth, *While God Is Marching On: The Religious World of Civil War Soldiers* (Lawrence: University Press of Kansas, 2001), 177.

192 **"That there were bad men":** Woodworth, *While God Is Marching On*, 179.

192 **"It is sad to contemplate":** George C. Rable, *God's Almost Chosen Peoples: A Religious History of the American Civil War* (Chapel Hill: University of North Carolina Press, 2010), 91.

193 **There was a natural:** Woodworth, *While God Is Marching On*, 184–85.

193 **"I feel for one":** Woodworth, 189.

193 **On his twentieth birthday:** Elisha Hunt Rhodes, *All for the Union: The Civil War Diary and Letters of Elisha Hunt Rhodes*, ed. Robert Hunt Rhodes (New York: Crown, 1991), 52.

193 **Army life was incompatible:** Rable, *God's Almost Chosen Peoples*, 95–97.

194 **"We have no religious services":** Rable, 119.

195 **While the Confederacy lost access:** Robert J. Miller, *Both Prayed to the Same God: Religion and Faith in the American Civil War* (New York: Lexington Books, 2007), 42.

195 **When in 1863 troops:** Woodworth, *While God Is Marching On*, 167.

196 **He later learned they were:** Woodworth, 167–71.

197 **Other activists in the Sanitary:** Rable, *God's Almost Chosen Peoples*, 219–20.

197 **Though in theory every regiment:** Woodworth, *While God Is Marching On*, 149–51.

199 **Nevertheless, almost two thousand four hundred:** John W. Brinsfield, William C. Davis, Benedict Maryniak, and James I. Robertson Jr., eds., *Faith in the Fight: Civil War Chaplains* (Mechanicsburg, PA: Stackpole Books, 2003), 129–210; and Robert J. Miller, *Both Prayed to the Same God*, 98–101. See also Warren B. Armstrong, *For Courageous Fighting and Confident Dying: Union Chaplains in the Civil War* (Lawrence: University Press of Kansas, 1998).

199 **"The men who offered themselves":** A. Noel Blakeman, ed., *Personal Recollections of the War of Rebellion: Address Delivered Before the New York Commandery of the Loyal Legion of the United States, 1883* (New York: G. P. Putnam's Sons, 1912), 341.

200 **In reality, it is impossible:** James H. Moorhead, *American Apocalypse: Yankee*

Protestants and the Civil War, 1860–1869 (New Haven, CT: Yale University Press, 1978), 70.

200 "great national baptism": Bradley J. Longfield, *Presbyterians and American Culture: A History* (Louisville, KY: Westminster John Knox Press, 2013), 112.

200 Similar revivals, often larger: William W. Bennett, *A Narrative of the Great Revival which Prevailed in the Southern Armies during the Late Civil War between the States of the Federal Union* (Philadelphia: Claxton, Remsen & Haffelfinger, 1877), 324.

200 Some bursts of revivalism: Gardiner H. Shattuck Jr., *A Shield and a Hiding Place* (Macon, GA: Mercer University Press, 1988), 73–74.

200 One day, soldiers filed: Lemuel Moss, *Annals of the United States Christian Commission* (Philadelphia: J. B. Lippincott, 1868), 491.

201 "A great many have been": Woodworth, *While God Is Marching On*, 214.

201 "quite a number": Woodworth, 214.

201 Within days, he felt: Woodworth, 217.

201 In a diary entry dated: Rhodes, *All for the Union*, 115.

202 Several months later, the men: Woodworth, *While God Is Marching On*, 229.

202 Soldiers from all parts: Woodworth, 231–33, 241.

202 Some, like Rhodes, were devout: Rhodes, *All for the Union*, 233.

203 "I feel confident": James P. Byrd, *A Holy Baptism of Fire & Blood: The Bible & the American Civil War* (New York: Oxford University Press, 2021), 231.

203 As he slipped away, Whipple: Phillip Shaw Paludan, *A People's Contest: The Union & Civil War, 1861–1865* (Lawrence: University Press of Kansas, 1988), 365.

203 Soldiers demonstrated a wide range: Rable, *God's Almost Chosen Peoples*, 161–62.

204 It was a common refrain: Woodworth, *While God Is Marching On*, 29–31.

204 Understandably, many men turned: Rable, *God's Almost Chosen Peoples*, 161–62.

205 "These are trying times": David Rolfs, *No Peace for the Wicked: Northern Protestant Soldiers and the American Civil War* (Knoxville: University of Tennessee Press, 2009), 81–82.

205 Others, including many border: Chandra Manning, *What This Cruel War Was Over: Soldiers, Slavery, and the Civil War* (New York: Vintage Books, 2007), 23.

205 But as the conflict raged: Manning, *What This Cruel War Was Over*, 45.

206 A young man from Illinois: Manning, 93.

206 Even soldiers who remained: Manning, 50.

206 Soldiers also grew deeply resentful: Manning, 50, 97–101.

207 Many soldiers also encountered: Woodworth, *While God Is Marching On*, 202–4.

208 "Song by a Florida slavegirl": Hay Diary, April 19, 1863.

208 "Say my brother": Hay Diary, April 27, 1863.

208 "Genl. Hunter sitting": Hay Diary, May 23, 1863.

210 "I have tried to keep": Rhodes, *All for the Union*, 238.

CHAPTER 10: NATIONAL REGENERATION

211 **John Helm, who knew:** John B. Helm to WHH, June 27, 1865, *HI.*

212 **That both revivals and political:** Richard J. Carwardine, *Evangelicals and Politics in Antebellum America* (New Haven, CT: Yale University Press, 1993), 12–13.

212 **"give you light and direction":** Carwardine, *Evangelicals and Politics,* 24.

212 **Churches in the antebellum period:** Carwardine, 24.

212 **"They are known to be":** Carwardine, 121.

213 **Democrats were churchgoers:** Carwardine, 65.

213 **In 1856, Democrats:** Carwardine, 268.

214 **Gilbert Haven, the Methodist:** James P. Byrd, *A Holy Baptism of Fire & Blood: The Bible & the American Civil War* (New York: Oxford University Press, 2021), 42.

214 **John Wentworth, the mayor:** Victor B. Howard, *Religion and the Radical Republican Movement, 1860–1870* (Lexington: University Press of Kentucky, 1990), 8–10.

214 **George Julian, a radical antislavery:** Carwardine, *Evangelicals and Politics,* 297.

215 **Even in Springfield:** David B. Chesebrough, *"No Sorrow like Our Sorrow": Northern Protestant Ministers and the Assassination of Lincoln* (Kent, OH: Kent State University Press, 1994), 8.

216 **As late as September 1861:** George M. Frederickson, "The Coming of the Lord: The Northern Protestant Clergy and the Civil War Crisis," in *Religion and the American Civil War,* ed. Randall M. Miller, Harry S. Stout, and Charles Reagan Wilson (New York: Oxford University Press, 1998), 118.

216 **Now, according to Gilbert Haven:** Gilbert Haven, *National Sermons, Speeches, and Letters on Slavery and Its War [. . .]* (Boston: Lee and Shepard, 1869), 383.

216 **They took it as proof:** James H. Moorhead, *American Apocalypse: Yankee Protestants and the Civil War, 1860–1869* (New Haven, CT: Yale University Press, 1978), 127.

216 **"will that every vestige":** *Minutes of the General Assembly of the Presbyterian Church in the United States of America* (Philadelphia: Presbyterian Board of Publication, 1864), 298–99.

217 **"character of the war":** James M. McPherson, *Battle Cry of Freedom: The Civil War Era* (New York: Oxford University Press, 1988), 558.

217 **A Congregationalist minister from Salem:** Israel E. Dwinell, *Hope for Our Country: A sermon preached, in the South church, Salem, October 19, 1862* (Salem, MA: Charles W. Sweeney, 1862), 16–17.

217 **For many devout evangelicals:** George Leon Walker, *The Offered National Regeneration: a sermon preached in the State Street Church, Portland, on the occasion of the national fast, September 26, 1861* (Portland, ME: Little, Bro. 1861), 82.

217 **God would now:** Howard, *Religion and the Radical Republican Movement,* 25–28, 36, 52–55.

218 **"deemed it alike":** Howard, 54.

218 **Speaking at an AME church:** Frederick Douglass, "A Day for Poetry and Song," December 28, 1862, in *Frederick Douglass: Selected Speeches and Writings,* ed. Philip S. Foner, rev. ed. (Chicago: Lawrence Hill Books, 1999), 523–24.

218 **In acknowledgment of the document's:** Frederick Douglass, "Another Word to the Colored Man," April 1863, in Foner, *Frederick Douglass,* 531.

218 **"contest with oppression":** Frederick Douglass, "Men of Color, to Arms!," in Foner, 526.

218 **By early 1864, Douglass:** Frederick Douglass, "The Mission of the War," January 13, 1864, in Foner, 554–66.

219 **Support for emancipation proved:** Howard, *Religion and the Radical Republican Movement,* 25–28.

220 **Protestant voters broke ranks:** Howard, 40–44.

222 **When the American Baptist:** Lincoln to George B. Ide, James R. Doolittle, and A. Hubbell, May 30, 1864, CW 7:368.

222 **"I wish that [General Henry] Halleck":** William Tecumseh Sherman, *Home Letters of General Sherman,* ed. M.A. DeWolfe Howe (New York: Charles Scribner's Sons, 1909), 272.

222 **"seems to imagine that he":** Arthur C. Cole, "President Lincoln and the Illinois Radical Republicans," *Mississippi Valley Historical Review* 4 (March 1918), 431.

223 **"Lord God Almighty":** Howard, *Religion and the Radical Republican Movement,* 63.

224 **"the instrument with which":** Howard, 71.

224 **For the first time, leading:** Howard, 81–82.

225 **"Peace through Victory":** *New York Times,* September 19, 1864.

225 **"The hand of God":** George C. Rable, *God's Almost Chosen Peoples: A Religious History of the American Civil War* (Chapel Hill: University of North Carolina Press, 2010), 353.

226 **In a special election version:** David B. Chesebrough, *"No Sorrow like Our Sorrow,"* 14.

226 **William D. Potts, a clergyman:** William D. Potts, *Freemen's Guide to the Polls. And a Solemn Appeal to American Patriots* (New York: published by the author, 1864), 13.

228 **Even the president acknowledged:** Benjamin F. Butler, *Private and Official Correspondence of General Benjamin F. Butler During the Period of the Civil War* (Norwood, MA: Plimpton Press, 1917), 5:35.

228 **In late August, Lincoln:** Lincoln, "Memorandum concerning His Probable Failure of Re-election," August 23, 1864, CW 7:514.

228 **Reflecting Democrats' disgust:** *The Lincoln Catechism wherein the Eccentricities & Beauties of Despotism Are Fully Set Forth: A Guide to the Presidential Election of 1864* (New York: J. F. Feeks, 1864), 12, 14.

229 **Days later, Ulysses S. Grant:** John G. Nicolay to Therena Bates, September 11, 1864, JGN-LC, box 7.
230 **It seemed, as John Hay:** John Hay to John G. Nicolay, September 11, 1863, JH-BU, reel 5, frame 1448.
230 **"It is a little singular":** Hay Diary, November 8, 1864.
230 **a great majority of evangelical voters:** Richard J. Carwardine, *Lincoln: A Life of Purpose and Power* (New York: Vintage Books, 2006), 307.
231 **Years later, the devout Congregationalist:** Howard, *Religion and the Radical Republican Movement*, 1.

CHAPTER 11: NO SORROW LIKE OUR SORROW

234 **cheered passage:** Victor B. Howard, *Religion and the Radical Republican Movement, 1860–1870* (Lexington: University Press of Kentucky, 1990), 92–93.
235 **"bedraggled and drenched":** Ronald C. White Jr., "Lincoln's Sermon on the Mount: The Second Inaugural," in *Religion and the American Civil War*, ed. Randall M. Miller, Harry S. Stout, and Charles Reagan Wilson (New York: Oxford University Press, 1998), 210.
238 **Neither before nor since:** White, "Lincoln's Sermon on the Mount," 208–28.
239 **"contemned and insulted God":** Lincoln to George B. Ide, James R. Doolittle, and A. Hubbell, May 30, 1864, CW 7:368.
239 **"wear as well as":** Lincoln to Thurlow Weed, March 15, 1865, CW 8:333.
240 **"the religion that sets men":** "The President's Last, Shortest, and Best Speech," CW 8:356.
241 **"intensely crowded audience":** David B. Chesebrough, *"No Sorrow like Our Sorrow": Northern Protestant Ministers and the Assassination of Lincoln* (Kent, OH: Kent State University Press, 1994), xviii.
242 **"The sight was novel":** Richard White, *The Republic for Which It Stands: The United States during Reconstruction and the Gilded Age, 1865–1896* (New York: Oxford University Press, 2017), 13–14.
243 **"The sun is less bright":** *Sermons Preached in Boston on the Death of Abraham Lincoln: Together with the Funeral Services in the East Room of the Executive Mansion at Washington* (Boston: J. E. Tilton, 1865), 146.
243 **Ministers struggled to find:** George Dana Boardman, *An Address in Commemoration of Abraham Lincoln, President of the United States, Delivered in the Meeting House of the First Baptist Church of Philadelphia, on the Day of His Funeral at the National Capitol, April 19, 1865* (Philadelphia: Sherman, 1865), 52.
243 **"There has been, on this":** Morgan Dix, *The Death of President Lincoln: A Sermon Preached in St. Paul's Chapel, New York, on Wednesday, April 19, 1865* (Cambridge, MA: Riverside Press, 1865), 6–7.
244 **In East Saginaw, Michigan:** Chesebrough, *"No Sorrow like Our Sorrow,"* 3.
244 **"Why did a just":** George C. Rable, *God's Almost Chosen Peoples: A Religious*

History of the American Civil War (Chapel Hill: University of North Carolina Press, 2010), 377.

244 **"We, as a people, feel"**: Jacob Thomas, *Sermon Preached in the African Methodist Episcopal Zion Church* (Troy, NY: Young & Benson, 1865), 44.

244 **Had Lincoln's assassin**: Michael Burlingame, *Abraham Lincoln: A Life* (Baltimore: Johns Hopkins University Press, 2008), 2:829.

245 **"as when a dear old"**: Elias Nason, *Eulogy on Abraham Lincoln: Late President of the United States, May 8, 1865 [. . .]* (Boston: William V. Spencer, 1865), 5.

245 **"never did a ruler"**: Gilbert Haven, *Sermons, Speeches, and Letters on Slavery and Its War [. . .]* (Boston: Lee and Shepard, 1869), 561.

245 **"In such a juncture"**: Chesebrough, *"No Sorrow like Our Sorrow,"* xviii.

246 **"taint of this assassination"**: Chesebrough, 42.

246 **Alonzo Quint, a Congregationalist minister**: Alonzo Hall Quint, *Three Sermons Preached in the North Congregational Church, New Bedford, Massachusetts [. . .]* (New Bedford, MA: Mercury Job Press, 1865), 32–33.

246 **"representing treason, disloyalty"**: Marvin R. Vincent, *A Sermon on the Assassination of Abraham Lincoln, Sunday Morning April 23, 1865, First Presbyterian Church, Troy* (Troy, NY: A. W. Scribner), 8.

247 **"We have lost all sentiment"**: Theodore L. Cuyler, "Sermon IX," in George Bancroft, et al. *Our Martyr President, Abraham Lincoln: Voices from the Pulpit of New York and Brooklyn* (New York: Tibbals & Whiting, 1865), 314.

247 **"Since they had not succeeded"**: Samuel Coulter Baldridge, *The Martyr Prince. A Sermon on the Occasion of the Assassination of President Lincoln, April 23, 1865* (Cincinnati: Jos. B. Boyd, 1865), 10.

247 **"every officer educated"**: Matthew Simpson, *Funeral Address Delivered at the Burial of President Lincoln, at Springfield, Illinois, May 4, 1865* (New York: Carlton & Porter, 1865), 12.

248 **"Events are God's teachers"**: Seth Sweetser, *A Commemorative Discourse on the Death of Abraham Lincoln* (Worcester, MA: John Wilson and Son, 1865), 26.

248 **Reflecting the careful balancing**: William Eleazar Barton, *The American Pulpit on the Death of Lincoln* (Chicago: Open Court, 1937), 618.

248 **"died because his work"**: Chesebrough, *"No Sorrow like Our Sorrow,"* 69.

248 **"Let us look for"**: Cuyler, "Sermon IX," in Bancroft, et al., *Our Martyr President*, 312.

248 **"the kindest, gentlest"**: *New York Times*, April 16, 1865.

249 **Above all, church leaders believed**: Charles S. Robinson, *The Martyred President: A Sermon Preached in the First Presbyterian Church [. . .]* (New York: John F. Trow, 1865), 29.

249 **"Republican institutions have been vindicated"**: Henry Ward Beecher, "Abraham Lincoln," in *Patriotic Addresses: In America and England, from 1850 to 1855, on Slavery, the Civil War, and the Development of Civil Liberty in the United States* (New York: Fords, Howard & Hulbert, 1891), 100.

249 **"upon every American like"**: Richard White, *The Republic for Which It Stands*, 11.

250 **"Let Abraham Lincoln be known"**: E. S. Atwood, *The Nation's Loss: A Discourse Delivered on the Sunday After the Assassination of President Lincoln, South Church, Salem, April 16, 1865* (Salem, MA: Salem Gazette, 1865), 27.

CHAPTER 12: THE UNRAVELING

252 **"You become a Christian"**: Washington Gladden, *Being a Christian: What It Means, and How to Begin* (New York: Congregational Sunday School and Publishing Society, 1876), 61.

253 **"We must make men believe"**: George McKenna, *The Puritan Origins of American Patriotism* (New Haven, CT: Yale University Press, 2007), 198.

255 **"engineer and architect"**: George M. Marsden, *Fundamentalism and American Culture: The Shaping of Twentieth-Century Evangelism, 1870–1925* (New York: Oxford University Press, 1980), 24.

255 **"whether God made"**: Lyman Abbott, *Reminiscences* (Boston: Houghton Mifflin Company, 1914), 459.

256 **"the only errors"**: *A Documentary History of Religion in America to 1877*, Edward S. Gaustad and Mark A. Noll, eds. (Grand Rapids, MI: William B. Eerdmans Publishing Company, 1983), 369.

BIBLIOGRAPHY

ARCHIVES AND COLLECTIONS

Abraham Lincoln Papers, Library of Congress, Washington, DC.

CW: Lincoln, Abraham. *The Collected Works of Abraham Lincoln*. Abraham Lincoln Association. New Brunswick, NJ: Rutgers University Press, 1953. Online edition. Abraham Lincoln Association: 2006. https://quod.lib.umich.edu/l/lincoln.

Hay Diary: Michael Burlingame and John R. Turner Ettlinger, eds., *Inside Lincoln's White House: The Complete Civil War Diary of John Hay*. Carbondale: Southern Illinois University Press, 1999.

HI: Herndon, William Henry. *Herndon's Informants: Letters, Interviews, and Statements about Abraham Lincoln*. Edited by Douglas L. Wilson and Rodney O. Davis. Urbana: University of Illinois Press, 1997.

JGN-LC: John G. Nicolay Papers. Library of Congress, Washington, DC.

JH-BU: John Hay Papers. Brown University Library, Providence, RI.

PRIMARY AND SECONDARY SOURCES

Abbott, Lyman. *Reminiscences*. Boston: Houghton Mifflin Company, 1914.

American and Foreign Anti-Slavery Society. *The Thirteenth Annual Report of the American and Foreign Anti-Slavery Society, with the Addresses and Resolutions*. New York: American and Foreign Anti-Slavery Society, 1853.

Angle, Paul M. *"Here I Have Lived": A History of Lincoln's Springfield*. New Brunswick, NJ: Rutgers University Press, 1935.

Appleby, Joyce. "New Cultural Heroes in the Early National Period." In *The Culture of the Market: Historical Essays*, edited by Thomas L. Haskell and Richard F. Teichgraeber III, 163–888. New York: Cambridge University Press, 1996.

Armstrong, Warren B. *For Courageous Fighting and Confident Dying: Union Chaplains in the Civil War*. Lawrence: University Press of Kansas, 1998.

Atwood, E. S. *The Nation's Loss: A Discourse Delivered on the Sunday after the Assassination of President Lincoln, South Church, Salem, April 16, 1865*. Salem, MA: Salem Gazette, 1865.

Baird, Robert. *Religion in the United States of America*. Glasgow: Blackie and Son, 1844.

Baker, Jean H. *Mary Todd Lincoln: A Biography*. Rev. ed. New York: W. W. Norton, 2008.

Baldridge, Samuel Coulter. *The Martyr Prince. A Sermon on the Occasion of the Assassination of President Lincoln, April 23, 1865*. Cincinnati: Jos. B. Boyd, 1865.

Bancroft, George, et al. *Our Martyr President, Abraham Lincoln: Voices from the Pulpit of New York and Brooklyn*. New York: Tibbals & Whiting, 1865.

Barton, William E., D. H. Rutledge, A. Lincoln Free, and George M. Marsh. "Abraham Lincoln and New Salem." *Journal of the Illinois State Historical Society* 19, no. 3/4 (October 1926–January 1927): 74–101.

Barton, William Eleazar. *The American Pulpit on the Death of Lincoln*. Chicago: Open Court, 1937.

Beecher, Henry Ward. *Patriotic Addresses: In America and England, from 1850 to 1855, on Slavery, the Civil War, and the Development of Civil Liberty in the United States, by Henry Ward Beecher*. New York: Fords, Howard & Hulbert, 1887.

Beecher, Lyman. *Autobiography, Correspondence, Etc. of Lyman Beecher*. Edited by Charles Beecher. 2 vols. New York: Harper, 1865.

Bennett, William W. *A Narrative of the Great Revival which Prevailed in the Southern Armies during the Late Civil War between the States of the Federal Union*. Philadelphia: Claxton, Remsen & Haffelfinger, 1877.

Blakeman, A. Noel, ed. *Personal Recollections of the War of Rebellion: Address Delivered Before the New York Commandery of the Loyal Legion of the United States, 1883*. New York: G. P. Putnam's Sons, 1912.

Blight, David W. *Frederick Douglass: Prophet of Freedom*. New York: Simon & Schuster, 2018.

Blue, Frederick J. *Salmon P. Chase: A Life in Politics*. Kent, OH: Kent State University Press, 1987.

Boardman, George Dana. *An Address in Commemoration of Abraham Lincoln, President of the United States, Delivered in the Meeting-House of the First Baptist Church of Philadelphia, on the Day of His Funeral at the National Capitol, April 19, 1865*. Philadelphia: Sherman & Co., 1865.

Bourne, George. *The Book and Slavery Irreconcilable*. Philadelphia: J. M. Sanderson & Co., 1816.

Boyer, Paul. *Urban Masses and Moral Order in America, 1820–1920.* Cambridge, MA: Harvard University Press, 1978.

Brinsfield, John W., William C. Davis, Benedict Maryniak, and James I. Robertson Jr., eds. *Faith in the Fight: Civil War Chaplains.* Mechanicsburg, PA: Stackpole Books, 2003.

British and Foreign Antislavery Society, *Proceedings of the General Antislavery Convention Called by the British and Foreign Antislavery Society.* London, 1841.

Burlingame, Michael. *Abraham Lincoln: A Life.* 2 vols. Baltimore: Johns Hopkins University Press, 2008.

———. *The Inner World of Abraham Lincoln.* Urbana: University of Illinois Press, 1994.

——— ed. *An Oral History of Abraham Lincoln: John G. Nicolay's Interviews and Essays.* Carbondale: Southern Illinois University Press, 1996.

Butler, Benjamin F. *Private and Official Correspondence of General Benjamin F. Butler during the Period of the Civil War.* 5 vols. Norwood, MA: Plimpton Press, 1917.

Butler, Jon. *Becoming America: The Revolution Before 1776.* Cambridge, MA: Harvard University Press, 2001.

———, Grant Wacker, and Randall Balmer. *Religion in American Life: A Short History.* New York: Oxford University Press, 2000.

Byrd, James P. *A Holy Baptism of Fire & Blood: The Bible & the American Civil War.* New York: Oxford University Press, 2021.

Cady, John F. "The Religious Environment of Lincoln's Youth." *Indiana Magazine of History* 37, no. 1 (March 1941): 16–30.

Campbell, James T. *Songs of Zion: The African Methodist Episcopal Church in the United States and South Africa.* Chapel Hill: University of North Carolina Press, 1998.

Cartwright, Peter. *The Autobiography of Peter Cartwright: The Backwoods Preacher.* Edited by W. P. Strickland. New York: Carlton & Porter, 1857.

Carwardine, Richard J. *Evangelicals and Politics in Antebellum America.* New Haven, CT: Yale University Press, 1993.

———. *Lincoln: A Life of Purpose and Power.* New York: Vintage Books, 2006.

———. "Lincoln, Evangelical Religion, and American Political Culture in the Era of the Civil War." *Journal of the Abraham Lincoln Association* 18, no. 1 (Winter 1997): 27–55.

———. "'Simply a Theist': Herndon on Lincoln's Religion." *Journal of the Abraham Lincoln Association* 35, no. 2 (Summer 2014): 18–36.

Chappell, David L. *A Stone of Hope: Prophetic Religion and the Death of Jim Crow.* Chapel Hill: University of North Carolina Press, 2004.

Chesebrough, David B. *"No Sorrow like Our Sorrow": Northern Protestant Ministers and the Assassination of Lincoln.* Kent, OH: Kent State University Press, 1994.

Cole, Arthur C. "President Lincoln and the Illinois Radical Republicans." *Mississippi Valley Historical Review* 4, no. 4 (March 1918): 417–36.

Cole, Jean Lee, ed. *Freedom's Witness: The Civil War Correspondence of Henry McNeal Turner*. Morgantown: West Virginia University Press, 2013.

Coleman, Charles H. *Abraham Lincoln and Coles County, Illinois*. New Brunswick, NJ: Scarecrow Press, 1955.

Corrigan, John. *Business of the Heart: Religion and Emotion in the Nineteenth Century*. Berkeley: University of California Press, 2002.

Cross, Whitney R. *The Burned-Over District: The Social and Intellectual History of Enthusiastic Religion in Western New York, 1800–1850*. Ithaca, NY: Cornell University Press, 1982.

Current, Richard N. *The Lincoln Nobody Knows*. New York: Hill and Wang, 1958.

Daggett, David. *An oration, pronounced in the brick meeting-house, in the city of New-Haven, on the Fourth of July, A.D. 1787*. New Haven, CT: T. and S. Green, 1787.

Davis, Rebecca Harding. *Bits of Gossip*. Boston: Houghton Mifflin, 1905.

Dix, Morgan. *The Death of President Lincoln: A Sermon Preached in St. Paul's Chapel, New York, on Wednesday, April 19, 1865*. Cambridge, MA: Riverside Press, 1865.

Dixon, James. *Personal Narrative: A Tour through a Part of the United States and Canada*. New York: Lane and Scott, 1849.

Donald, David Herbert. *Lincoln*. New York: Simon & Schuster, 1996.

Dwinell, Israel E. *Hope for Our Country: A sermon preached, in the South church, Salem, October 19, 1862*. Salem, MA: Charles W. Sweeney, 1862.

Edwards, Jonathan. *The Works of Jonathan Edwards, A.M.* Edited by Edward Hickman. 2 vols. London: John Childs & Son, 1839.

Evans, Linda Jeanne. "Abolitionism in the Illinois Churches, 1830–1865," PhD diss., Northwestern University, Evanston, IL, 1981.

Faust, Drew Gilpin. *This Republic of Suffering: Death and the American Civil War*. New York: Vintage Books, 2008.

Finney, Charles Grandison. *Sermons on Various Subjects*. New York: S. W. Benedict, 1835.

Fish, Henry Clay. *The Valley of Achor a Door of Hope; or The Grand Issues of the War*. New York: Sheldon, 1863.

Foner, Eric. *The Fiery Trial: Abraham Lincoln and American Slavery*. New York: W. W. Norton, 2010.

———. *Free Soil, Free Labor, Free Men: The Ideology of the Republican Party before the Civil War*. New York: Oxford University Press, 1970.

Foner, Philip S., ed. *Frederick Douglass: Selected Speeches and Writings*. Rev. ed. Chicago: Lawrence Hill Books, 1999.

Foster, Eden Burroughs. *Four Pastorates: Glimpses of the Life and Thoughts of Eden B. Foster*. Lowell, MA: George M. Elliott, 1883.

Frederickson, George M. "The Coming of the Lord: The Northern Protestant Clergy and the Civil War Crisis." In *Religion and the American Civil War*, edited by

Randall M. Miller, Harry S. Stout, and Charles Reagan Wilson, 110–30. New York: Oxford University Press, 1998.

———. *The Inner Civil War: Northern Intellectuals and the Crisis of the Union.* Rev. ed. Urbana: University of Illinois Press, 1993.

Gac, Scott. *Singing for Freedom: The Hutchinson Family Singers and the Nineteenth-Century Culture of Reform.* New Haven, CT: Yale University Press, 2007.

Gardner, George W. *Treason and the Fate of Traitors: A Sermon Preached in the First Baptist Church [. . .].* Boston: Davis and Farmer, 1862.

Gaustad, Edward S. and Mark A. Noll, eds. *A Documentary History of Religion in America to 1877.* Grand Rapids, MI: William B. Eerdmans Publishing Company, 1983.

Gaylord, William Luther. *The Soldier God's Minister: A Discourse Delivered in the Congregational Church, Fitzwilliam, N.H. [. . .].* Fitchburg, MA: Rollstone Job Printing Office, 1862.

"General Order 100: Instructions for the Government of Armies of the United States in the Field, prepared by Francis Lieber, LL.D., Originally Issued as General Orders No. 100, Adjutant General's Office, 1863." Washington, DC: Government Printing Office, 1898.

Gienapp, William E., and Erica L. Gienapp, eds. *The Civil War Diary of Gideon Welles, Lincoln's Secretary of the Navy: The Original Manuscript Edition.* Urbana: University of Illinois Press, 2014.

Gladden, Washington. *Being a Christian: What It Means, and How to Begin.* New York: Congregational Sunday School and Publishing Society, 1876.

Goen, C. C. *Broken Churches, Broken Nation: Denominational Schisms and the Coming of the Civil War.* Macon, GA: Mercer University Press, 1985.

Guelzo, Allen C. "Abraham Lincoln and the Doctrine of Necessity." *Journal of the Abraham Lincoln Association* 18, no. 1 (Winter 1997): 57–81.

———. *Fateful Lightning: A New History of the Civil War & Reconstruction.* New York: Oxford University Press, 2012.

Guyatt, Nicholas. *Providence and the Invention of the United States, 1607–1876.* New York: Cambridge University Press, 2007.

Harmon, George D. "The Pennsylvania Clergy and the Civil War." *Pennsylvania History* 6, no. 2 (April 1939): 86–102.

Hatch, Nathan O. *The Democratization of American Christianity.* New Haven, CT: Yale University Press, 1989.

———, and Mark A. Noll, eds. *The Bible in America: Essays in Cultural History.* New York: Oxford University Press, 1982.

Haven, Gilbert. *Sermons, Speeches, and Letters on Slavery and Its War [. . .].* Boston: Lee and Shepard, 1869.

Herndon, William H., and Jesse W. Weik. *Herndon's Lincoln: The True Story of a Great Life.* North Scituate, MA: Digital Scanning, 1999.

Holland, J. G. *Holland's Life of Abraham Lincoln.* Lincoln: University of Nebraska Press, 1998.

Holzer, Harold. *Lincoln at Cooper Union: The Speech That Made Abraham Lincoln President.* New York: Simon & Schuster, 2004.

Hovey, Charles E., and Elijah P. Lovejoy. "Two Old Letters: One from Elijah P. Lovejoy, 1837; the Other from Gen. Charles E. Hovey, 1858." *Journal of the Illinois State Historical Society* 2, no. 4 (January 1910): 44–48.

Howard, Victor B. *Religion and the Radical Republican Movement, 1860–1870.* Lexington: University Press of Kentucky, 1990.

Howe, Daniel Walker. *The Political Culture of the American Whigs.* Chicago: University of Chicago Press, 1979.

Johnson, Paul E. *A Shopkeeper's Millennium: Society and Revivals in Rochester, New York, 1815–1837.* New York: Hill and Wang, 1978.

Keller, Ralph A. "Methodist Newspapers and the Fugitive Slave Law: A New Perspective for the Slavery Crisis in the North." *Church History* 43, no. 3 (September 1974): 319–39.

Laderman, Gary. *The Sacred Remains: American Attitudes toward Death, 1799–1883.* New Haven, CT: Yale University Press, 1996.

Levasseur, Auguste. *Lafayette in America in 1824 and 1825; or, Journal of Travels, in the United States.* 2 vols. New York: White, Gallagher & White, 1829.

The Lincoln Catechism wherein the Eccentricities & Beauties of Despotism Are Fully Set Forth: A Guide to the Presidential Election of 1864. New York: J. F. Feeks, 1864.

Longfield, Bradley J. *Presbyterians and American Culture: A History.* Louisville, KY: Westminster John Knox Press, 2013.

Manning, Chandra. *What This Cruel War Was Over: Soldiers, Slavery, and the Civil War.* New York: Vintage Books, 2007.

Marsden, George M. *Fundamentalism and American Culture: The Shaping of Twentieth-Century Evangelism, 1870–1925.* New York: Oxford University Press, 1980.

Maynard, Nettie Colburn. *Was Abraham Lincoln a Spiritualist?* Philadelphia: Rufus C. Hartranft, 1891.

McClellan, George B. *Letter of the Secretary of War, Transmitting Report on the Organization of the Army of the Potomac.* Washington, DC: Constitutional Union Office, 1864.

McDannell, Colleen. *The Christian Home in Victorian America, 1840–1900.* Bloomington: Indiana University Press, 1986.

McKenna, George. *The Puritan Origins of American Patriotism.* New Haven, CT: Yale University Press, 2007.

McKivigan, John R. *The War against Proslavery Religion: Abolitionism and the Northern Churches, 1830–1865.* Ithaca, NY: Cornell University Press, 1984.

McLoughlin, William G., Jr. *The Meaning of Henry Ward Beecher: An Essay on the Shifting Values of Mid-Victorian America, 1840–1870.* New York: Alfred A. Knopf, 1970.

————. *Modern Revivalism: Charles Grandison Finney to Billy Graham.* New York: Ronald Press, 1959.

McPherson, James M. *Battle Cry of Freedom: The Civil War Era.* New York: Oxford University Press, 1988.

Miller, Robert J. *Both Prayed to the Same God: Religion and Faith in the American Civil War.* New York: Lexington Books, 2007.

Miller, William Lee. *Lincoln's Virtues: An Ethical Biography.* New York: Alfred A. Knopf, 2002.

Moorhead, James H. *American Apocalypse: Yankee Protestants and the Civil War, 1860–1869.* New Haven, CT: Yale University Press, 1978.

Morgan, Edmund S. *The Puritan Dilemma: The Story of John Winthrop.* New York: Little, Brown, 1958.

Moss, Lemuel. *Annals of the United States Christian Commission.* Philadelphia: J. B. Lippincott, 1868.

Nason, Elias. *Eulogy on Abraham Lincoln: Late President of the United States, May, 8, 1865 [. . .].* Boston: William V. Spencer, 1865.

Nevins, Allan. *The Ordeal of the Union.* 8 vols. New York: Charles Scribner's Sons, 1947–1971.

Newman, Richard S. *Freedom's Prophet: Bishop Richard Allen, the AME Church, and the Black Founding Fathers.* New York: New York University Press, 2008.

Nicolay, John G., and John M. Hay. *Abraham Lincoln: A History.* 10 vols. New York: Century, 1890.

Noll, Mark A. *The Civil War as a Theological Crisis.* Chapel Hill: University of North Carolina Press, 2006.

————. "Lincoln's God." *Journal of Presbyterian History* 82, no. 2 (Summer 2004): 77–88.

————, ed., *God and Mammon: Protestants, Money, and the Market, 1790–1860.* New York: Oxford University Press, 2002.

Paine, Levi L. *Political Lessons of the Rebellion: A Sermon Delivered at Farmington, Connecticut, on Fast Day, April 18, 1862.* Farmington, CT: Samuel S. Cowles, 1862.

Paludan, Phillip Shaw. *A People's Contest: The Union & Civil War, 1861–1865.* Lawrence: University Press of Kansas, 1988.

Patton, W. W. "A Paper Read Before the Maryland Historical Society, Baltimore." December 12, 1887. Baltimore: Peabody Publication Fund, 1888.

Phelps, Elizabeth Stuart. *The Gates Ajar.* Boston: Fields, Osgood, 1868.

Pierson, George Wilson. *Tocqueville and Beaumont in America.* New York: Oxford University Press, 1938.

Potter, David M. *The Impending Crisis: America before the Civil War, 1848–1861.* New York: Harper & Row, 1976.

Potts, William D. *Freemen's Guide to the Polls. And a Solemn Appeal to American Patriots.* New York: published by the author, 1864.

Presbyterian Church in the USA. *Minutes of the General Assembly of the Presbyterian Church in the United States of America*. Philadelphia: Presbyterian Board of Publication, 1864.

———. *Minutes of the Presbyterian General Assembly: General Assembly of the Presbyterian Church in the United States, 1789–1820*. Philadelphia: Presbyterian Board of Publication, 1820.

Quint, Alonzo Hall. *Three Sermons Preached in the North Congregational Church, New Bedford, Massachusetts [. . .]*. New Bedford, MA: Mercury Job Press, 1865.

Rable, George C. *God's Almost Chosen Peoples: A Religious History of the American Civil War*. Chapel Hill: University of North Carolina Press, 2010.

Raboteau, Albert J. *Slave Religion: The "Invisible Institution" in the Antebellum South*. New York: Oxford University Press, 1978.

———. *Canaan Land: A Religious History of African Americans*. New York: Oxford University Press, 1999.

Reynolds, David S. *Abe: Abraham Lincoln in His Times*. New York: Penguin Press, 2020.

Rhodes, Elisha Hunt. *All for the Union: The Civil War Diary and Letters of Elisha Hunt Rhodes*. Edited by Robert Hunt Rhodes. New York: Crown, 1991.

Robinson, Charles S. *The Martyred President: A Sermon Preached in the First Presbyterian Church [. . .]*. New York: John F. Trow, 1865.

Rolfs, David. *No Peace for the Wicked: Northern Protestant Soldiers and the American Civil War*. Knoxville: University of Tennessee Press, 2009.

Schneider, A. Gregory. *The Way of the Cross Leads Home: The Domestication of American Methodism*. Bloomington: Indiana University Press, 1993.

Scott, Sean A. *A Visitation of God: Northern Civilians Interpret the Civil War*. New York: Oxford University Press, 2011.

Sellers, Charles. *The Market Revolution: Jacksonian America, 1815–1846*. New York: Oxford University Press, 1991.

Sermons Preached in Boston on the Death of Abraham Lincoln: Together with the Funeral Services in the East Room of the Executive Mansion at Washington. Boston: J. E. Tilton, 1865.

Shattuck, Gardiner H., Jr., *A Shield and a Hiding Place*. Macon, GA: Mercer University Press, 1988.

Sherman, William Tecumseh. *Home Letters of General Sherman*. Edited by M. A. DeWolfe Howe. New York: Charles Scribner's Sons, 1909.

Simpson, Matthew. *Funeral Address Delivered at the Burial of President Lincoln, at Springfield, Illinois, May 4, 1865*. New York: Carlton & Porter, 1865.

Smith, John Cotton. *Two Discourses on the State of the Country*. New York: John A. Gray, 1861.

Smith, Timothy L. *Revivalism & Social Reform: American Protestantism on the Eve of the Civil War*. Rev. ed. Baltimore: Johns Hopkins University Press, 1980.

Stewart, James Brewer. *Holy Warriors: The Abolitionists and American Slavery*. Rev. ed. New York: Hill and Wang, 1996.

———. *Joshua Giddings and the Tactics of Radical Politics*. Cleveland: Press of Case Western Reserve University, 1970.

Stone, Andrew Leete. *Emancipation: A Discourse Delivered in Park Street Church, on Fast Day Morning, April 3, 1862*. Boston: Henry Hoyt, 1862. www.loc.gov /item/92838832.

Stout, Harry S. *Upon the Altar of the Nation: A Moral History of the Civil War*. New York: Penguin Books, 2006.

Stowe, Harriet Beecher. *A Key to Uncle Tom's Cabin [. . .]*. Boston: John P. Jewett, 1854.

Sturtevant, Julian M. *Julian M. Sturtevant: An Autobiography*. Edited by Julian M. Sturtevant Jr. New York: F. H. Revell, 1896.

Sweet, William Warren. *The Methodist Episcopal Church and the Civil War*. Cincinnati: Methodist Book Concern Press, 1912.

Sweetser, Seth. *A Commemorative Discourse on the Death of Abraham Lincoln*. Worcester, MA: John Wilson and Son, 1865.

Thomas, Benjamin P. *Lincoln's New Salem*. Carbondale: Southern Illinois University Press, 1954.

Thomas, Jacob. *Sermon Preached in the African Methodist Episcopal Zion Church*. Troy, NY: Young & Benson, 1865.

Thompson, Robert Ellis. *A History of the Presbyterian Churches in the United States*. New York: Christian Literature, 1895.

Tocqueville, Alexis. *Democracy in America*. 2 vols. New York: Knopf Doubleday, 1990.

Vincent, Marvin R. *A Sermon on the Assassination of Abraham Lincoln, Sunday Morning April 23, 1865, First Presbyterian Church, Troy*. Troy, NY: A. W. Scribner, 1865.

Walker, David. *Appeal to the Coloured Citizens of the World*. Boston: published by the author, 1830.

Walker, George Leon. *The Offered National Regeneration: a sermon preached in the State Street Church, Portland, on the occasion of the national fast, September 26, 1861*. Portland, ME: Little, Bro., 1861.

Walters, Ronald G. *American Reformers, 1815–1816*. New York: Hill and Wang, 1978.

Whipple, Charles E. *Relations of Anti-Slavery to Religion. No. 19, Anti-Slavery Tracts*. New York: American Anti-Slavery Society, 1856.

White, Richard. *The Republic for Which It Stands: The United States during Reconstruction and the Gilded Age, 1865–1896*. New York: Oxford University Press, 2017.

Whitney, Henry Clay. *Life on the Circuit with Lincoln*. Boston: Estes and Lauriat, 1892.

Wiley, Bell Irvin. *The Life of Billy Yank: The Common Soldier of the Union*. Baton Rouge: Louisiana State University Press, 1952.

Wilson, Douglas L. *Honor's Voice: The Transformation of Abraham Lincoln*. New York: Vintage Books, 1999.

———. *Lincoln before Washington: New Perspectives on the Illinois Years.* Urbana: University of Illinois Press, 1997.

Winkle, Kenneth J. *The Young Eagle: The Rise of Abraham Lincoln.* Dallas: Taylor Trade, 2001.

Wood, Gordon S. *The Radicalism of the American Revolution.* New York: A. A. Knopf, 1992.

Woodworth, Steven E. *While God Is Marching On: The Religious World of Civil War Soldiers.* Lawrence: University Press of Kansas, 2001.

Wyatt-Brown, Bertram. "The Antimission Movement in the Jacksonian South: A Study in Regional Folk Culture." *Journal of Southern History* 36, no. 4 (November 1970): 501–29.

———. *Lewis Tappan and the Evangelical War against Slavery.* Cleveland: Press of Case Western Reserve University, 1969.

Zeitz, Joshua M. *Lincoln's Boys: John Hay, John Nicolay, and the War for Lincoln's Image.* New York: Viking, 2014.

———. "Remembering the Gettysburg Address." *New York Times.* November 21, 2013.

INDEX